AMERICAN WORKERS, AMERICAN UNIONS,
1920–1985

THE AMERICAN MOMENT
Stanley I. Kutler, Consulting Editor

The Twentieth-Century American City
Jon C. Teaford

American Workers, American Unions, 1920–1985
Robert H. Zieger

American Workers, American Unions, 1920–1985

Robert H. Zieger

THE JOHNS HOPKINS UNIVERSITY PRESS
Baltimore and London

The Johns Hopkins University Press
701 West 40th Street
Baltimore, Maryland 21211
The Johns Hopkins Press Ltd, London

The paper in this book is acid-free and meets
the guidelines for permanence and durability
of the Committee on Production Guidelines for
Book Longevity of the Council on Library Resources.

Library of Congress Cataloging-in-Publication Data

Zieger, Robert H.
    American workers, American unions, 1920–1985.

    (The American moment)
    Bibliography: p.
    Includes index.
    1. Trade-unions—United States—History—20th century.
I. Title. II. Series.
HD6508.Z53   1986   331.88′0973   85-24102
ISBN 0-8018-3126-1 (alk. paper)
ISBN 0-8018-3128-8 (pbk. : alk. paper)

Contents

Editor's Foreword

Labor unions have dramatically declined in membership and influence in the 1980s. Do workers still need unions? Has a new era arrived? Have management's concerns with benefits and a satisfactory workplace environment, particularly in the new high-tech industries, preempted union appeals? Perhaps the much-vaunted high-tech workplace made traditional union concerns outmoded. Two decades earlier, organized labor was both courted and feared as a political force. By 1985, political candidates began to question whether such support was a liability. The question, in short, was whether unions had become irrelevant.

Future economic developments will answer that question. Robert Zieger's narrative of organized labor since 1920, however, illuminates the upward cycle of the history of unions and summarizes the present state of decline as the product of both success and excess. His account offers a refreshing reminder of the struggles by American workers for decent working conditions and, above all, for an opportunity to insure that they, too, would share in the fruits of the capitalistic system. Whatever sense of security and well-being workers may feel today owes much to organized labor's efforts and victories from the Depression years of the 1930s through the unprecedented quarter-century of prosperity that followed World War II.

Zieger's engaging history reflects the sense of commitment within labor organizations, shared alike by the leadership and the rank-and-file workers. It was a heady time of passion, energy, and, above all, solidarity. Success, however, resulted in new problems. The unions' institutional maturity was accompanied by bureaucratization that sometimes left a gulf between officials and workers. Corruption and ties with organized crime in some unions have affected the perception of the movement as a whole. Blatant racism within enclaves of the labor movement has blurred the unions' solid achievements in civil rights and social justice. Eventually, these difficulties, as well as altered marketplace and economic considerations, have contributed to the present decline of labor unions.

The tale of labor's rise and currently troubled state of affairs is both exhilarating and melancholy; above all, it has a central place in understanding the modern American economy as well as social classes and stratification. Zieger's account forcefully reminds of that drama and that importance.

THE AMERICAN MOMENT is designed to offer a series of narrative and analytical discussions on a variety of topics in American history. Books in the series are both topical and chronological. Some volumes will survey familiar subjects—such as Puritanism, the American Revolution, the Civil War, and New Deal, and the Cold War—and blend necessary factual background with thoughtful, provocative interpretations. Other volumes—with topics such as women and reform movements, urban affairs, ethnicity, sports, and popular culture—will chart new or less familiar terrain. All will provide narrative and interpretation to open significant new dimensions and perspectives on the American past.

Stanley I. Kutler
UNIVERSITY OF WISCONSIN
MADISON, WISCONSIN

Preface

American Workers, American Unions, 1920–1985 is a book about organized labor. An opening chapter describes the state of the working
class in the 1920s and the impact of the Great Depression on it. A brief
final chapter touches on labor's tribulations in the 1970s and 1980s. The
core of the book examines the revival of unionism in the 1930s, organized labor's role in World War II, ideological and political conflicts
that rocked the labor movement after the global conflict, and the fate of
unionism in the affluent fifties and the turbulent sixties.

While I draw upon the research of social historians who have
taught us so much about families, communities, and cultural life, my
focus is on the unions as central institutions in American life. More than
any other agent, they have spoken legitimately for working people as a
class. While the American idiom avoids ideological formulations and
while unions have, both by preference and necessity, stressed practical
goals over transformational programs, the fact remains that no force in
American life in the twentieth century rivals the unions as the embodiment of the public and collective aspirations of working people. For
those who find a need to affix a label to *American Workers, American
Unions,* let me suggest that it is best described not as "social history," as
that term is commonly understood, nor as "institutional history," that
dreary-sounding category. Rather, I think of the book as the civic history of American workers since 1920.

Throughout American history, the labor movement has enjoyed
little public esteem. Feared by the Right as un-American and radical,
reviled by the revolutionary Left as reformist and opportunistic, American unions have endlessly struggled to attain strength and power. A
skeptical press, indifferent or hostile political parties, and an intransigent business class have usually kept the unions on the defensive. In
retrospect, it is true, labor's victims of yesteryear sometimes achieve post-
humous martyrdom, but often those who honor the dead do so in such a
manner as to denigrate the contemporary labor movement—a lump in

the throat for Joe Hill, a cynical sneer for Lane Kirkland. Walter Reuther's colleagues nodded knowingly when he declared in a 1958 speech that "in America we are being tolerated. We have not been fully accepted."

For a time, however, it seemed that organized labor had overcome its isolation. In the 1930s, a sympathetic government and union-supporting legislation helped give the union movement a new lease on life. The period from Franklin D. Roosevelt's inauguration in March 1933 through the presidency of his successor, Harry S. Truman, ending in January 1953, was one of massive, permanent growth of union membership. For the first time, the nation's central industrial core and its main transport networks became solidly organized. Mass organization dovetailed with heightened laborite political activity to such an extent that the Democratic party took on a strong working-class orientation, and working people continued to support the Democrats even after death removed the magic of Roosevelt's name from the ballot.

Depression-decade legislation underwrote labor organization and created the rudiments of a modern social welfare system in the United States. The expanding network of government programs and the impact of global conflict drew ordinary working people as never before into the national economy. Union leaders, bargaining now with once-disdainful corporate powers, asserted their views at the centers of political and economic decision-making. Successful unions, gains in collective bargaining, and bold labor initiatives in the political arena rewrote the script of public debate on economic, social, and political issues. In the thirties, forties, and early fifties, organized labor stood at center stage as it never had before (or would thereafter). "The United States," declared one of the country's leading labor economists in 1948, "is gradually shifting from a capitalistic community to a laboristic one—that is, to a community in which employees rather than businessmen are the strongest single influence."

American Workers, American Unions focuses on this period of maximum public interest in the affairs of the unions. The mass organizing and dramatic strikes of the 1930s, the bold rhetoric of the inimitable John L. Lewis, the turbulence in the shops and factories during World War II, and the pathbreaking developments in political activity and collective bargaining after the war kept organized labor at the heart of public attention for two decades. A rising labor movement raised basic questions about work and authority. Labor leaders, some of them imbued with anticapitalist ideas, urged the extension of democracy from the ballot box to the shop floor and corporate boardroom. Militant laborites linked their own struggles with those of disfranchised and segregated black Americans. Global conflict triggered sharp ideological debate throughout the labor movement and led some unionists to the brink of defiance of the government. After the war, a conservative backlash resurrected fundamental questions about the nature of class relations, while laborites themselves struggled with basic problems of radicalism and toleration of dissent. Throughout this period, the unions and their strikes, controversies, ideological struggles, and political efforts were rarely off the front pages of the nation's newspapers.

With the fifties and sixties came a certain retreat from these concerns. The economic expansion of the fifties and the absence of overt expressions of class conflict edged organized labor from the center of public attention. In the sixties, questions of civil rights, war, and student dissent took center stage. Still, it was during these decades that organized labor grew most powerful in collective bargaining and political influence, its leaders and partisans attempting to find an appropriate idiom by which to relate labor's heritage of struggle to these new and passionate concerns.

Some of those active in the thirties and forties remain. Ronald W. Reagan, for example, was president of the Screen Actors Guild, AFL, in the late 1940s. Mostly, however, the men and women who rebuilt the labor movement and whose lives were so decisively shaped by the struggles against fascism, the controversies over Communism, the efforts to extend union influence, and the innovations in collective bargaining and political action have passed from the scene. Still, their story and the story of the labor movement at flood tide is worth remembering.

In part, this is because the foundations of basic institutions were laid in this period. The modern labor movement itself, for example, sprang directly from the New Deal years. The current American party system retains many of the features and patterns of allegiance taken on in the thirties. The social welfare state and the military-industrial nexus are likewise products of the New Deal–World War II era.

At the same time, though, it is precisely because the idiom of the thirties and forties, and increasingly, of the fifties and sixties, is so different from that of our own that the concerns of an earlier era need to be brought freshly to the attention of a rising generation. The questions that labor's men and women, their allies, and their critics grappled with—questions about the economic dimensions of democracy, the tensions between class identity and national loyalty, and the political implications of union strength—remain. The vividness with which these matters stand out in retrospect may help to clarify the terms of public debate today, when the clutter of the present so often seems to trivialize our discourse. Understanding and even arguing with the past can help us to see where we are and to sense the continuities that we can ignore but never escape. "There are," declares the great English scholar Leonard Schapiro, "no such things as 'answers' in history, but the continuous attempt to find them is part of the duty of responsible citizens."

The genesis and preparation of *American Workers, American Unions* owes much to the encouragement and advice of Stanley Kutler, series editor, and Henry Tom of Johns Hopkins University Press. Le Roy Ashby, Joe Bloch, Douglas Fraser, Howell Harris, Patrick Maney, Sam Merrill, Alan Raucher, Bernard Sternsher, and Melvyn Dubofsky read parts of the manuscript and offered valuable commentary. Ginny Corbin typed it with her usual skill and enthusiasm. Carolyn Moser was an acute and understanding copyeditor. Gay Zieger once again was my listener, critic, champion, and friend.

AMERICAN WORKERS, AMERICAN UNIONS,
1920-1985

American Workers in Prosperity and Depression, 1920–1933

The years between the Armistice ending the Great War in 1918 and the inauguration of Franklin D. Roosevelt were truly ones of boom and bust for American workers. Accelerating economic, technological, and social change through the middle 1920s followed a postwar period of convulsive upheaval and depression. The economic advances of the later twenties helped workers to achieve unparalleled prosperity. Even though chronic insecurity, grossly unequal distribution of income, and grim working conditions flawed the good times, the period 1923–1929 did set a kind of benchmark for working people. Thus, when the economy fell apart in the early 1930s, workers responded vigorously, if fitfully. Although most no doubt considered the Depression primarily a private and familial disaster, thousands of workers protested, demonstrated, and struck. Many more trooped to the polls to defeat incumbents and elect new leaders, hoping that a changing of the guard would bring back good times. In prosperity and depression, American workers struggled to retain the rising material standards that the modern economy had introduced into their lives. Rarely voicing explicitly radical solutions, they nonetheless expected the system they had worked so hard to build and run to pay off for them. Neither victims nor celebrants of American capitalism, the American working class sought through private pursuits and public protest to resume its interrupted march.

PROSPERITY

By the end of the 1920s, American workers had reason to feel both proud and resentful. The 49 million wage and salary workers who ran the mills, mines, shops, factories, and trains were the country's greatest resource. Possessing an enormous array of skills and aptitudes, accustomed to hard work, receptive to technological change, they formed the heart of an economic system that achieved record levels of production. Although careful observers noted that rapid mechanization was undermining traditional skills, the basic industrial literacy of the American population continued to provide the essential human capital that operated and maintained a vast economic machine.

Between 1919 and 1929, American workers constructed 3.5 million new homes. They electrified 9 million residences. They installed 6 million telephones and turned out over 7 million radios. Autoworkers produced over 20 million motor vehicles, among them a stream of trucks and tractors that accelerated the mechanization of American agriculture. Workers made products of all descriptions, from basic steel and cotton fabric to a dazzling variety of rubber, glass, paper, metal, wooden, and electrical items. Together with the vast outpouring of foodstuffs and fibers from the nation's ever-productive farms, this tidal wave of goods confirmed and extended the country's status as the world's leader, by far, in almost every major economic category.

Moreover, even as production rose, the number of workers engaged in mining, manufacturing, and agriculture decreased. The number of gainfully employed Americans grew from 41.6 million in 1919 to nearly 49 million ten years later. But at the end of the twenties, 47 percent of them toiled in agriculture, mining, and manufacturing, whereas at the beginning of the decade over 58 percent had. Reflecting the increased scale of industrial enterprises, the number of workers per establishment almost doubled between the beginning of the century and 1930. The postwar decade also exhibited a quickening trend toward white-collar, clerical, and service employment. Between 1919 and 1929, the proportion of workers employed in these trades rose from 32 percent to over 35 percent; in the latter year, 17 million Americans worked in trade, finance, service, and related white-collar pursuits, as compared with just over 12 million in mining and manufacturing. Thus, even during the heyday of mass production industrialism, employment in traditional blue-collar pursuits had begun to level off while the expanding service and clerical sector mushroomed.

Foreign immigration to the United States declined sharply in the 1920s, reflecting the impact of restrictive legislation. However, the mechanization of agriculture combined with the expansion of service employment and clerical work to change drastically the sexual and racial composition of the labor force. Female employment, much of it funneled into office, clerical, and governmental work, grew from 8.3 million in 1920 to 10.6 million in 1930, an increase of 27 percent. By 1930, about a quarter of all workers were female, an increasing proportion of them married. Changes in agricultural production drove thousands of southern rural workers off the farms and into the service trades and factories of the North and West. Between 1915 and 1928, over 1.2 million Afro-

Americans migrated from the South. Both black workers and female workers experienced severe inequalities in opportunity and wages, as racial and sexual discrimination reinforced deeply etched patterns of segmentation in labor markets.

Still, according to the world's standards American workers, whatever their race, sex, or occupation, were handsomely rewarded for their efforts. In the most authoritative survey of wages conducted in the 1920s, economist Paul Douglas estimated that in 1926 average annual earnings stood at $1,473, a gain in real wages of nearly 40 percent in comparison with annual average earnings of $682 in 1914. Other studies carried the data down to 1929 and confirmed that real wages, virtually stationary between 1890 and 1915, leapt by 38 percent between the beginning of World War I and 1929. Hours of employment in manufacturing slid downward, from over 59 in 1900 to just over 50 in 1926.

Throughout the late 1920s surveys of consumer habits marveled at the wide range of purchases made by working-class people, many of them involving durable goods such as radios, washing machines, and even automobiles. The country made impressive strides in the decade in such humble, but profoundly important, categories as indoor plumbing, per capita living space, and extent of home ownership. Consumer credit, not long before the privilege of the well-to-do, flowed enticingly into working-class homes, permitting these expensive improvements and purchases. All experts agreed that by the end of the 1920s, the nation's working people had greater access to health care, recreational and cultural facilities, public services, and education than ever before.

The improving living standards of workers led celebrants of American life to suggest that the country had at last found the cure to recurrent labor unrest. Throughout the half century after 1870, America had led the world in work stoppages. Moreover, strikes in this country were more savage and bloody than anywhere else. Hundreds were killed in the great railroad uprising of 1877. Throughout the rest of the nineteenth century, police and private guards had freely resorted to the truncheon and the rifle. Nor did the twentieth century usher in a new era. In 1914, Colorado militiamen shot down striking coal miners, burned out their families, and left a trail of bloodshed and savagery across the southern part of the state reminiscent of the genocidal Indian wars. Escalating labor unrest throughout the World War I years triggered massive coal, rail, meatpacking, and public employees' strikes after the Armistice. In September 1919, over 300,000 steelworkers walked off their jobs, helping to make that year the most strike-torn one in American history. While less lethal than earlier conflicts, the postwar strikes were bitter enough. Private police and public authorities openly employed tear gas, billy clubs, and firearms to break up meetings, threaten leaders, and destroy labor organizations. Declared one shocked journalist, "The greatest of all wars between organized labor and capital seems to have begun." William Jennings Bryan warned that it threatened to become "a war of extermination."

But by the late 1920s, the days of confrontation and bloodshed seemed to have ended. In 1919, there were more than 3,600 strikes involving more than 4 million workers (a number equal to almost 21% of the labor force), but ten years later workers staged only 900 stoppages, involving but 289,000 strikers (a mere 1.2% of the labor force). The 604 strikes occurring in 1928 represented the fewest on record since 1884. Truly it seemed that rising prosperity had broken the cycle of labor unrest and violence. Certainly, Herbert Hoover, architect of the economic policies of the decade that Republicans identified as central to economic growth, thought so. Campaigning for the presidency in 1928, he reminded a working-class audience that seven years earlier "discontent and agitation against our Democracy [had been] rampant. Fear of the future haunted every heart." But economic growth and wise governmental policies, he asserted, had tamed the threat, quelled the fear, and brought peace and prosperity to American workers.

Not all observers, however, shared Hoover's optimism. The same academic studies that revealed the gains workers had made also documented their sharp limitations. Yes, conceded students of wage rates, real wages had been rising. But most of the data revealed that the great bulk of the gains had occurred before 1923. Indeed, by the end of the decade workers could claim only a meager 2.0 percent increase in weekly real wages as compared with their 1919 pay. Every index showed massive increases in productivity: 1929 figures showed a 72 percent per man hour gain in manufacturing performance over the decade, for example. Thus it seemed clear that workers were producing vastly more goods with only modest increases in compensation.

True, much of this gain involved mechanization. One study showed that during the twenties the amount of horsepower used per worker increased by 50 percent in manufacturing, 60 percent in mining, and 75 percent in railroading. But mechanization did not mean easier work. Workers and independent observers alike believed that the pace of work, set as it was increasingly by the capacities of machines and the calculations of employer-hired time-study experts, was quickening dramatically. Since an increasing proportion of productive work consisted of machine-paced operations and a decreasing proportion lay in skilled, worker-paced operations, the testimony of workers as to the

fatigue, boredom, and pressure of modern mechanical operations be-
spoke a reality of industrial employment.

There were other burdens as well. Throughout the 1920s unemployment was a constant ghost at the feast, rarely dipping below 5 percent. By mid-1929 it edged up to at least 8 percent, and well-informed
labor sources argued persuasively that 13–15 percent was a more accurate estimate. Nor did workers have recourse to public assistance or
unemployment insurance, as these innovations in welfare state practice
remained in their infancy in the United States long after they had become established in other industrial countries.

Of course, high wages partially compensated for insecurity and
hard work. Even here, however, the picture was spotty. Throughout the
decade, observers pointed to the dangers of using only statistical aggre-
gates in describing workers' incomes. For one thing, well before 1929,
whole industries fell on hard times. Throughout the decade hundreds of
thousands of coal miners and cotton spinners suffered unemployment,
short-time work, and eroded wage standards. Moreover, wage differentials in the United States widened appreciably in the 1920s, with the
result that workers with greater skills or in favored pursuits commanded
the lion's share of the overall wage gains made.

Rising standards of living also posed problems. It was one thing to
contrast the favorable wages and real income of 1929's industrial
workers with those of their counterparts two decades earlier but quite
another to realize that modern appliances, housing, medical care, and
other products of an industrial society increasingly defined as necessities
had to be paid for. Increasingly effective school attendance laws were no
doubt progressive and in the long run aided working-class children, but
in the short run they dried up a traditionally crucial source of family
income and helped to drive working-class wives into the labor force. In
1929, one survey showed that the average Detroit-area Ford worker
earned about $1,712—a princely sum in comparison with standards else-
where. Yet the necessities of urban living called for an outlay by the same
average family of $1,720. True, about a third of those surveyed reported
savings, averaging about 8 percent of their incomes; but 44 percent of
the Ford workers reported that their expenses exceeded income by
about the same amount. Nor did extravagance account for the shortfall:
In the last boom year of the 1920s, only 7 percent of Ford workers went
away on vacation, and these spent an average of $37 on their holidays.

Workers in auto, electrical, and other mass production industries
stood in the higher ranges of worker compensation. For millions, the
story was grimmer. In 1929, 21 percent of the nation's families earned

less than $1,000 and 42 percent less than $1,500, an amount barely adequate to sustain a family of four even outside the major industrial centers. At least half of the nation's families, preponderantly working-class, faced the vagaries of a notably unstable economic system and the periodic likelihood of unemployment without savings of any kind. In short, life for the vast majority of industrial workers, whatever the remarkable advances in recent years, consisted of long hours, hard work, careful calculation of every nickel spent, and little surplus cash for leisure, recreation, or cultural pursuits.

"The essence of the work was speed," observes historian Ronald Schatz of the experiences of men and women who made refrigerators for General Electric. The assembly line rolled endlessly. "You could drop over dead," recalled one electrical worker, "and they wouldn't stop the line." Coil winders in motor construction tasks did not have the line to pace their work, but they did have to contend with production-obsessed managers and payment plans carefully calibrated to require ceaseless effort. "It was such a monotonous job! Oh, just repetitive. . . . You didn't have to use your head at all," lamented a woman who spent eight years winding coils for GE.

In industries such as electrical appliance and auto, the modernity of the product and the widely hailed adoption by employers of new methods and machines created a public impression of smooth efficiency and calm scientific rationality on the shop floor. But, remarks historian David Montgomery, few workers perceived it thus. For many, "the plant resembled a bedlam: Arbitrary and pretentious men in white shirts shouted orders, crept up behind workers with stop watches," and sought always to gain greater control over the production process. Workers in auto, electrical appliance, rubber, and other mass production industries waged sporadic guerrilla warfare with their foremen and production supervisors over the speed of the line and the pace of work.

Even the declining strike statistics were misleading. As some contemporary observers—and many historians, with the benefit of hindsight—noted, the sharp decline in disputes reflected temporary circumstances rather than the arrival of a new age of permanent industrial peace. After all, a record wave of strikes had swept through the World War I years and into the early 1920s. The defeat of these strikes had not resolved the grievances that triggered them. The steel magnates had crushed the fledgling unions in the 1919–20 strike, but the industry's arbitrary personnel, compensation, and disciplinary practices remained intact. By the late 1920s, the nation's 700,000 coal miners, ordinarily a militant army, had been subdued, their union almost destroyed. However, few who observed the poverty, resentment, and sullen hostility of the miners and their families believed that the mining regions had seen the last of labor conflict.

Throughout the teens and into the early twenties, the new mass production industries, such as rubber, auto, metals fabrication, and electrical goods, had seethed with sporadic strikes that had often turned violent and bitter. On the surface, this pattern of conflict did not carry over into the new era of prosperity. But few of the cities affected—such as East Pittsburgh, where in 1916 electrical workers had struck Westinghouse, or Bridgeport, where wartime strikes of brass and metal workers had defied employers and government—were without their nucleus of organizers and agitators. These men and women, at least, were eager to rekindle the spark of unionism.

Even in the quiet years of the 1920s, strikes broke out in the southern textile mills. Repression and violence punctuated these grim encounters. Some observers saw in such company-dominated mill towns as Elizabethton, Tennessee, and Gastonia, North Carolina, throwbacks to the "bad old days" of class conflict and repression. According to this view, southern textiles and some of the isolated mining regions that also suffered through violent strikes in this period were vestiges of an otherwise-dying era. For others, however, the tyranny, paternalism, and misery of these villages and mines and the continuing struggle of mill hands and miners to sustain their unions were merely the latest chapters in a story that stretched back a hundred years. The southern textile strikes and their violent denouement, according to some veteran labor observers, were no fading echo of a vanished past. Rather, they provided a glimpse of things to come.

By the end of the 1920s, the American working class was a study in apparent contradictions. In terms of income, style of life, and status, it did indeed form a class. As sociologists Robert and Helen Lynd observed in their study of Muncie, Indiana, the "division into working class and business class . . . constitutes the outstanding cleavage" in the city. This division "is the most significant single cultural factor tending to influence what one does all day long throughout one's life; whom one marries; when one gets up in the morning; . . . whether one drives a Ford or a Buick; . . . whether one sits about evenings with one's necktie off; and so on indefinitely throughout the daily comings and goings of a . . . man, woman, or child."

Yet this class did not act like a class in the European sense of the term. Composed of many diverse ethnic and national groups, often divided especially on the matter of race, toiling in hundreds of industries and trades, participants in a profoundly individualistic social order, the members of the American working class did not commonly *think* of themselves as a class. Seen from one angle of vision, they formed the solid bedrock of American industrial and economic strength, their skills, discipline, and tenacity the key factors in running, improving, and maintaining a machine civilization. Seen from another angle, this class dissolved into a kaleidoscope of regional, ethnic, and industrial fragments. Their skills and brawn energized the system, but public acclaim commonly went to the entrepreneur and the corporate executive. Incredibly advantaged in terms of income and access to goods and services insofar as the vast human majority was concerned, they actually struggled on the narrow edge of making do; and in declining industries, rural areas, and agricultural employment they lived lives of economic desperation. Seemingly absorbed into a smoothly running economic and social system, their unions crushed or hapless, they nonetheless were heirs to a rich, indeed legendary, heritage of protest and activism. So in March 1929, as Herbert Hoover assumed the presidency, he faced a working class proud of its contributions, loyal to its understanding of the promise of American life, expecting better things of a bright future, and keenly aware of the struggles and defeats of the past.

DEPRESSION

In the fall of 1929, the bottom dropped out of the stock market. This financial crisis further damaged an economy already struggling with sluggish inventories, rising unemployment, and disastrous agricultural conditions. In an economic system chronically prone to boom and bust cycles, bad times were familiar. Optimistic words from the White House, the *Wall Street Journal*, and the prestigious academic rostrums at first encouraged belief that the downturn would be short.

But by the fall of 1930, even government officials acknowledged that unemployment had soared over the 15 percent mark. Plunging farm prices brought closures and bankruptcies to rural America. Massive bank failures abroad deepened the crisis at home. Landlords called on police to evict penniless tenants. For the first time since the 1921 depression, bread lines appeared in large cities. Relief agencies were swamped. In Michigan, the Ford Motor Company laid off all but 37,000 of its 128,000 workers, and American Federation of Labor (AFL) president William Green grew alarmed at what he saw in Detroit. "The men are sitting in the park all day long and all night long," he reported. There were "hundreds and thousands of them, muttering . . . out of work, seeking work."

By the winter of 1932–33, the disaster had become a catastrophe. Unemployment hit the 25 percent mark. A 1932 California study reported that joblessness was creating "a new class of poor . . . among the ranks of young, sturdy, ambitious laborers, artisans, mechanics, and professionals"—the very lifeblood of the future of the country. Rootless, homeless people wandered the countryside in uncountable numbers. The Southern Pacific Railroad reported that in 1932 alone its agents had ejected nearly 700,000 people from its freights. Slums of cardboard, lumber scraps, tin sheeting—the detritus of an industrial society—spread along the wastelands and outskirts of major cities. Historian Arthur M. Schlesinger, Jr., has provided an unforgettable portrait of a people at the brink of despair: "Every week, every day, more and more workers joined the procession. . . . The shadows deepened in the dark cold rooms, with the angry father helpless and ashamed, the distraught children too often hungry or sick, and the mother, so resolute by day, so often . . . lying awake . . . at night, softly crying." In 1931, the commissioner of the Casket Manufacturers' Association added a grim statistic to the Niagara of numbers that suggested a nation's agony: Since 1929, the number of indigent deaths, requiring cheap public burials, had doubled. And, he added, throughout rural America the people had reverted to building homemade coffins.

Working people faced this frightening depression with diverse responses. At no time, even in the direst days of 1932 and early 1933, did the American working class pose a direct threat to the country's economic and political system. Even in the worst of times, workers perceived too many positive features in American life, had too many alternatives available with which to express protest or find a modicum of succor, and too well knew the dangers of confrontation to form the basis for sustained antigovernment activity of either right- or left-wing variety. American workers were far from docile or lacking in outrage, but their response to the depression simply was not system-threatening.

Millions of people—no one knew how many—took to the road, some for a week or two, others for months, even years. This huge country with its lack of internal controls on migration had throughout the period of industrialization provided the sheer physical space and the economic and social diversity to lure the unemployed and the down-and-out onto the road. For a hundred years, migratory labor in the wheat fields, on construction gangs, and along the railroads had provided hard livings for transient workers. In some quarters, the tramp or the bindlestiff was a romantic figure, a working-class counterpart to the Deerslayer or the Mountain Man. In reality, life on the road, whether it led to sporadic employment or chronic disappointment, was harsh. Its heroism consisted of sustaining life, enduring hunger and privation, and surviving the harrowing loneliness. But the ease with which a man (or a woman: in 1933 the U.S. Women's Bureau estimated that 60,000 females were on the road) could drift off into the vast reaches of the country drew hundreds of thousands of workers into the transient life. There was always the rumor of work in the next town, of harvest hands needed in the distant valley; and if the pull of opportunity was not always strong, the sense of despair and failure made return to abandoned families and familiar communities increasingly uncertain.

Most workers stayed put, however. For them, any solution to hard times outside the family was unthinkable. Just as the grudging prosperity of the 1920s had depended on family incomes, so the success in weathering the storm rested on the family's ability to continue as a unit. This was especially true among immigrants, those close to the family-based rural economies of the old country. People of southern and eastern European derivation displayed particular determination to cope with the sudden terror through family resources. In the great industrial valleys of Pennsylvania and Ohio, where the depression all but sealed up the steel mills, metal fabricating shops, and electrical appliance factories, the Poles, Slovenes, and Lithuanians who provided the labor for these facilities drew inward. Young people delayed marriages. Boys and girls left school to find work. Mothers sought out washing and took in boarders. More fortunate brothers and sisters lent and shared their meager resources. Far more than native Americans, immigrants and near-immigrants sought survival in familial rather than in individual strategies. Thus, while for some workers the depression acted as a catapult, tossing them into a huge, unfocused internal migration, for millions in the industrial core it acted as a magnet, pulling them back into the paternal family, reducing opportunities while providing the grim sustenance of mutual need. In either case, however, behavior was private—individual and familial—not political and communal.

Millions needed public relief. Unable to move or correctly perceiving the hopelessness of relocation, having exhausted family resources, they trickled into the various public relief and private charity agencies. As the depression deepened, the trickle became a flood, and case loads of harried welfare workers and volunteers doubled, quadrupled. In Detroit, the city Department of Public Relief saw its rolls expand from 156,000 people in October 1929 to 728,000 just six months later. Homeless people by the hundreds slept in a downtown park each night, while some families burrowed in the ground, using branches to cover the openings in the holes they dug. In the winter of 1930, city facilities sheltered 5,000 and fed 10,000 each day . A year later, the city Welfare Department added 300 families each day to the rolls, a majority of whom had never before applied for assistance. Lacking adequate statistics, welfare workers in dozens of communities simply recorded the staggering dimensions of this tidal wave of human suffering, almost all of them noting with alarm that large numbers of their charges had no record of previous application.

President Hoover and his advisors, committed to traditional American values of local self-help and voluntarism, encouraged private charity to supplement state and local efforts. In the fall of 1931, Walter S. Gifford, president of American Telephone and Telegraph and chairman of the president's Organization on Unemployment Relief, launched a publicity campaign to encourage private charitable donations. "Between October 18 and November 25," declared one appeal, "America will feel the thrill of a great spiritual experience" as fortunate folk chipped in to provide for the distressed. Husbands and wives, for example, would grow closer together in the glow of giving. Despite these appeals, private charity, which had in 1929 contributed about 25 percent of the total national expenditures for relief, by 1932 contributed only 20 percent.

The overwhelming crisis ruthlessly exposed the primitive character of public assistance in America. The burden fell on state and local authorities, particularly the latter. But no general program of unemployment relief or regular income supplements underlay local emergency efforts. The purpose of the system was to isolate the relatively small (it was thought) number of chronic incompetents or distressed individuals in a community and provide them with a combination of close supervision and niggardly aid. In some large cities more sophisticated systems had emerged, and the needy could find generous and sensitive help from newly trained social workers, but even here the relief system was geared to deal with the small handful of misfits. The existing bureaucracies, public or private, simply could not handle the deluge of distress.

At root, the problem was financial. Industrial and commercial depression cut tax revenues even while it created mass misery. Agricultural depression and a glutted housing market drove down receipts from property taxes. Some cities paid their employees with scrip and begged charity vouchers from grocers to distribute to the poor in lieu of cash. Few cities could help with housing, medical care, dental work, or utilities. By the winter of 1931–32, whole families in New York had to make do with $2.39 per week in aid. In one Ohio city—hardly atypical—authorities permitted only 6.42 cents a day for recipients' food allowances. In the auto centers of Michigan, Ford and other manufacturers responded to city officials' pleas for assistance by providing space for temporary shelters for the homeless, food and medical vouchers against future earnings for unemployed autoworkers, free use of vacant company land for gardening, and recreational space for workers now experiencing increased leisure time. In general, industrialists, frightened themselves by their sudden plunge from prosperity to chaos, turned to their sorely beset employees for most charitable initiatives. Thus, employers launched work-sharing plans and collected contributions from employees to be distributed to the needy as company largess.

The impact of all this was at once measurable and incalculable. Cold statistics told part of the story. Marriage rates plummeted; suicide rates soared. Prostitution, alcoholism, juvenile crime, and other social pathologies flourished. If starvation per se was not statistically significant, malnutrition, its close cousin, surely was widespread, though difficult to quantify because its effects were often delayed or felt through susceptibility to disease. In the heyday of the auto industry in the 1920s, Henry Ford had made promises to certain disabled workers, pledging lifetime employment. As Ford slashed manpower, the disabled were among the first to go. Shocked and incredulous at their doubly desperate plight, they appealed to the Flivver King and his wife, Clara, famous for her warmth and sympathy. "Won't you try and do something for my husband . . . at least let me work in his place," pleaded one worker's distraught wife. "We have three children and have tried so many times to get back [to the Ford employment office] that we are about desperate," wrote another supplicant.

But most workers did not supplicate. They endured. They did what they had to, and sometimes that meant appeal to relief agencies and employers. And often these appeals contained a sense of self-blame, of individual failure, predictable attitudes in a society that defined individual worth in terms of work and achievement and that prided itself on its adherence to individualistic values of thrift and hard work. But if traditional values could lead to self-blame and self-doubt, they could also spur protest and even rebellion. The 1920s had created expectations of material gains, opportunities, a better life. Corporate America and its political spokesmen had promises to keep. In the past, working-class America had never been long quiescent.

PROTEST

Indeed, protest flared throughout the depression era. The years of the early 1930s were particularly turbulent. While most workers and their families relied primarily on individual and family resources, thousands took to the streets. Protests, demonstrations, relief riots, and anti-eviction actions provided an activist counterpoint to the dreary cycle of unemployment and despair. Thus, in March 1930 hundreds of thousands of unemployed workers tramped through the streets of New York, Detroit, Washington, San Francisco, and other cities in a mass protest organized by the Communist party's Unemployed Councils.

Most outbursts, however, were local and spontaneous. Outraged neighbors and relatives drove off moving men and faced down police officers and landlords seeking to evict impoverished renters. Embittered relief applicants lashed out at insensitive officials and case workers. In 1931, over 400 relief protests broke out in Chicago, followed by an additional 550, or an average of 10 a week, in 1932.

Incidents erupted in city after city. In January and February 1932, for example, authorities in the Bronx tried to carry out a wave of evictions. On February 2, as police guided furniture movers into the dwellings of families unable to pay their rent, a thousand people gathered in the street. Reported the *New York Times*, "Women shrieked from the windows. . . . Fighting began simultaneously in the house and on the street." In Chicago, groups of activists marched through the streets of the black community, mobilizing anti-eviction crowds, confronting a police force notorious for brutality. Horace Cayton, a young black sociologist, found himself in the middle of a Chicago protest one day in 1931. He joined an anti-eviction crowd as it filed past a restaurant he happened to be patronizing. Two squad cars quickly appeared, and officers with drawn revolvers faced the protestors, who stopped but did not disperse. Police reinforcements quickly appeared, and fifteen or twenty bluecoats charged the assemblage, wielding billy clubs and night sticks. "They stood like dumb beasts," Cayton wrote of the protesters, "no one ran, no one fought or offered resistance, just stood, an immovable black mass." A Chicago rent riot in August of that year resulted in three deaths, inflaming the entire black community and eventually forcing civic authorities to find municipal employment for evictees.

Two of the most dramatic mass protests occurred in 1932. The winter of 1931–32 brought only deepening crisis and greater individual hardship. The violent encounters between hunger marchers and police in Michigan in March and between army veterans and the United States cavalry in July revealed a mixture of desperation and repressiveness that seemed frightening indeed.

In the winter of 1931–32, the Communist-led Detroit Unemployed Council began to mobilize a march to confront auto magnate Henry Ford with a petition. The council had been active for two years in anti-eviction, relief, and unemployment work in and around Detroit. Its leaders sought to link protest over the plight of the unemployed with the deteriorating conditions within Ford's facilities, and particularly inside the gigantic River Rouge complex in adjacent Dearborn. Thus, the

"Ford Hunger March," as the demonstration was billed, asserted Ford's responsibility for unemployment, mass poverty, and lack of aid for the afflicted. But it also called vivid attention to the grievances of Ford's employees, stressing the intensification of the work pace, the spiraling accident rates, the discrimination against black workers, the violent intimidation of union supporters, and the frightening insecurity experienced by autoworker families lacking access to medical facilities.

Just as he had personified the motor age, Ford also epitomized for many the callousness and injustice of employers' reactions to the depression. He had cut his payroll by 75 percent. Since his plants lay outside the city, he paid no taxes in Detroit, where most of his employees lived. Despite his great personal wealth, he acknowledged no personal responsibility for the plight of the distressed. Any charitable initiatives that Ford did launch were characterized by maximum publicity, niggardly benefits, and stern repayment requirements. In addition, he constantly carped at harassed public authorities as they tried desperately to cope with the spreading misery. Instead of assistance, Ford offered homilies and on more than one occasion observed publicly that those who truly wanted to work could find employment if they sincerely sought it out.

On March 7, marchers gathered on the city's west side. Gaining strength as they proceeded in the direction of the Rouge complex, they numbered over 3,000 as they approached the boundary separating Detroit from the industrial suburb of Dearborn. This city, notorious as a Ford-controlled barony, housed the company's headquarters and the Rouge plant itself. Dozens of Dearborn police met the marchers at the city limits and ordered them to turn back. When the protesters refused, the police fired tear gas bombs into their midst. But the swirling winter winds blew the acrid fumes back into Dearborn and the distraught police, now pelted with rocks and frozen chunks of dirt by the irate marchers, fled toward the nearby Rouge.

The marchers surged across an open field to the plant's employment gate. Dearborn firemen hooked up their powerful hoses to mains inside the plant and sprayed the front ranks with icy jets of water. The police again tried tear gas, while angry demonstrators continued their barrage of missiles. Shots rang out, killing two marchers outright and wounding others. As march leaders attempted to reorganize their forces for a retreat in the face of this murderous assault, an automobile careened through the crowd toward the gate. It bore Harry Bennett, easily recognizable to the marchers as head of Ford's union-busting "Service Department." As Bennett's automobile entered the plant those inside mistook a bloody wound he had suffered from a house brick thrown by a demonstrator for a gunshot wound. The police opened up on the crowd with rifle, pistol, and machine-gun fire. Dozens of marchers fell wounded, and the rest fled from the scene, attempting to assist their fallen comrades. By evening, the casualty list included four dead, two dozen of the wounded in police custody, and dozens more who had made off despite their injuries.

On March 12, now numbering 20,000, marchers again took to Detroit's streets. They bore the dead down Woodward Avenue from the Institute of Arts to Grand Circus Park. There they gathered to hear speeches eulogizing the martyrs and denouncing Ford, the police, and capitalist repression in general. A funeral cortege carried the bodies out along Michigan Avenue to Woodmere Cemetery, where the slain hunger marchers were buried at a site overlooking the billowing smokestacks of the sprawling Rouge complex.

Later that spring, the scene of mass protest shifted to Washington, D.C. In May and June thousands of World War I veterans from around the country started out for the capital. They sought passage by Congress of a bill that would prepay a bonus due them for their wartime service. Unemployed, without resources, these men were by 1932 in the prime of life. They were the generation of the 1890s, citizens of a buoyant American republic, heroes of the American Expeditionary Force of 1917–18, men with families, growing children who needed food and shelter. Why should they have to wait till 1945, the statutory date for payment of this bonus; why could not Congress advance the bonus? For thousands of veterans—young men who at age 35–40 would normally be hitting their full stride in careers and vocations—this promised government money represented their only financial resource.

The movement to petition Congress sprang spontaneously among groups of veterans around the country. They rode the rails, hitchhiked, or simply walked to the nation's capital, occasionally clashing with railroad detectives and local police, but always proclaiming their peaceful and patriotic intentions. By mid-June, about 20,000 of them, now dubbed the Bonus Expeditionary Force, had reached Washington. They camped across the Anacostia River from the Capitol, bivouacking in quasi-military formations. Even when the Senate defeated the Bonus Bill on June 18, they remained orderly, greeting the news with solemn disappointment but joining in the singing of "America" before dispersing from the Capitol steps.

After defeat in the Senate, some left. Many, however, had literally no place to go. Wives and children joined them in the poorly drained, pestiferous encampment on the Anacostia Flats. By now, internal disputes had begun to rack the BEF. A small but articulate Communist group sought to use the situation to raise consciousness and provide an illustration in class politics. Walter W. Waters, the self-proclaimed chief of the BEF, attacked the Communists in terms that sounded uncomfortably akin to the rhetoric of European fascism. The *BEF News* denounced an unresponsive Congress, which adjourned in mid-July and thus sealed the fate of the bonus plan. Turning its frustration on the veterans themselves, the *News* called for unspecified action on their part. "A dog in the gutter will fight to feed its pups," the camp newspaper declared, but the veterans "have cringed and fawned and begged for crumbs. . . . Are you truly curs and cowards?" For officials in the Washington city government and the Hoover administration, these words sounded like the tocsin of revolution. Pressure mounted to use the United States Army against its veterans, to disperse the lingering remnants of the BEF. On July 28, police clashed with veterans who had occupied an abandoned downtown building, killing two men. City officials called for federal troops, and with President Hoover's approval, Secretary of War Patrick Hurley ordered in the army.

Late in the afternoon of the twenty-eighth, with General Douglas MacArthur in personal command, four troops of cavalry, backed with six tanks and an infantry column, clattered into the city. Sabers drawn, ample supplies of tear gas at the ready, they cleared the downtown buildings and then moved on the disorderly colony at Anacostia. There they burned the shanties and flushed men, women, and children out of the tents and hovels. The tear gas hugged the ground in the low-lying areas, undisturbed in the heavy Washington summer air. An eleven-week-old baby, born in the camp, died the next day as a result of the gassing. The veterans and their families, some still defiant, others thoroughly whipped, trickled off into the Maryland countryside. For General MacArthur, resplendent in his cavalry breeches and flourishing his riding crop, it had been a heroic action against a "mob" exhibiting "the essence of revolution." The *Washington News*, no friend of revolution, saw it differently: "What a pitiful spectacle is that of the great American government . . . chasing unarmed men, women, and children with Army tanks. . . . If the Army must be called out to make war on unarmed citizens, this is no longer America."

In the protests and demonstrations that punctuated these early depression years, Communists, Socialists, and other anticapitalist radicals often provided leadership. They sought to convert unfocused neighborhood militancy into organized popular defense organizations. The Communist Unemployed Councils and similar Socialist bodies tried to use the people's experience with oppression and poverty to lead them to a recognition of the system's fundamental inequities. At the same time, radical activists pressured authorities for concessions and reforms, thus hoping to earn the allegiance of distressed families. The wide range of protest—the demonstrations, anti-eviction actions, relief riots, and street marches—never coalesced into a mass movement or achieved the kind of political consciousness Communists and Socialists sought. Yet these protests made it abundantly clear that working people would fight for their homes, that those in power could not count on permanent quiescence, and that if traditional leadership did not respond to the crisis, working people could turn to corps of energetic, articulate radicals for support.

UNIONS AND POLITICS

Whatever the drama and violence of marches and demonstrations, politics and trade union activity provided the most enduring avenues for worker response to the depression. Workers' votes punished the majority Republican party's candidates in state, local, and congressional elections in 1930. And in 1932, they helped to defeat the troubled Hoover administration and bring Franklin D. Roosevelt and the Democratic party to power. Meanwhile, organized labor began to shed the stunned lethargy with which it had initially responded to the crisis and to demand major changes in public policies. Workers began to lash out at the deteriorating conditions that had made the depression a nightmare even for those able to retain their jobs.

Political action offered both advantages and limitations to distressed working-class people. The ballot box was the most sanctioned and even sanctified means by which angry citizens could protest and seek change. In theory at least, casting a ballot was safe, even patriotic; it entailed no risks. In reality, millions of Americans were voteless. In the South a combination of terror and legalistic manipulations drove blacks and many poor away from the polls. In other states arcane residence and registration requirements discouraged political action. Black citizens in the South and immigrant populations in northern cities, both overwhelmingly working class, found the vaunted American promise of free elections a dead end rather than a pathway to freedom. Nonetheless, millions of workers could vote and did participate in the congressional elections of 1930 and the presidential campaign of 1932, adding their ballots to the majorities that undermined Republican strength in 1930 and that massively repudiated Hoover in 1932. Indeed, thousands of workers turned their backs on both major political parties. In the presidential election of 1928, the candidates of the Communist and Socialist parties received a total of just under 300,000 votes (90% of these for the Socialist, Norman Thomas) from among the 38 million voters casting ballots that year. Four years later, the combined total of the two left-wing parties leaped to almost one million (880,000 of them Socialist) in a slightly larger voter turnout. Even so, this increase of over 300 percent could hardly encourage radicals. After all, in 1912 Eugene V. Debs, the Socialist party candidate, had gained almost 900,000 supporters at a time when the electorate numbered barely 15 million. As one veteran socialist noted after the 1932 election, "Everything that the Socialists predicted in the way of breakdown of the capitalist system is coming to pass." Yet support for the traditional parties remained overwhelming.

The distinctive character of the American political system undercut potential support for radical parties. The country's vast geographical dimensions, its highly decentralized system of government, its winner-take-all method of conducting elections, and over a century of practice and tradition buttressed the two-party system. And the polyglot nature of American society helped insure that the two parties remained shifting coalitions of diverse interests and groups rather than vehicles for working-class politics. Through the nineteenth century, especially on the local level, working people had indeed created political organizations to control their communities and voice their interests. During the first two decades of the twentieth century, workers had enthusiastically participated in socialist politics that gained representation in scores of cities and in rural and mining areas in the Southwest. During the 1910s, two Socialist congressmen sat in the House of Representatives, sent by working-class constituencies in Milwaukee and New York City.

For the most part, however, working-class voters had given their support to the Democratic party. Usually this affinity had little to do with economic issues but was based rather on ethnocultural concerns. Historically, the Democratic party had been less threatening than its Republican rival to the cultural traditions of Catholic and Jewish immigrants. Its leaders, especially in the large eastern and middle western cities into which so many newcomers flocked, were less inclined than their GOP counterparts to interfere with the religious, social, and educational practices of immigrant groups. They were more likely to absorb political leaders from the various ethnic groups into the party's hierarchy. And since the Democratic party was extraordinarily decentralized, having virtually no national structure at all, the fact that a less tolerant, increasingly xenophobic southern wing also used the Democracy for its vehicle in national politics made little difference to northern urban workers of Italian, Polish, or Jewish extraction.

Even this indirect, ethnoculturally based affinity of immigrant workers for the Democratic party was weak. Through the 1920s, powerful GOP machines in Philadelphia and Chicago rested on immigrant, working-class votes. Skilled workers in the construction trades and on the railroads often voted Republican, identifying the GOP's probusiness reputation as a positive force in maintaining high levels of employment and wages. Indeed, in 1928 prominent labor leaders all but wrote off the Democratic party. The secretary-treasurer of the American Federation of Labor observed that "party spirit has disappeared as far as the great mass of workers is concerned," while mineworkers' chief John L. Lewis declared that Herbert Hoover "is the foremost industrial statesman of modern times."

The flow of voters from the Republican party into the Democratic fold between 1928 and 1932 had only a tenuous class character. Political analysts charted the defection of Republican voters and the entry of new elements into the balloting largely in terms of geographical regions and ethnic groups rather than in terms of class backgrounds. Still, careful observers noted that the increasingly anti-Republican trend in local and state elections and in the 1930 congressional races was strongest in the large cities with their immigrant and working-class masses. Franklin Roosevelt's great victory in 1932, while in good part a continuation of previous trends and a result of Roosevelt's uncanny ability to unite the diverse elements in the often-chaotic Democratic party, contained a large, if temporarily submerged, element of working-class support.

Even successful politics, however, did little in the short run to help devastated families and jobless workers. The political and legislative processes were maddeningly slow in operation and often ambiguous in results. For example, the GOP suffered sharp setbacks in the 1930 congressional races, but the Republicans continued to hold the presidency and a majority in the Senate. Moreover, the new Congress did not meet until thirteen months after the election. As a result, even the rather cautious efforts of progressives in both parties to pass relief measures and programs to employ the jobless became tangled in the endlessly complex intricacies of a divided government. The years between 1930 and 1933, in the words of historian Jordan Schwartz, remained an "interregnum of despair" insofar as hopes for governmental response to economic crisis was concerned.

Nor could Roosevelt's supporters point with any confidence to specific proposals by their candidate that might promise better times. An enormously charming and compassionate man, as deft a politician as ever led a party, Roosevelt hammered away at the dismal record of his opponent. Although he had compiled a progressive record during two terms as governor of New York, in the 1932 presidential campaign he carefully avoided controversial proposals, for he knew that only a monumental blunder on his part could rescue the doomed Hoover. Thus, although workers stood aloof from radical political options and generally supported the optimistic but essentially programless Roosevelt, they could hardly feel that he and his party offered immediate relief. Surely the confident, even jaunty FDR, backed as he would be by solid Democratic majorities in both houses, offered a stirring contrast to the defeated, embittered Hoover. But for the time being the American people would have to be content with the bracing words of Roosevelt's inaugural address. They could only hope that this patrician with the common touch might succeed in bringing the country back to life.

If political action was an uncertain means of working-class protest, the trade union movement appeared no more promising. At a time of mass unemployment, labor unions naturally retreated into defensive postures, hoping to protect existing memberships and to prevent wage cuts and layoffs. Perhaps unions with close ties to anticapitalist parties, such as characterized most European labor movements, might have combined defensiveness at the workplace with advocacy of broad social goals. But American unions, as represented in the American Federation of Labor (AFL), had distanced themselves from the country's weak socialist movement. In the early 1930s, the AFL, which embraced about 85 percent of the country's organized workers, adhered to a policy of "voluntarism," opposing relief and welfare legislation and stressing the need for workers to depend on their own economic strength. Under the impact of the depression, the AFL unions attempted to convince employers that maintenance of wage standards would help keep mass purchasing power afloat, thus providing the consumer demand needed to ride out the slump. Labor chiefs vigorously opposed proposals for federal unemployment relief and other social welfare measures, programs long since endorsed by the socialist and labor movements of Western Europe. Intrusion of the federal or state government into unemployment compensation, declared one AFL leader in December 1930, would be "a resort fraught with the direst of consequences . . . [and] prey to abuse and chicanery."

Nor could the AFL point to militant organizing and mass activism. Since the war, its membership had plummeted, declining from nearly 5 million in 1919 to under 3 million in 1933. Moreover, the workers who remained organized belonged to unions largely outside the great mass production industries. Steel, autos, rubber, textiles, and other mass employment sectors contained but a handful of union members. Construction, local transport, and the entertainment and printing trades provided over 60 percent of all AFL members. Having suffered a crushing defeat in its effort to organize steel in 1919–20, the AFL had languished in torpor and apathy throughout the 1920s. Its only gesture toward mass organizing was an abortive campaign in the auto industry that collapsed almost as soon as it had begun when employers ignored the AFL's plea for worker-employer harmony under the AFL banner.

Worsening conditions did not improve the organizing climate. Strikes remained infrequent. But gradually AFL officials discovered the limits to voluntarism. Certainly, radical unionists, both in AFL unions and in the few separate Socialist and Communist organizations, kept up a drumbeat of demands on the government to come to the aid of the jobless and destitute. Even mainline AFL union leaders began to speak out. In 1931 George Berry of the Printing Pressmen, a union traditionalist, broke with voluntarism, declaring that "our capitalistic system requires a radical reorganization." At the AFL convention that year traditionalists and innovators clashed in heated debate over the need for federal action on unemployment, and in 1932 the AFL openly endorsed federal funding of unemployment compensation, a drastic break with a half century of pure voluntarism. After the 1932 election, AFL president William Green, as cautious and circumspect a unionist as the nation had ever produced, declared that "we have been irresistibly forced to take new positions . . . and to adjust ourselves to the changed order." Two months later he told a congressional committee that if Congress did not enact legislation in behalf of working people, the labor movement would call "a universal strike." These were bold words indeed for a man whose blandness and conservatism were legendary. And when one senator protested that Green seemed to be threatening class war, Green began to sound like a red radical. Class war? Yes, he admitted, "it would be that. . . . That is the only language that a lot of employers ever understand—the language of force."

Whatever Green's newfound rhetoric, organized labor called no general strike. Communist-sponsored unions in metalworking, mining, and textiles enrolled a few thousand members and conducted several hapless strikes. The Socialist-led Amalgamated Clothing Workers of America struggled to keep itself afloat, as its roster of dues payers, which once held almost 180,000 names, shrank to 7,000 in 1933. In the early 1930s the construction unions, the very heart and soul of the AFL, lost 336,000 members. And even those unions that did attempt to press forward in the midst of the crisis found few recruits. Even where workers were interested, few could afford to pay dues, however low. John Burke, president of the Pulp and Paper Workers union, spoke for many of his colleagues in the labor movement in the summer of 1930 as he watched his ranks melt away. "The only thing the unions can do during these times," he lamented, "is to hang on and . . . try to save our organization."

In January 1933, two months after Roosevelt's victory and two months before his inauguration, strikes broke out in key automobile plants in Detroit. Workers at Briggs, the largest auto body manufacturer in the country, responded to the latest in a series of wage cuts by walking out, first at one plant, then another. Soon workers at a rival body manufacturer joined them. By early February, some 12,000 body workers were out. Their strike idled another 100,000 autoworkers, dependent on a steady supply of bodies to keep the production lines going.

Briggs workers had deep grievances. Throughout the 1920s, the company's plants had been notorious for their miserable working conditions and unsafe operations. In 1927, an explosion and fire at one Briggs facility killed at least twenty-one workers. Detroit trolley conductors ruefully dubbed the Mack Avenue plant "the slaughterhouse" as they called off the stops. With the onset of the depression, the company slashed wages repeatedly and accelerated the pace of operations. "If poison doesn't work, try Briggs," a bit of Detroit working-class gallows humor, captured the reality of the company's reputation. The dangerous conditions, the killing pace of operations, and the repeated wage cuts triggered this wave of walkouts and sustained a strike that lasted over six weeks through the cold Michigan winter.

In the end, the forces of law and property prevailed. The presence of Communists among the strikers' leadership facilitated the inevitable red-baiting. Divisions among the strikers, the recruitment of scabs, police harassment, and the ability of the company to achieve near-normal levels of production eventually drove the workers back into the plants— if indeed they could avoid the blacklist and regain their jobs. In a sense, the Briggs walkout was simply another chapter in the same old story in Detroit and other mass production centers. Powerful corporations, reinforced by compliant public authorities and an antilabor press, had once again crushed an embryonic labor organization. But to some of the Briggs workers, historian Joyce Shaw Peterson observes, things seemed different this time. The Briggs strike, she believes, "seemed to workers in the auto industry qualitatively and quantitatively different from other auto walkouts." Years later, one of the strike leaders reflected back on the experience. "In one sense," Leon Pody admitted, "the strike was a lost cause." But he and other strikers drew strength and comradeship from the experience. They had, after all, gained some concessions in the early weeks of the strike, and they had curtailed the operations at Briggs and other auto plants for over a month. Workers, veterans of the strike later recalled, began to feel a sense of their own power.

"There is no such thing as a lost strike," declares an old working-class adage. Most likely, these hopeful words sustained few Detroit strikers as they picked up the pieces after their defeat in the winter of 1933. Still, a display of worker solidarity, however brief, offered hope for the future. Perhaps the new administration, elected with the widespread support of working-class voters, could stop the slide and begin the recovery.

Rebirth of the Unions, 1933–1939

In 1932, Professor George Barnett, one of the nations's leading students of the labor movement, painted a doleful picture of organized labor's prospects. Wracked by the depression and suffering under timid and unimaginative leadership, unions, he believed, were exercising "lessening importance . . . in American economic organization." Indeed, Barnett saw "no reason to believe that American trade unionism will so revolutionize itself . . . as to become in the next decade a more potent social influence than it has been in the past decade." The cumbersome phraseology carried a harsh judgment: The day of the unions had passed. Rarely has so expert an authority been so wrong.

UNIONS REVIVED

The revival of the labor movement was as unexpected as it was dramatic. Between 1932 and 1939, membership soared from under 3 million to almost 9 million. Workers everywhere surged into unions. Whereas the AFL's strength normally lay in the construction, hand craft, and entertainment trades, by the end of the 1930s powerful new organizations in mass production industries embraced hundreds of thousands of recruits. The unparalleled expansion of the labor movement involved the revival of such venerable organizations as the United Mine Workers and such other long-established AFL affiliates as the Carpenters, Machinists, and Teamsters. But the rise of new organizations in steel, automobiles, rubber, electrical appliances, and other core industries and the emergence of a new national federation, the Congress of Industrial Organizations (CIO), truly transformed the labor movement.

In the past, organized labor had experienced several remarkable surges of growth. In Jacksonian America, workingmen's parties and unions had flourished for a season. Again, in the 1880s the Knights of

Labor had reached hundreds of thousands with its gospel of mass organization and workers' power. And during World War I union membership had mushroomed as labor moved into previously unorganized industries and in 1919 made a bold bid to capture the steel industry.

The upsurge of the 1930s, however, was different. It swept up workers in every geographical area and in every trade and industry. It persevered through misfortunes, setbacks, and repression. Workers and union leaders exhibited an ability to match struggles on the shop floors and picket lines with effective political action. Unlike earlier episodes of union growth, this one generated permanent mass organizations, capable of asserting and defending workers' rights on both the political and economic fronts.

Underlying this remarkable achievement lay the determination of working people to resist the victimization and distress that the depression had brought. Throughout the 1930s, unionists, journalists, government observers, and academic experts puzzled over the mood of working people. Did the economic crisis breed resignation and self-blame? Would it spark resentment and radicalism? Would the broken promises of the golden twenties cause embittered workers to abandon the American system; would they embrace some authoritarian alternative, as the German and Italian people appeared to be doing?

In a nation of over 140 million people there could be no simple answer to these questions. Yet the pattern of workers' behavior in the 1930s did permit some conclusions. Throughout the decade workers were uncommonly militant. They resisted further erosion of their standards and struggled to create and sustain organizations to buttress their position and safeguard their working conditions and pay packets. They made clear political choices, voting in heavy numbers and casting their ballots for Franklin D. Roosevelt and politicians closely identified with his policies. They showed little interest in radical parties or unions, and they overwhelmingly avoided extremism.

This particular brand of working-class militancy was complex, and it was far from universal. Many workers continued to regard unions as foreign and distasteful. Ethnic and sexual rivalries often weakened activism. Workers calculated an investment in union dues as carefully in terms of benefits anticipated as they did any other family purchase. Close observers detected a strong strain of cautious defensiveness behind even the most militant activism. Pennsylvania steelworkers, for example, saw the new union as an opportunity to create a system of security to support traditional family values, regarding the broader purposes of the labor movement as irrelevant. Workers wanted stability, protection from arbitrary personnel policies—freedom (in the words of a New York State paper worker) from "the petty tyrannies of our supts. and foremen during the depression."

The desire for the union contract lay at the heart of the militancy of the 1930s. Workers felt mystified at complex, ever-shifting systems of payment. They resented the favoritism, arbitrariness, and cruelty of hiring practices that forced workers to abase themselves for preference in employment and that discarded older workers in favor of presumably more vigorous younger ones. Workers in the 1930s resolved to limit managerial authority and to safeguard their standards and status with clear contractual safeguards. One union activist observed bitterly that his employer "refuses to sign a contract for labor when every piece of machinery or stick of wood is bought through a written contract. Certainly," he argued, "buying labor is just as important." Much of the activism of the 1930s aimed at changing this situation.

This seemingly humble goal, however, aroused bitter opposition. Its achievement required huge organizing campaigns, unprecedented political activism, massive strikes, and great sacrifices. Some critics believed that "mere" contractual relationships only solidified the basic capitalist system. Collective bargaining, argued some leftists, only led to cooptation of workers by employers. Only revolutionary struggle that refused to compromise with illegitimate capitalist authority merited working-class commitment.

But things looked different to American businessmen. Utilization of labor without restriction was central to the innovative heart of the American economy, they believed. Earlier in the century, aggressive employers under the banner of the open shop had broken the power of many established craft unions precisely so that engineers and managers could impose their version of efficient, unrestricted production. Union work rules, contractual grievance and seniority rights, and other union-imposed regulations and customs, they believed, stifled the creative genius of the American system.

Moreover, it was an article of faith among employers that few workers genuinely desired union representation. The craft unions, charged critics, benefitted only a small cadre of highly skilled workers. So America's largest and most powerful corporations, as well as her smaller shops and factories, fiercely resisted unionism. While some industrialists preferred accommodation to open conflict, most regarded industrial unionism with the same fear, suspicion, and determination to resist that their predecessors accorded to craft unionism.

Early in the Roosevelt administration, workers began to give evidence of their newfound activism. Enthusiastic reaction to passage of the National Industrial Recovery Act on June 16, 1933, revealed discontents and hopes seething beneath the surface of working-class life. Section 7(a) of the new law declared that workers had the right to bargain collectively with their employers through representatives of their own choosing. The law implied that it was illegitimate for employers to stifle unions, interfere with efforts to form unions, or refuse to enter into bargaining relationships. The primary purpose of the Recovery Act was to stimulate economic recovery through a National Recovery Administration (NRA). This body relied on business groups and trade associations to develop codes of fair competition that would be binding on all firms enjoying their protection. Despite the decidedly probusiness cast of the NRA, however, its establishment gave hope to thousands of workers and stimulated the formation of unions under the promised protection of Section 7(a).

The most dramatic growth spread through the nation's soft coal regions. John L. Lewis, president of the United Mine Workers of America (UMW), had watched his once-powerful miners union shrink from membership of a half million in 1919 to under 80,000 in the early 1930s. Lewis himself seemed to personify the combination of ruthlessness, cynicism, and ineptitude that caused observers such as Professor Barnett to despair of organized labor's future prospects.

But Lewis had helped to draft the labor section of the Recovery Act. A series of strikes in the impoverished Appalachian coal fields in 1931 and 1932 had reaffirmed the coal miners' legendary militancy. He believed that Section 7(a) could provide the spark needed to revive his union and perhaps the entire labor movement. He committed the UMW's shaky finances to rebuilding the union. Scores of organizers invaded the coal towns, mining camps, and backwater hollows preaching the gospel of the UMW and the NRA.

"The President wants you to join the union," organizers told recruits, stretching the truth but effectively linking the campaign with the popularity of Franklin Roosevelt. Reports from Ohio, Kentucky, West Virginia, and New Mexico poured in. By the end of June, Pennsylvania alone claimed 128,000 new members. Veteran organizer Van A. Bittner declared that Logan County, West Virginia, scene of a bloody civil war in the early 1920s, had become union territory. Nor did workers require much convincing, for, as Lewis's long-time critic John Brophy observed, coal miners "moved into the union *en masse*. . . . They organized themselves for all practical purposes."

Results in the needle trades, like coal mining traditionally a bastion of unionism, were almost as impressive. The two most vigorous organizations in the garment industry were the International Ladies Garment

Workers Union (ILGW) and the Amalgamated Clothing Workers union (ACW). Their leaders, David Dubinsky of the ILGW and Sidney Hillman of the ACW, were Jewish immigrants with roots in the socialist organizations associated with Jewish working-class culture. Both rejected the AFL's disdainful attitudes toward female, immigrant, and unskilled workers, and both believed that trade unionism had to move beyond AFL voluntarism. But both organizations had had to struggle through the 1920s and had fought to maintain standards in an anti-union era. Meanwhile, Communist dissidents, eager to enlist garment workers in the crusade to bring to America the revolutionary transformation that in 1917 had swept Russia, waged sharp battles to control important locals. The depression devastated the garment trades and the unions, pushing both the ILGW and the ACW toward disaster. In 1933, Hillman's union, which held almost 180,000 members in 1920, now claimed 60,000 but collected dues from only 7,000. Dubinsky's Ladies Garment Workers declined from 120,000 to under 40,000 on paper, and key locals faced disintegration.

Both leaders grasped the opportunities that the new legislation offered. Through the summer of 1933, the Amalgamated fought successful organizing campaigns in New York, Boston, Philadelphia, and Rochester. It recruited thousands of new members in hitherto unorganized segments of the men's clothing trade, extending its influence into the shirt shops of rural Pennsylvania, New Jersey, and Connecticut. In some of the small mining towns, garment factories provided low-wage employment for miners' wives and children, and in these places Amalgamated organizers linked up with Lewis's resurgent UMW locals to recruit whole families into the revitalized labor movement. By the end of 1933, Hillman's organization had doubled its membership.

The ILGW expanded even more impressively. Taking on Philadelphia ladies garment manufacturers even before passage of the NIRA, in May 1933, the ILGW won a major strike in that city. Another walkout in August rebuilt the union in the decisive women's dress industry in New York City. Strikes and organizing campaigns in New York and outlying areas extended the ILGW's gains, and when the union's convention met in May 1934, Dubinsky pointed proudly to membership rolls topping 200,000.

These stunning gains reached far beyond the industries themselves. All three unions had traditions of mass industrial organization. All three featured bold, energetic leadership. Moreover, the three reborn organizations teemed with activist workers unusually loyal to their unions and to the cause of trade unionism in general. "The rebuilding of the UMW, the Amalgamated, and the ILGWU in 1933," observes Irving Bernstein, "was of the utmost significance . . . to the future of the American labor movement. These developments formed an axle upon which trade unionism was to turn for most of a decade."

But labor's gains went far beyond these areas of traditional strength. Indeed, the most remarkable development of the early New Deal years was the explosion of organizing throughout the nation and in industries and trades with little previous unionism or with long records of defeat and despair. Steel and iron workers signed up with the AFL affiliate with jurisdiction over the industry, the Amalgamated Association of Iron, Steel, and Tin Workers (AA). Pulp and paper workers—some veterans of agonizing strike defeats in the 1920s, others new recruits—flocked into two established AFL unions in the industry. "I have so many calls for organizers," declared the Pulp Workers' president in July, "that I have neither the men nor the money to take care of all of them." By August, the union had depleted its stock of dues books and payment stamps. AFL unions in the construction trades, which normally recruited very selectively, found themselves besieged with applications from workers of every description.

Whole categories of workers with no previous record of activism sought unionism. From Filipino fruit pickers to newspaper editorial employees, and from Hollywood actors to dry cell battery workers, thousands signed up. Workers in auto plants, rubber factories, and electrical appliance shops joined despite their lack of previous laborite experience. In all, the AFL gained about 500,000 members in 1933 and added 400,000 in 1934.

This vast new recruitment created difficulties for the Federation's staid leadership. The flood of new members overwhelmed cautious union bureaucrats, comfortable in their tenure and now threatened by the sudden influx. The AA, for example, could not cope with the newly militant contingent of steelworkers, and the opportunity to bring mass organization to the furnaces, mills, and fabricating shops slipped through their fingers. Tens of thousands of new union enthusiasts worked in trades not easily classified under the AFL's antiquated system of jurisdiction. The unions that held the bulk of power in the AFL simply could not deal with recruits from the mass production industries, most of whom toiled in semiskilled or unskilled jobs. Machine operators and assemblers in the auto plants, for example, were not machinists in the usual sense of the term, for typically they served no apprenticeship, held no journeyman's card, and could not claim conditions of autonomous, independent craftsmanship. Were these semiskilled operatives eligible for membership in the International Association of Machinists? If so, their vast numbers would overwhelm the traditional membership, whose highly prized skills had enabled the union to gain impressive pension and wage benefits. If not, what AFL affiliate could properly claim these hopeful new recruits? Most large AFL affiliates faced this problem. For example, would the thousands of unskilled and semiskilled workers in the expanding electrical appliances industry be enrolled as full members in the venerable International Brotherhood of Electrical Workers? What of the large numbers of lumber and sawmill workers seeking organization and falling under the jurisdiction of the haughty United Brotherhood of Carpenters and Joiners? The policies and structures of the most powerful AFL unions were geared to the needs of skilled workers and seemed unable to accommodate the newly organizing masses.

To what AFL organization, for example, would the thousands of rubber workers in Ohio, Maryland, Massachusetts, and Alabama belong? What of the groups of button makers, pen and pencil workers, casket makers, onion pickers, warehouse loaders, salt miners, and new activists in a hundred other trades and occupations from Florida to Washington state who sought union representation in the heady days of 1933 and 1934? The AFL, a sober, tradition-bound organization, had never before needed to respond to such an upheaval of union sentiment. Its leadership, delighted but perplexed at this sudden turn of fortunes, hastily issued charters to hundreds of groups, packing them into so-called "federal labor unions," organizations directly run by the AFL itself. In due time AFL officials would sort out these recruits and dole them out to the appropriate craft unions.

In accordance with AFL policies, a shop that had organized as one integrated body would find that AFL functionaries wanted to break up this unity. Established unions insisted that particular groups of workers, regardless of the auspices under which they were first organized, be turned over to the AFL affiliate that normally represented those with similar skills or functions. AFL traditionalists believed that if they retreated from this policy, they would undermine the strength of the established unions, many of which had gained success by tight control of the job market. For workers in mass production industries, however, this approach made no sense. If AFL policies prevailed, the comradeship and strength of union solidarity would give way to fragmentation, as workers in the same shop found themselves suddenly dispatched to the Teamsters, Carpenters, or Sheet Metal Workers.

In addition, Federation officials, wedded as they were to policies of restraint, caution, and legalistic notions of correct union behavior, soon found that these new recruits demanded action. For newly organized workers, the act of joining a labor union often required courage. They expected to remain together in the same local union, regardless of the diverse jobs workers performed. And they expected their bold step of joining a union to pay off, at least in the form of vigorous leadership on the part of AFL officials. When Federation functionaries responded— as they usually did to the demands of newly organized locals—with counsels of delay, restraint, and moderation, disaffection spread almost as quickly as enthusiasm had earlier.

1934: CONFLICT ABOUNDING

Throughout 1934, this tension between an established bureaucratic labor movement and volatile new recruits underlay an extraordinary spasm of labor unrest and violence. Work stoppages in that year totaled over 1,800 and involved over 1.5 million strikers. These were the highest figures for work stoppages since the early 1920s. In part, the strike wave resulted from the mild economic upturn that the enthusiastic initial public reaction to the NRA had created. In part also, it reflected worker discontent with the limitations of labor policy under the new federal recovery program. Many of the walkouts were routine labor-management confrontations, but some of the strikes convulsed whole communities and industries. In the summer of 1934, several key strikes exhibited a lethal bitterness rarely matched in American history.

In May, for example, thousands of unionists and their allies confronted police and national guardsmen in Toledo, Ohio. Throughout the day of May 24, soldiers and strikers charged and countercharged on the streets outside the Auto-Lite factory, focal point of a strike of auto parts workers enrolled in a federal labor union. Guardsmen hurled tear gas into the crowd. They fixed bayonets and drove it back, only to yield as unionists and sympathizers retook their ground, attempting to force strikebreakers out of the plant. After hours of savage street fighting, the ill-trained troops leveled their rifles and fired into the crowd, killing two and wounding scores. Even so, fighting lasted into the night, and the next day Ohio governor George White dispatched more guardsmen while the Toledo Central Labor Union, representing eighty local unions, debated calling a general strike.

Later that summer, violence erupted in San Francisco and Minneapolis. In the Bay City, striking longshoremen linked up with rank-and-file Teamsters and cargo handlers to paralyze the waterfront. When police began to escort strikebreakers to the piers, a pitched battle erupted. Police bullets killed two strikers. A mass public funeral on July 9 brought the city to a standstill. Thousands upon thousands of strikers and supporters marched through the city, accompanying the hearse to the strains of the march from Beethoven's *Eroica* symphony. Historian Charles Larrowe describes the scene: "Tramp—tramp—tramp—grave and grim, on they came; there seemed no end to the procession. Long after the trucks bearing the coffins had passed . . . the phalanxes of the marchers escorting the bodies . . . continued."

Two weeks later, conflict shook Minneapolis. A newly expanded Teamsters' local, embracing hundreds of truckers, freight-handlers, and produce loaders, struck in protest over the cargo and freight companies' refusal to bargain. The strike brought commerce to a halt, with the highly disciplined strikers permitting only deliveries of essential medical and emergency food supplies. With the aid of local police, the cartage company resolved to crack the street barricades and resume deliveries. On Friday afternoon, July 20, one large yellow truck, escorted by fifty armed policemen, rolled into the central market area to unload a few token boxes. As it moved slowly off, a vehicle bearing club-wielding pickets cut it off. The police blasted away at the car with shotgun fire and then turned their weapons on the strikers filling the surrounding streets. As other pickets moved up to aid their fallen comrades, an eyewitness reported, "They flowed directly into the buckshot fire. . . . And the cops let them have it as they picked up their wounded. Lines of living, solid men fell, broke, wavering." He saw one man "stepping on his own intestines, bright and bursting in the street, and another holding his severed arm in his right hand." A troubled calm fell upon the city, as the strikers counted their losses—two dead and sixty-seven wounded.

The summer's agony ended in September with the massive strike of textile workers in New England and the South. The AFL's weakly organized United Textile Workers, unable to compel employers to recognize its unions but goaded by rank-and-file impatience, reluctantly called its people out of the mills. Over 400,000 cotton and fabric workers responded. Local police and national guardsmen clashed with angry pickets, as mill owners recruited strikebreakers to maintain production and crush the unions. At Trion, Georgia, on September 5, a union supporter and a sheriff's deputy died in an exchange of gunfire. In neighboring South Carolina the next day, bullets killed six pickets. A crowd of 10,000 gathered on the eighth in the small mill town of Honea Path to bury the dead. Two more textile workers died and twenty more fell wounded as riots and demonstrations swept through the dreary textile towns in Rhode Island, Connecticut, Massachusetts, and Maine.

The upheavals of 1934 held important lessons for working-class activists. The AFL too often provided only dilatory and unresponsive leadership. Lack of solid organization too frequently led to defeat. The NRA, seemingly so promising as an instrument of worker power, proved unable to enforce its vague mandate to encourage collective bargaining. Yet the San Francisco longshoremen, the Minneapolis truckers, and the Toledo strikers learned that strong local organizations, determined leaders, and mass support could bring gains. Despite the ineptitude of AFL officials, the antagonism of employers and local authorities, and the weakness of NRA functionaries, workers won at least partial victories in these strikes.

THE WAGNER ACT

The limitations of the machinery established under the NRA to enforce Section 7(a) became starkly apparent during the 1934 turbulence. Though the legislation declared that workers had the right to create unions free of employer control, it provided no means of enforcement. In theory, a Labor Advisory Board (LAB) heard complaints and brought them to the attention of NRA code compliance authorities. These officials in turn could recommend that NRA director General Hugh Johnson strip offending companies of code protection. Presumably, this would put the offender at great competitive disadvantage, and hence the threat of removal of the NRA's emblem of compliance, the Blue Eagle symbol, would induce employers to honor the provisions of Section 7(a).

In reality, this mechanism almost never operated. The grossly understaffed LAB could not keep track of the widespread violations. Nor did its functionaries have high regard for labor unionists, considering them ignorant and self-serving, impediments to the board's work. Sneered one LAB official, unionists were so "green and lacking in insight" that their inclusion in NRA proceedings was mere "window dressing." Moreover, NRA officials in general regarded Section 7(a) as an unfortunate provision, an embarrassment rather than an integral part of the recovery program. Code-enforcement authorities believed that workers' interests were best protected in the codes themselves, which stipulated wage minimums, limitations on hours of work, and other labor provisions. Unions did not fit into the picture, whatever the apparent language of Section 7(a). When union growth brought with it strikes and confrontations, NRA officials reacted impatiently. Labor unrest merely delayed recovery. Where the union was strong, officials accommodated themselves reluctantly to its power. Where it was weak or illorganized, they ignored or bypassed it. Despite the apparent promises of Section 7(a), the actual policy of NRA officials was, in the words of historian Cletus Daniel, "antiunion in theory" and often "it proved antiunion in practice."

At least NRA administrator Johnson and most of his key advisors seemed to share this view. Unionists, however, had friends in the Roosevelt administration, especially in Congress. Astute Democrats saw a resurgent labor movement as an ally of their party and as a critical element in economic recovery. Senator Robert F. Wagner, for example, emerged as a leading critic of the NRA's uncertainty in regard to Section 7(a). The New York Democrat believed that only a revitalized labor movement could protect workers' rights. Moreover, he held that mass purchasing power provided the essential stimulus to economic recovery; strong unions, Wagner argued, would raise wages and thus provide a powerful engine of economic growth. So when employers violated workers' rights and when NRA officials responded ineffectually, Wagner threatened congressional action.

The president had no fixed views on these matters. If anything, he leaned toward the more paternalistic approach of Johnson and the NRA hierarchy. Certainly, he found the strike wave of 1934 distracting. He dispatched representatives to trouble spots, hoping to quell unrest by appeasing or cajoling the aggrieved parties and thus get workers back to their jobs so that the recovery program could proceed without further delay. But Wagner was a power in the Democratic party, and Roosevelt had no desire to alienate him or an expanding labor movement. On August 5, 1933, he created the National Labor Board (NLB), a seven-member panel charged with investigating and resolving labor disputes arising under the NRA. The board was empowered to conduct elections among workers to determine whether they wanted union representation. Presumably, once the NLB held an election, employers would abide by the results and would enter into a bargaining relationship if the union won. In a typically Rooseveltian stroke, the president named Wagner to the new agency, thus neatly sidetracking the senator's threatened legislative investigation.

But neither the NLB nor a successor agency, the National Labor Relations Board, which replaced it in June 1934, proved effective. While the personnel of these labor boards were more sympathetic to unionism than were NRA functionaries, they remained essentially powerless. They could bring disputing parties together. They could recommend settlements. They could conduct elections. But in the final analysis, they had only the power that the law itself, the original National Industrial Recovery Act, granted. NLB investigators and board members simply had no means of forcing employers to recognize unions or to engage in collective bargaining.

These limitations proved particularly damaging in cases involving the discharge or harassment of union activists. Employers found that the firing of a vocal rank and filer or the layoff of a local union officer invariably had a chilling effect on workers' enthusiasm for organization. If the union could not protect these militants by securing reinstatement, ordinary workers drew back from signing a union card or wearing a union button. Yet laborites turning to the labor board for relief found little satisfaction. However sympathetic, the agents of these bodies could only try to persuade employers to reconsider. Even when they did gain reinstatement, aggrieved activists rarely received back pay, nor did employers suffer any punishment.

A determined employer had many devices with which to thwart the apparent intent of Section 7(a). Even where a union won a representation election, neither the law nor any NRA regulation required that the employer deal only with the majority organization. He could, and many did, claim that those workers who voted against the union also deserved consideration, and many employers entered into talks with representatives of the "loyal" (i.e., anti-union) employees as well as with those of the pro-union faction. Playing one side off against the other, employers could reward the "loyal" employees with minor concessions while protracting negotiations with the bona fide (or trade union) group. One Wisconsin employer offered advice to a colleague threatened with the virus of unionism. String out negotiations, he counseled. "I cannot help but feel that if you follow such a stalling procedure . . . this thing will wash out." Since nonunion employees, who paid no dues and faced no management displeasure, received minor benefits from a benign employer, unionists would rapidly grow disillusioned. "The employees," he counseled, "are quick to lose interest because in joining the union their natural expectancy is that they are going to secure some immediate benefits." Soon, he predicted, "they rapidly [will] start dropping out of the union." The labor board had no remedy for these tactics.

In 1934, autoworkers grew particularly disillusioned with the NRA. Through the summer and fall of 1933, thousands of workers in auto and auto parts plants had joined dozens of new federal labor unions. AFL president William Green dispatched veteran organizers to advise and direct these raw recruits, who in turn often chafed under the unimaginative leadership of these old-timers. Throughout its brief history, the auto industry had fought all unions. Union sentiment had flared up in the wake of World War I, and small groups of left-wing activists and skilled tradesmen kept a union presence alive through the 1920s and early depression years. As the 1933 Briggs strike had revealed, lack of viable unions was not necessarily a result of worker satisfaction or docility. So the surge of autoworkers into the federal unions came as no surprise to veteran activists and observers.

Joining the union was one thing. Wrenching a signed contract or even merely protecting rank-and-file activists was quite another. Some employers, notably the huge Ford Motor Company, refused even to participate in the NRA and openly pursued blatantly anti-union policies. Even NRA participants—including such powerful corporations as General Motors, Chrysler, Bendix, Auto-Lite, Briggs, and scores of other parts and body manufacturers—fought the union menace without quarter. Throughout late 1933 and into 1934, these employers waged no-holds-barred warfare against the new locals, firing activists, imposing company-controlled organizations, and refusing to bargain.

In 1934, impatient autoworkers threatened to push the timid AFL leadership into an auto strike. The Roosevelt administration, cooperating closely with fearful AFL leaders and obliging industry officials, sought to resolve the conflict by creating a special body, the Automobile Labor Board, to deal with labor disputes in this critical industry. Without the vigorous support of the AFL—and perhaps realizing that a mass strike against the auto giants had little hope of success—autoworkers grudgingly acquiesced. But the board's limited power and ineffectual personnel did nothing. Employers continued their assaults on the disintegrating unions without penalty. By the summer of 1934, autoworkers by the thousands had abandoned the federal unions. Lamented one local leader in July: "Since March our membership has fallen away in appalling numbers. . . . Our treasuries have been drained. . . . The few remaining loyal members are discouraged."

In all, the AFL lost some 600 of its new federal labor unions in 1934 and early 1935. Once a shining promise of a reborn labor movement, the NRA had become in the eyes of thousands of workers the "National Run Around." Since the NRA's recovery program seemed increasingly ineffectual in general, the muddled labor policies of the Roosevelt administration merely appeared to conform to the pattern of failure increasingly evident in this early phase of the New Deal.

In the spring of 1935, Senator Wagner resumed the initiative in the formulation of labor policy. Convinced of the fatal weaknesses of Section 7(a), he introduced a bill that would reinforce its encouragement of labor organization and collective bargaining. The proposed legislation would establish a powerful new federal agency to safeguard and enforce workers' rights. At the root of Wagner's initiative rested his conviction that labor organization would boost wages and that in the resultant rise of mass purchasing power lay the key to economic recovery.

The Wagner proposal envisaged broad changes in federal labor relations machinery. It would create a three-member National Labor Relations Board (NLRB). This new agency, unlike the similarly named boards that functioned under the NRA, would wield broad powers of investigation and enforcement. The bill included a list of "unfair labor practices," prohibiting specific activities such as financing of company unions, employment of spies, arbitrary firing of activists, and refusal to bargain. Perhaps most important, it mandated representation elections upon workers' request, laid down ground rules for the conduct of those elections, and required that employers engage in collective bargaining exclusively with the party victorious in the election. In all, the Wagner bill reinforced the basic concept of Section 7(a) and lodged primary responsibility for federal activity in labor relations in an independent agency armed with substantial powers of investigation and enforcement.

Through the spring of 1935, the proposal's fate remained uncertain. Organized labor's representatives, of course, supported it in testimony before the Senate Committee on Labor and Education. Despite the law's clear endorsement of unionism and collective bargaining, however, some labor and liberal spokespeople remained wary. Veteran AFL leaders feared that the law would weaken the federation's traditional voluntarism. If labor now relied on a federal agency to gain membership, they worried, the unions might soon find that they were becoming mere appendages to the government. Some radical unionists opposed the legislation's provision for exclusive bargaining rights, believing that it would eliminate dissenting organizations and increase the already bureaucratic nature of mainstream union governance. Business and corporate groups lashed out at Wagner's proposal, arguing that it would violate individual rights, create a top-heavy bureaucracy, and interfere with traditional labor-management relationships. They resented the "unfair labor practices" provision, which, they claimed, singled out and prejudged businessmen as virtual criminals. The Roosevelt administration, still wedded to the top-down approach to recovery embodied in the NRA, gave Wagner no encouragement. Indeed, the president even sent Secretary of Labor Frances Perkins to Capitol Hill to delay congressional action.

On May 27, 1935, however, the United States Supreme Court declared the National Industrial Recovery Act unconstitutional. This bombshell decision dismantled the entire NRA operation. For laborites, it meant that the provisions of Section 7(a), uncertain and disappointing as they were, no longer applied. The events of 1934 had clearly revealed that the potential for labor unrest and even for violent confrontation lay close to the surface; thus, the destruction of the Recovery Act and the sudden elimination of its dispute machinery strengthened Wagner's hand. Doubts about the new legislation faded as administration officials and congressional leaders contemplated the specter of unregulated labor-management confrontation. President Roosevelt clambered aboard the labor law express, seeking to identify the administration with the suddenly popular and seemingly indispensable proposal. Mainstream labor leaders, increasingly aware of the gains they had made under 7(a), swallowed their reservations. Business representatives remained adamant, but on July 5, the National Labor Relations Act became law.

The National Labor Relations (or Wagner) Act was one of the seminal enactments in American history. Building on a half century of experimentation on both state and federal levels, it established basic machinery in the realm of labor relations. It shifted the focus of labor conflict away from violent confrontation toward the hearing rooms and courts. Prior to the passage of the Wagner Act, literally hundreds of workers had been killed and thousands injured in a long history of disputes stretching back into the nineteenth century. After its enactment—and especially after the United States Supreme Court passed favorably on its constitutionality, as it did in March 1937—deaths and serious injuries in labor disputes became rare. In effect, the Wagner Act declared it public policy to encourage collective bargaining through independent unions. It promised that the government would guarantee a fair procedure for determining bargaining rights and for the disposition of charges of unfair practices. While strikes and picket lines remained important, workers could turn to the National Labor Relations Board, operating under clearly specified rules and procedures, to protect their rights. For their part, employers now had to contend with an agency armed with powers that made intimidation, delay, and union-breaking far more costly.

The law was not magic, however. Veteran unionists counseled against complacency. "American workers," declared one long-term union leader, "should not lean too much on the Wagner Labor Disputes Law or any other law." Indeed, until the Supreme Court passed on its constitutionality, the Wagner Act had only limited effect. Many employers, utterly convinced that the Court would strike the new legislation down, continued to fight the unions without restraint. When Court approval finally came, the NLRB did indeed prove a vigorous supporter of union goals, and it played an important role in sustaining union gains during the late 1930s. Still, recruitment of members, building local organizations, and demonstrating strength at the workplace remained the task of the unions. Despite the reassuring presence of the NLRB, the words of the old miners' song remained as true as they ever had been: "You've got to go down and join the union/Join it for yourself/Ain't nobody there to join it for you/ You've got to go down and join the union for yourself."

Nor was the new law without drawbacks for labor unionists. The voluntaristic stance of the old AFL had a point to it. However sympathetic, the NLRB remained outside union control. In an unfriendly administration, its appointees could well use its complex machinery to discourage union growth. The broad powers of the board, while safely enlisted on the unions' side as long as Wagner, Roosevelt, and the New Deal remained in place, could prove two-edged. Moreover, even a friendly board had to operate in a broadly political context. As the board exercised its powers and as difficult questions of interpretation and application of the law emerged, lawyers and bureaucrats stepped to the foreground, often rendering rulings and decisions that brought drastic changes to the collective bargaining process, to the patterns of organization and recruitment, and even to the basic nature of the unions themselves. Thus, for example, is fell to the board to determine appropriate bargaining units. Under what circumstances, rival union organizers, employers, and ordinary workers asked, should all workers in a given plant or shop or group of establishments in a given region or company—be considered a distinct unit for the purposes of holding representation elections and for subsequent bargaining? When was it appropriate for a group of distinctive craftsmen, or specialized workers, to be considered as a separate unit? Such seemingly arcane and pedestrian questions really struck at the heart of the matter of union character, and board decisions caused labor organizations to make profound changes in their structures, policies, and organizing strategies to accommodate the rulings. As some of the AFL's old-line leaders had cautioned, organized labor soon found that basic decisions regarding the future and direction of the labor movement were being made by government bureaucrats and board lawyers, not by the workers' representatives themselves.

JOHN L. LEWIS AND THE CIO

For John L. Lewis the debate over government labor policy remained secondary in 1935 to the crisis that he perceived in the labor movement itself. He believed that the AFL had frittered away the golden opportunity to organize the vast mass production industries. True, at its October 1934 convention, it had adopted a bold-sounding resolution calling for organization of steel, auto, rubber, and other core industries. But Lewis knew from his long experience as a member of the AFL's ruling Executive Council that traditionalist leaders would block any real program of mass organization. Fearful that new recruits would jeopardize power arrangements within their unions, yet unwilling to waive their theoretical jurisdictional claims, such crusty veterans as William Hutcheson of the Carpenters union, Arthur Wharton of the Machinists, Matthew Woll of the Photo Engravers, and Gustave Bugniazet of the Electricians insisted that newly recruited workers be divided up among the established unions after the initial organizing campaign. There they could receive wise counsel, cautious advice, and firm direction from tried and true veterans. New recruits from steel, auto, and rubber, AFL patriarchs believed, were headstrong and foolish. They had no deep attachment to the labor movement and wanted only immediate results. Their inexperience and impatience played into the hands of the corruptionists and radicals forever lurking on the fringes of the labor movement. Mass production workers had to be recruited very carefully and had to be kept under tight control. Otherwise this "rubbish" (as Teamsters president Daniel Tobin once referred to unskilled workers) might destroy the AFL.

But Lewis's Mine Workers had always recruited on an industrial basis, as had the needle trades unions as well as organizations in food processing, paper-making, and some other trades. For these organizations, the solidarity of workers regardless of skill levels or trade had brought great benefits. Moreover, the simple fact of the matter was that modern industry, in which the vast majority of workers toiled, had been making nonsense out of traditional definitions of skill. To John L. Lewis, the equation was starkly clear: as things stood in 1935, the AFL could not organize the central core of American industry. And this inability to organize the millions of workers in this central core doomed the labor movement to political and economic irrelevance. Thus, regardless of federal labor policy, organized labor had to change its course. Wagner Act or no Wagner Act, somebody had to challenge the AFL's backward officialdom.

Late in 1935, Lewis made his move. Fifty-five years old, Lewis had led the UMW since 1919. With his imposing bulk, his mane of thick, graying hair, and his bushy eyebrows, Lewis could be an awesome figure, especially in contrast with the bland men who held power in the AFL. Lewis's larger-than-life physical appearance combined with his stentorian voice to remind reporters of a Shakespearean actor. And Lewis, though he customarily read almost nothing other than newspapers and union documents, obliged by salting his oratory with carefully chosen and well-rehearsed snippets of biblical and classical rhetoric. Some veteran labor reporters and union leaders dismissed Lewis as a power-hungry fraud, pointing to his poor record in the 1920s, his persecution of honorable union rivals, and the monumental ego that made him a stranger to self-doubt. But Lewis's mixture of vainglory, vision, and vigor struck a chord in the mid-1930s. Armed with seemingly absolute self-assurance and buttressed by the financial and organizational power of his reborn UMW, Lewis stepped forth at the AFL's October 1935 convention to challenge the federation's officialdom and to assert the claims of industrial workers.

AFL conventions were tedious affairs. Guest speakers, pious clergymen, and stodgy union chiefs droned on from a dais lined with venerable labor leaders and honored public officials. Floor debate rarely disturbed the somnolent convention hall. Delegates from the affiliated unions and from the city and state federations, bedecked with gaudy convention badges, paid little attention to the proceedings, which largely rubber-stamped the resolutions emanating from the tradition-bound Executive Council. Normally lasting at least two weeks, AFL conventions did well by the barkeeps and restaurant owners, for trade unionists tended to be heavy drinkers and big tippers. Labor reporters paid little attention to the scheduled events and attempted to remain alert enough at the endless card-playing and drinking sessions to pick up the odd scrap of gossip that might contain the germs of a story.

Amid this dull routine, Lewis was always a welcome distraction. Striding confidently into a room, surrounded by a worshipful entourage of relatives, bodyguards, and yes-men, the Mine Workers' chief automatically drew journalists into his circle. He was always good for a pithy quote, dressed up with unexpected and high-sounding phrases from the Bard or the Book of Job. And in the 1930s, Lewis truly stood for something. He did have a vision of a powerful, activist labor movement, reinforced with millions of recruits from the steel mills, auto plants, warehouses, and rubber, glass, and cement factories. So when Lewis spoke, as he did frequently at Atlantic City, people paid attention. Though the industrial union forces lost vote after vote on the convention floor as Executive Council resolutions intoned the wisdom and propriety of AFL policies and reaffirmed traditional views of mass production workers, Lewis's sharp dissents became the focus of attention. As the convention drew to a close, an air of troubled expectancy pervaded the hall.

The climax came on October 18. Amid desultory debate relating to the precise jurisdictional rights of federal unions, the powerful traditionalist president of the Carpenters' union, William L. Hutcheson, sought to silence an industrial union advocate through raising a point of order. "This thing of raising points of order all the time on minor delegates," Lewis interjected, "is rather small potatoes." The sixty-one-year-old Hutcheson shot back with choice epithets, calling Lewis, among other things, a "bastard." Lewis's biographers, historians Melvyn Dubofsky and Warren Van Tine, describe what happened next: "Lewis jumped to his feet. Quick as a cat, he leaped over a row of chairs toward Hutcheson, jabbed out his right fist, and sent the carpenters' president sprawling against a table." Hutcheson, his faced bloodied, soon left the convention floor. Meanwhile, reported a journalist, "Lewis casually adjusted his tie and collar, relit his cigar, and sauntered slowly through the crowded aisles," having, literally, dealt AFL traditionalism a staggering blow.

On November 9, Lewis convened a meeting of AFL leaders eager to pursue industrial unionism. Dubinsky, Hillman, and Charles Howard, president of the International Typographical Union (ITU), joined the UMW chief, as did the presidents of four smaller AFL affiliates. The group established a Committee for Industrial Organization (CIO), whose publicly announced purpose was to operate through the AFL to encourage industrial unionism. Lewis and the United Mine Workers provided much of the financial and organizational support for the new body. Although ACW and ILGW members contributed large sums and although Hillman and Dubinsky were influential within the CIO, everyone looked to Lewis as the heart and soul of this new initiative.

The AFL establishment immediately denounced this CIO. Green and his colleagues viewed it as a dual union, that is, a direct rival and threat to the established labor movement. Both Lewis and Hillman dismissed the AFL's complaints. Lewis ostentatiously resigned from the AFL Executive Council, and Hillman had little but contempt for the corrupt and ineffective AFL unions in the clothing field. CIO leaders refrained, however, from severing ties with the AFL, even after the federation's leaders pushed through suspension proceedings in August and October 1936. Lewis publicly ridiculed Green, calling his manhood and intelligence into question in thunderous and orotund press releases. Still, the CIO leaders believed that they could continue to claim sympathetic support among second- and third-level AFL unionists, many of whom shared their disappointment with the Federation's leadership, if the dissidents remained at least nominally attached to the AFL. Also acting as a brake on the more impetuous CIO enthusiasts was Dubinsky. The diminutive head of the ILGW, while generous in support of CIO activities, opposed plans to leave the federation. Indeed, when in November 1938 the CIO at last held a convention, adopted a constitution, and changed its name to Congress of Industrial Organizations, thereby institutionalizing its break with the AFL, Dubinsky refused to go along.

Well before this final break, however, the CIO had begun to function as a separate body. Throughout 1936 and 1937 it provided a dramatic contrast to the old federation. In February of 1936, for example, CIO director John Brophy dispatched representatives to Akron, Ohio, where the AFL United Rubber Workers (URW) confronted the powerful Goodyear Company in a mass strike. While cautious AFL representatives clucked with disapproval over the rubber workers' militancy, the CIO people joined the strikers on the frigid picket lines, addressed their meetings, and provided good copy for the newspaper reporters covering the strike. Although CIO representative Adolph Germer himself grumbled over the rubber workers' disdain for proper procedures, the CIO nonetheless projected an image of forceful commitment to mass organization in Akron, while the confused AFL representatives dropped out of the picture. Few were surprised when in June 1936 the URW defied its AFL advisors and cast its lot with the CIO.

Through 1936, the CIO made spectacular gains on both the organizing and political fronts. In June, Lewis and his associates created a new organization, the Steel Workers Organizing Committee (SWOC), to bring unionism to the nation's half-million steel workers. With Lewis's lieutenant, Philip Murray, in charge, SWOC represented a bold innovation in organizing strategy. Bypassing established unions with jurisdictional claims among steel mill workers, SWOC organizers fanned out into the industrial heartland, encouraging local activists to take over AA locals, supporting CIO militants in company-sponsored unions, and gathering membership in the steel-making centers of Pennsylvania, Ohio, Indiana, and Illinois.

Politically, 1936 was decisive as well. The early success of CIO initiatives could not always hide a certain sense of desperation, even on the part of Lewis and Hillman. Time was running out. Industrial workers, so often disappointed by both the AFL and previous government policies, might well give up on organized labor. The CIO group believed that reelection of Franklin Roosevelt and increased Democratic majorities in Congress were critical to its success. Armed with the new labor legislation and supported by a triumphant New Deal, the CIO could capture millions of members in the auto, steel, rubber, and textiles industries. But a Roosevelt defeat—a prospect that in the summer of 1936 seemed all too possible—would usher in a hostile Republican administration that could gut the Labor Relations Act and bolster anti-union employers. Thus, Lewis and his colleagues threw unprecedented labor support behind the president. The UMW alone contributed over $500,000 to the Democratic war chest, an amount that dwarfed any previous labor commitment to any political campaign. Perhaps more important, throughout the industrial areas union officials and rank-and-file workers threw themselves wholeheartedly into the campaign, regarding it as a critical showdown between the forces of the liberal, prolabor New Deal and the GOP and its candidate, Kansas governor Alfred M. Landon.

FDR's spectacular reelection on November 3 galvanized working-class communities. Powerful corporate interests, including the leading figures in the steel and auto industries, had contributed heavily to anti-Roosevelt organizations. The Democrats' stunning victory carried into office hundreds of state and federal legislators, dozens of liberally inclined mayors and other local officers, and governors in key industrial states. It seemed a labor triumph, so massive and enthusiastic was support for FDR in working-class precincts.

Years later, Katherine Pollock Ellickson, Brophy's assistant, recalled the mixture of jubilation and apprehension that prevailed at the CIO's post-election gathering. Lewis stressed that "we must capitalize on the election. The CIO," he declared, "was out fighting for Roosevelt and every steel town showed a smashing victory for him." Hillman added that the CIO had to move quickly, for now "may be the last opportunity to organize" the industrial masses. The CIO leaders, Ellickson recalled, "had won at the ballot box. But could they win at the plants?"

VICTORY IN AUTOS AND STEEL

The answer—a resounding yes—came soon after. Early in 1937, CIO unions won monumental victories in the two most obstinate open shop industries, auto and steel. In February, the UAW capped an epic six-week confrontation with the General Motors Corporation (GM) in Flint, Michigan, with the achievement of a union contract. Barely three weeks later, SWOC, without a strike, brought U.S. Steel to terms. Following as they did on the heels of organized labor's sweeping electoral triumphs of 1936, the victories over GM and U.S. Steel touched off a wave of mass organization of remarkable intensity. By the spring of 1937, the CIO seemed to be at full tide.

The first great victory came in Flint, a city of 150,000 people lying sixty miles north of Detroit and linchpin of GM's nationwide production empire. On December 29, 1936, UAW militants shut down the huge Fisher Body plant, one of five major GM facilities in the bleak Michigan city. Employing 7,300 workers, Fisher One supplied bodies for the profitable Buick division. The UAW's strength in Flint had ebbed and flowed with the vagaries of union fortunes and government policies during the early New Deal years. The union could claim only about 10 percent of GM's 47,000 Flint workers as members, but this work stoppage and those in other Flint plants soon brought in thousands of new recruits. For the auto giant, the strike erupted at a particularly inopportune moment, for a mildly resurgent economy had begun to buoy the car market, leaving GM vulnerable in a long work stoppage.

For six weeks, UAW members occupied critical GM plants in Flint. Supported by mass picketing outside the factories and by a complex network of UAW services, this sit-down strike technique both demonstrated the workers' power to paralyze the operations and discouraged the usual kinds of strikebreaking. Although GM badgered public authorities to remove the workers, skillful UAW and CIO legal maneuvering permitted Michigan governor Frank Murphy, committed to a peaceful settlement, to pursue negotiations. As usual, the company could rely on a compliant local police force to do its bidding, and early on, the police did launch an attack on one of the occupied buildings. The sit-downers so savagely repelled this foray, hurling heavy door hinges and other metal parts from commanding upper-floor windows, that the police soon abandoned frontal assaults.

The Flint sit-down strike was one of the epic confrontations in American labor history. Pictures of the sit-downers—sprawled on the car seats that provided their bedding; hauling supplies up through the plant windows from the union food wagons; kissing their children, lifted up from the sidewalks by visiting wives—appeared in newspapers everywhere. Some of the wives created a Women's Emergency Brigade, whose colorfully clad members provided visible moral support and on more than one occasion interposed themselves between vulnerable strikers and mayhem-bent Flint police. With able UAW operatives such as Victor Reuther, Robert Travis, and Henry Kraus mobilizing strike support and orchestrating publicity outside the plants, and with John L. Lewis himself in Detroit handling negotiations with frustrated GM executives and anxious government officials, in the second week of February the two parties eventually reached a settlement. The contract, a humble document of barely one page, contained few concrete concessions for GM workers. But it did have the critical stipulation: the company agreed to recognize the UAW as bargaining agent for its members in the struck facilities.

On February 11, the sit-downers, many sporting beards and all beaming with joy, trooped from the plants. Thousands of autoworkers filled the streets in a celebration that lasted through the freezing winter night. Despite the grudging and partial character of the contract wrung from GM, unionists regarded the very fact of bringing the world's most powerful corporation to the bargaining table as a breathtaking victory.

"The GM sit-down strike of 1936–37," declares historian Sidney Fine, "was, all in all, the most significant American labor conflict in the twentieth century."

Victory in steel came in the spring. Through the latter half of 1936 and into 1937, SWOC built its organization in the plants of U.S. Steel and the so-called Little Steel companies. Corporations such as Jones and Laughlin, Republic Steel, and Inland Steel were "little" only in comparison with industry leader U.S. Steel, which in the mid-1930s held about 40 percent of the nation's steel-producing capacity and employed over 220,000 workers. The other corporations, industrial giants in their own right, had traditionally followed U.S. Steel's lead in most matters relating to pricing and labor policy. And the steel industry had a long record, from the notorious Homestead Strike of 1892 through the great 1919–20 strike, of violent opposition to organized labor. Thus, SWOC's success in recruiting about 125,000 steelworkers by the beginning of 1937 was an impressive start. At the same time, it did not guarantee success, for the figure represented only about 25 percent of the steelworkers, and if past practice continued, all the large corporations would fight this new union without quarter.

But the political and social climate in the New Deal years provided laborites with some new weapons. Roosevelt's victory stiffened the resolve of SWOC organizers in scores of mill towns whose voters had overwhelmingly cast their ballots for FDR. Democratic governors in key steel states such as Pennsylvania, Ohio, Indiana, and Illinois would perhaps not be so ready as their predecessors to intervene in behalf of the corporations. In June 1936, the United States Senate had created a special committee to investigate employer violations of workers' rights. This body, dubbed the LaFollette Committee after its chairman, Senator Robert M. LaFollette, Jr., of Wisconsin, sent investigators to probe into the use of espionage, the stockpiling of arms and munitions, and the domination of local authorities by antilabor corporations. The committee's activities attracted great public attention and provided a sense of governmental support for labor's organizing efforts rarely seen before.

The New Deal years had brought changes inside the mills as well. True, U.S. Steel and the others remained hostile to organized labor. Still, during the NRA period, the companies had created so-called Employee Representation Plans (ERPs) by which they hoped to fulfill their obligations under Section 7(a). These organizations, designed primarily to undercut true labor unions, operated under company auspices and usually under tight managerial control. By 1935, however, union sympathizers and other militant workers had gotten themselves elected to serve in dozens of these organizations, often called "company unions." With at least 90 percent of the workers in basic steel enrolled in these organizations, company unions, though disdained by trade unionists, had begun to attack management policies. Indeed, SWOC organizers often found the ERPs hotbeds of militancy. Throughout 1936 and 1937, local activists constantly pressed the steel companies for wage and other concessions, demands that put the employers in a double bind. If they granted concessions, SWOC members in the company unions escalated their demands and claimed that the companies were only trying to buy off union sentiment. If the companies turned a deaf ear, CIO supporters argued that only SWOC could force the steelmakers to come around.

By early 1937, the chairman of U.S. Steel's board, Myron Taylor, had grown weary of the incessant conflict in his mills. The company unions' purpose was to soothe labor unrest and to keep workers loyal and docile; instead, plant managers and foremen complained of escalating guerrilla warfare, fueled by SWOC's organizers and publicity. With the steel industry just approaching 1929 levels of production and with federal and state political authorities seemingly enlisted on the side of the union, Taylor began to believe that perhaps it was time to come to terms with organized labor.

Although most of the leaders of the Little Steel companies opposed concessions, in January and February of 1937 Taylor met frequently— and secretly—with John L. Lewis to discuss an agreement. Announced to the public on March 2, 1937, it broke with almost forty-five years of the steel corporation's anti-unionism and, in the words of historian Irving Bernstein, "converted the Steel Workers Organizing Committee from an aspiration to a trade union." Union gains were limited. Steelworkers won modest improvements in wages and hours of employment, along with sharply limited seniority rights. The contract created a grievance procedure, an important factor in giving SWOC locals a day-to-day presence in the mills. Most importantly, however, the contract conceded recognition of SWOC by the steel corporation. True, this recognition carried with it no guarantee that U.S. Steel and its subsidiaries would stop dealing with the ERPs. Nor did it provide for any form of union security, that is, any requirement that workers join or retain membership in the union for any specified period. It was, as with the GM-UAW agreement signed just two weeks earlier, important far beyond its specific provisions, however. In both cases a fledgling union had compelled an enormously powerful corporation to deal with its representatives and to acknowledge the right of its members to a contractual relationship with the company.

Initially, Philip Murray, SWOC head, believed that the agreement would quickly translate into agreements with the Little Steel companies.

After all, they had traditionally followed the industry giant's lead in labor policies. But Murray's expectations remained unfulfilled. Most of the other large steel companies resisted the new union, often bitterly. Hardliners such as Tom Girdler, president of Republic Steel, felt that Taylor and U.S. Steel had betrayed the industry. U.S. Steel had sold out to Lewis and the radical CIO; to follow the U.S. Steel–SWOC agreement, he believed, would be "a bad thing for our companies, for our employees; indeed for the United States of America." Rather than deal with SWOC, Girdler vowed, he would shut down and "raise apples and potatoes." When his peers chose Girdler as president of the powerful Iron and Steel Institute on May 27, weeks after SWOC had concluded its agreement with U.S. Steel subsidiaries, few believed that victory in Little Steel would be quick or painless.

For the moment, however, the CIO was triumphant. The months from the Roosevelt victory in 1936 through May of the following year was labor's time. The very term "CIO" carried a kind of magic. In the hulking steel mills and the vast auto factories of Flint and Detroit, workers asserted their power on the shop floor. Aggressive SWOC and UAW grievancemen, emboldened now by victory after victory, went after strawbosses and foremen. Whole communities seethed with fervor for the CIO. In May, when SWOC ended a strike by signing a preliminary contract with the Jones and Laughlin Steel Company covering 25,000 employees in Aliquippa, Pennsylvania, SWOC district organizer Joe Timko could not persuade the pickets to disperse. Indeed, they remained around the mills, spitting at and beating up workers suspected of scabbing. Eventually, he rounded up a marching band, found an American flag to wave aloft, and stationed himself in front of the musicians. The pickets fell in behind, and Timko led a parade of 20,000 unionists and supporters away from the J & L Mill. "The procession," says Bernstein, "spun out for twelve miles along the Ohio River."

The victories in basic industry spurred workers everywhere to claim the mantle of the CIO. Reported director John Brophy, "Hundreds of groups of all types are clamoring for charters." Workers were "besieging" CIO organizers. "We have had to turn down hundreds of requests," he reported, on the grounds that the new organization had to concentrate on the basic industries. Still, UAW and SWOC representatives found themselves bringing into their local unions all sorts of workers— clerks, waitresses, bank tellers, cigar makers, dairy employees. The UAW even signed up a group of corsetmakers.

A wave of sit-down strikes rippled through the stores, shops, restaurants, and hotels of downtown Detroit, normally the preserve of staid businessmen and sober financiers. In the wake of its victory over

GM, the UAW added members by the thousands, climbing from barely 30,000 to over 200,000 by the end of 1937. SWOC mushroomed as well, adding as many as 30,000 new members a week in April and May and claiming over 300,000 by June 1. The CIO leadership, astonished by these developments, began to create a whole apparatus, remarkably parallel to that of the despised AFL, for enrolling thousands of workers who toiled in jobs outside the basic auto, steel, and rubber industries into permanent CIO organizations.

THE CIO SURGES ON

In addition to the CIO's impressive numerical growth, the new organization brought an exciting new dimension to the labor movement. Industrial unionism itself, while hardly unknown in the AFL, became a dynamic force, embodying the aspirations of hundreds of thousands of mass production workers. The distinctive CIO style of unionism quickly challenged employers' authority in the day-to-day operations in the plants and shops. Typically in AFL organizations, a paid business agent looked after workers' interests, often through quiet arrangements with the employer or contractor. Even where directly elected union officials handled workers' complaints, in AFL unions top-ranking officers, often remote from the actual workplace, settled up with the boss and then handed down the decision to a passive work force.

CIO grievance-handling, however, functioned as a direct extension of organizing. Work groups or departments elected their stewards and grievancemen. These men and women, many of them long-term union activists seething with resentment against anti-union employers and heavy-handed supervisors and foremen, prided themselves on their militancy. With the coming of the CIO, struggles for shop-floor power rippled through scores of industrial plants, as triumphant activists now tried to redefine basic relationships. Stewards sought to demonstrate the union's ability to compel changes both to their own constituents and to workers who had not yet joined the union. As foremen tried to step up production or impose discipline, these activists pulled the switches, led unionists off the job, and launched chronic mini-sit-downs, job actions which workers called "quickies." This "brass knuckles unionism" especially characterized such organizations as the Auto Workers and the Rubber Workers, in which local unions had grown directly from grassroots activism.

The CIO also exhibited distinctiveness in its approach to black workers. For generations, Afro-Americans had been the forgotten or despised stepchildren of the labor movement. Many AFL affiliates excluded or discriminated against black workers. Indeed, black Americans often regarded the labor movement as an enemy of their people while praising such employers as Henry Ford, who at least provided some industrial jobs to Detroit-area blacks. In the labor conflicts of the late nineteenth and early twentieth centuries, employers had often recruited black workers to break strikes, a role that the labor movement's disdain and the limited economic opportunities available to blacks encouraged. True, some unions, notably the United Mine Workers, had recruited membership on a multiethnic basis and had even boasted of some black officers. A tenuous thread of multiracial labor activity stretched back to before the Civil War in some sectors. Still, in general black workers understandably regarded the resurgence of the labor movement in the 1930s with suspicion and even hostility.

CIO leaders were well aware of this. They understood too that the employment of blacks in basic industry often had the result of placing them at critical junctures in production processes. They could not organize the great packinghouses of Chicago, for example, unless they organized the kill floors. It was here, amid the filthy conditions and backbreaking toil, that the whole production process began. And it was here, in these fatiguing, low-wage jobs, that black workers commonly toiled. Nor could they build stable unions in steel without recruiting the workers, many of them black, who labored among the coke ovens, where noxious fumes, foul conditions, and heavy physical demands exacted a harsh toll. In metalworking, the foundries—hot, dirty, physically exhausting, and downright dangerous—were central to the production process and extensive employers of black labor. Throughout the industrial heartland, CIO organizers knew, black workers performed their tasks in key areas of the plant. Organizing them was critical to the success of the new unions.

Other factors highlighted the role of blacks as well. Even where blacks did not provide the key to the production process, their presence as potential strikebreakers dictated their recruitment. Younger and better educated than their counterparts in the AFL, CIO organizers and leaders were less provincial, less wedded to traditional racial attitudes. CIO activists often had experience with socialist and communist organizations, where racial egalitarianism was an article of faith. Of course, not all CIO organizers glowed with racial enlightenment, nor did black workers typically respond to CIO appeals uncritically. Indeed, Murray noted in the midst of the SWOC drive that "the organization of the negro steel workers will follow, rather than precede, the organization of white mill workers." In Ford's auto plants, where throughout the late 1930s the UAW fought bitter battles, many black workers in the foundries held back. But CIO organizations, often establishing close ties with black civic organizations, civil rights leaders, and churches, continued to stress the recruitment of black workers, for, as Murray acknowledged, "the negroes have become an increasingly important factor" and were essential to CIO success.

Also distinguishing the new labor federation was its commitment to political action. In the AFL tradition of voluntarism, unions entered into the political process cautiously and reluctantly. Labor's appropriate strategy, believed AFL founder and perennial president Samuel Gompers, rewarded labor's legislative friends and punished its enemies. The labor movement could not become tied to any political party, nor should it look to the state to provide basic benefits for workers. Labor organizations did not actively campaign for or finance specific parties or politicians. While the modern age encouraged closer attention to the political and legislative area, most of the AFL's activities under the Gompers formula consisted of resistance to antilabor bills and practices.

True, in state and local politics particular unions and union leaders expanded on this narrow definition of labor's political purposes. And it is also true that with the depression and the New Deal, the AFL had moderated its position regarding national politics. Still, the basic components of AFL voluntarism—detachment from day-to-day political activities, a limited view of the state's proper role, and suspicion that government activity would, in the long run, work against union interests—remained strong in the 1930s.

CIO leaders had many reasons for rejecting this narrow approach. Hillman and Dubinsky, for example, were at least nominal socialists whose ideology stressed the connection between political and economic affairs. Even Lewis, who still retained much of the traditional AFL perspective, had grasped the central importance for the labor movement of a friendly administration in Washington and in the state capitals. Unionists in mass production industries could not afford to disdain politics. While AFL craft unions could enforce high wage demands and provide generous benefits for their skilled members, CIO unionists spoke for vast thousands of unskilled and semiskilled workers. If a CIO union struck, employers, especially in the slackened labor market of the 1930s, could readily find replacements. Clearly, for the CIO the political environment, from the behavior of local police all the way up to the attitude and policies of the Chief Executive, were of central importance.

Nor could CIO unions create the sort of private welfare system that AFL unions, operating in part as fraternal societies, had often achieved. Mass production workers were transient, moving from place to place, job to job, industry to industry. The vast majority of industrial workers looked to government for the creation and expansion of a social welfare system, rather than to elite craft unions. This being the case, labor organizations that presumed to speak for their membership had to attempt as forcefully as possible to shape the political environment. Thus, ardent CIO support and financial commitment to Roosevelt and the Democrats in 1936 was no fluke; it grew directly from the very concept of industrial unionism.

In still another area, the CIO stood out. Under Lewis's direction, the CIO eagerly welcomed anticapitalist radicals into its fold. Neither Lewis nor any other major CIO leader had as an active part of his agenda any sort of revolutionary plan. Still, veteran unionists such as Lewis, Hillman, Murray, and Brophy realized that Communists, Socialists, and other radicals were often among the most energetic, committed, and effective organizers. People who exhibited long-term Socialist or Communist activism amid the hostile environment of the United States had paid their dues. Because of the misfortunes of the labor movement of the 1920s and early 1930s, the established unions could provide relatively few experienced and energetic organizers. Thus, Lewis and his colleagues turned to men and women schooled in the hard classroom of radical politics, people at once skilled in the techniques of organizing and battle-tested in the struggles of the pre–New Deal era.

In the early UAW, Communists played key roles in Flint and other organizing and strike campaigns. In SWOC, one estimate held that as many as 30 percent of the original cadre of organizers were either Communists or very close to the Communist party. In the electrical appliance industry, James Matles, Julius Emspak, William Sentner, and other Communists took leading roles from the beginning. Communists and those deeply sympathetic to the goals of the Party were prominent in CIO unions in shipping, longshoring, mine and metal working, and other areas as well. In 1937, Lewis appointed men with strong affinities with the Communist party as CIO general counsel and publicity director.

No aspect of CIO innovation was more controversial. Employers saw in the CIO's use of Communists and Socialists proof of its subversiveness. The AFL, which had increasingly distanced itself from all but the most moderate Socialists, attacked Lewis and the CIO relentlessly for their association with Communists. In 1938, a leading labor journalist published a widely read series of articles that indicted the CIO for its penetration by Communists. Lewis, however, remained unfazed. Communists and other radicals knew how to organize. Even anti-Communist functionaries attested to that. In the mid- and late 1930s, moreover, the Communist party, for reasons of international Communist policy, seemed to be cooling its revolutionary ardor. Indeed, radicals of every stripe were so eager to seize the opportunity to build the CIO and to organize mass production workers that they set aside their controversial politics, at least temporarily. In any event, Lewis was convinced that radicals who had spent so many years wandering in the wilderness could not in any fundamental way challenge him or usurp the CIO. When asked if he weren't fearful that the Communists might attempt to dominate the young organization, Lewis replied with typical hauteur: "Who gets the bird, the hunter or the dog?"

Thus, in its aggressive activism in the shops, its openness to black workers and to radical influences, and in its enthusiasm for political action, the CIO did indeed command attention. In November 1937, SWOC head Philip Murray pointed with pride to the achievements of the new organization. Six thousand new local unions had been born, he reported. Workers had chosen some 36,000 local officers in democratic elections. Twenty-eight thousand CIO grievancemen asserted industrial workers' rights on the shop floor. From a modest plan to encourage organization of neglected workers, the CIO had emerged in less than two years as a mass movement of over 4 million members. Asserted Murray, "We are the dominant labor force in this nation."

SETBACKS AND COMPETITION

And so it seemed in the hectic days of 1937. Before long, however, the tide began to turn. Developments within the labor movement, in the larger political and economic environment, and on the international scene began to drag against the CIO upsurge and to impose limits to the new organization's gains. The latter years of the 1930s, while on the whole a period of continued growth on the part of the labor movement, revealed sharp limitations in both the extent and character of the militant upsurge embodied in the early CIO.

As impressive as CIO victories were, the new organization failed to complete its conquest of basic industry. In auto, Ford remained unorganized. In steel, such important corporations as Bethlehem, Inland, Youngstown, and Republic fought SWOC as vigorously and, for the time being, as successfully as they had in the past. A CIO drive in textiles sputtered on inconclusively. CIO organizations created to recruit white-collar workers, government employees, and professionals made little progress. Even in areas such as auto, rubber, steel, and electrical appliances, where the CIO won its greatest victories, incomplete organization encouraged employers to resist bargaining.

In May 1937, Henry Ford's private police mercilessly beat UAW organizers attempting to pass out leaflets near the Rouge plant. In

Ford's factories around the country, his so-called servicemen—thugs often recruited directly from prison—regularly intimidated and assaulted unionists. Though the UAW brought ultimately successful unfair labor practices proceedings against Ford, the Ford workplaces remained a no-man's-land insofar as the UAW was concerned as these cases wound their halting way through the NLRB.

In steel, the aftermath of the great victory over U.S. Steel was one of the bloodiest episodes in American labor history. Unable to bring Little Steel to the bargaining table, in May 1937, SWOC struck. The companies recruited strikebreakers and sought to turn local opinion against the CIO. "Back-to-work" movements pitted strikebreakers against SWOC pickets throughout Pennsylvania and the Middle West. In ugly confrontations throughout the industrial heartland, eight steelworkers were killed on the picket lines. Dozens more were injured or arrested, as Little Steel slowly began to gain the upper hand, resuming production and forcing the weakened SWOC locals to call off the strikes.

On May 30, 1937, Memorial Day, the steel strike erupted in shocking carnage. As SWOC members and their families gathered outside a Republic Steel plant in south Chicago, scores of Chicago police confronted them. Housed and partially armed by Republic, the police tensed for action. For reasons never fully explained, the bluecoats began emptying their pistols into the crowd, which included women and children. Onlookers gaped in disbelief as scores of marchers fell to the ground, many shot in the back. Newsreel cameramen recorded the spectacle of frenzied policemen clubbing the wounded. Ten men died that day, contributing to the steel strike's ultimate total of eighteen. Fifty-eight suffered wounds, thirty of them from gunshot. Paramount News, whose cameraman had recorded the scene, suppressed the film, fearing that its showing in movie theaters might cause disturbances. *Life* magazine did run a picture spread, but the captions, in contradiction to virtually every eyewitness account, depicted the police as having acted only in self-defense.

Nor was all well within the CIO itself. As Lewis and Hillman drew farther away from the AFL and completed plans for the creation of a permanent, separate federation, Dubinsky held his 200,000 member ILGW back. Some members of the CIO staff believed that the man whom Lewis had appointed as general counsel, a brilliant young lawyer named Lee Pressman, was controlling important aspects of CIO policy. Since Pressman, along with Len De Caux, the Lewis-appointed director of publicity, was close to the Communist party, critics began to fear that the new labor federation was becoming an adjunct to an alien radical sect. As for Lewis himself, although he remained the towering figure and the courageous lion of the labor movement, Brophy and others in contact with him began to feel that he had become distracted from the affairs of the CIO. Always imperious, often secretive about his plans, Lewis seemed increasingly to surround himself with a small coterie of old cronies and relatives. His daughter Kathryn, serving as his private secretary, administrative assistant, and general factorum, guarded access to the UMW chief.

Disarray afflicted key CIO affiliates. Both the UAW and the URW bubbled with factionalism, both in their national offices and among the local unions. So bitter did the feuding become in the Autoworkers' union that Lewis had to dispatch Murray and Hillman to attempt to resolve the personal, ideological, and tactical conflicts that divided the executive board and threatened to rip the new union to shreds. Eventually, in 1939, CIO functionaries helped to oust the union's controversial president, Homer Martin, and to install a successor acceptable to most UAW officials. Meanwhile, rank-and-file unionists—without steady leadership at the top and still struggling to force the auto companies to deal with the local unions on grievances, work practices, and disciplinary matters—staged innumerable strikes and sit-downs. In the recessionary economic climate of 1938 and 1939, these confrontations often pitted UAW men in one department of a plant against those in another, while employers such as GM gained renewed optimism that the UAW might be only a passing phenomenon.

Things were less turbulent in SWOC but no more encouraging. Without Little Steel, SWOC could not achieve breakthroughs in bargaining with U.S. Steel. Membership in locals began to fall off. Heavily in debt to the United Mine Workers, SWOC found steelworkers reluctant to pay dues to a union that seemed stymied. Though SWOC, which was under firm central direction by Murray, did not exhibit the kind of grass-roots factionalism and shop-level conflict characteristic of the UAW, SWOC organizers grew increasingly apprehensive about the state of their locals and increasingly high-handed in their efforts to collect dues from apathetic local unionists.

A resurgent AFL also provided the CIO with cause for concern. As traditionalist leaders grasped the extent of the CIO victories, they began to shed some of their lethargy. While no AFL union could challenge the UAW in the auto industry, the International Association of Machinists did compete effectively with the upstart in the important aircraft industry. The Carpenters, Electrical Workers, Teamsters, and Boilermakers extended recruitment efforts, often clashing with new CIO affiliates. In areas such as meatpacking, paper making, food processing, service trades, and retail work, AFL affiliates found that hastily created CIO organizations could not generate the momentum and enthusiasm that the UAW, URW, and SWOC had.

By 1938, membership in AFL unions had surpassed that in CIO organizations. Outside of the basic mass production sectors, with their huge plants and enormous concentrations of workers, the AFL had many advantages in competition with the CIO. The older federation had an elaborate and long-established institutional structure. Central bodies existed in virtually every city, and well-established state federations were available to AFL organizers for political, legal, and organizing support. The CIO sought to create similar structures, but by 1939 it had done so only in its areas of heaviest concentration. As competition for members extended to smaller towns and to less centralized industries, the AFL was more than competitive.

The expansion of the International Brotherhood of Teamsters (IBT) illustrates the strengths that an awakened AFL could bring to competition with the CIO. For years, the IBT consisted of a loose federation of local unions, each seeking to control local hauling in the various cities. Milk wagon drivers, bakery wagon drivers, coal truck drivers, and other delivery men formed the heart of the local unions. The leadership of the international union, held since 1907 by Daniel Tobin, rarely interfered with these powerful local unions' internal affairs.

When the organizing fervor of the NRA swept through urban workers, Teamster locals often found themselves at the center of things. Since much economic activity depended on transport, truck and wagon drivers exerted great power in organizing campaigns and strikes. Moreover, in large cities warehouse, loading dock, and service workers, who came into daily contact with the truck drivers, often sought out IBT representation. While Tobin and other old-time leaders were reluctant to recruit these newcomers, militant young local leaders welcomed them. In Minneapolis, for example, the early surge of organization inspired by Section 7(a) brought an extraordinary group of young, bright radicals into effective control of Local 574. Activists such as Farrel Dobbs and Ray Dunn quickly realized that the conversion of their local union into a mass organization, consisting of all goods-handling workers, would add immeasurably to the power of the local. Moreover, such a program of mass organization coincided closely with their militantly socialist beliefs. By 1934, these able radicals had transformed Local 574 into a powerful working-class organization, one that effectively battled the employers and police in the great strike of that year and one whose radicalism and activism troubled the IBT's national leadership.

In other cities, even ideologically cautious unionists grasped the lesson of mass organization. In Detroit, for example, young James Hoffa led a spontaneous strike of grocery store loaders and helped to begin the expansion of Teamster recruitment in the warehouses, garages, and market areas of the Motor City. In effect, these militants were turning the once-limited IBT into an industrial union, one that recruited and bargained for workers in all areas relating to the loading, transportation, distribution, and disposition of goods. Moreover, by the end of the 1930s Hoffa, Pacific Northwest IBT leader David Beck, and others were using radical-inspired tactics to extend Teamster organization to over-the-road truckers, thus translating the public's increasing dependency on motor transport into the potential for enormous regional and even national power for the IBT and its fast-rising young leadership. What with its massive recruitment of "inside" workers—warehousemen, loaders, distributors—and of over-the-road truckers, by 1939 the IBT had grown to a powerful organization of some 440,000 members. These impressive numbers, the strategic positioning of the IBT in the nation's distribution system, and the organization's deep loyalties to the old Federation made it a potent instrument in the AFL's competition with the CIO.

By the end of 1937, however, any organizing had to take into account the deteriorating economic situation. The Roosevelt administration, alarmed by the mounting budgetary deficits that New Deal programs had accumulated, began cutting back sharply on public expenditures. The administration slashed relief rolls and curtailed public projects. Without the yeast of federal expenditures, the mild recovery of 1935–37 quickly collapsed. In the fall of 1937, unemployment surged upward. Through 1938, employers, faced with rising inventories and diminishing sales, stiffened their resolve to resist union demands and even pressed their workers for contract concessions. Recruitment grew difficult once again, especially for newer organizations which could not point to a long record of survival and resurgence.

The so-called Roosevelt Recession of 1937–38 was not labor's only grievance against its erstwhile friend. When asked by reporters about the bloody Little Steel strike, FDR, no doubt reflecting widespread public weariness over labor unrest, observed that if the employers and the unions did not soon resolve their differences, many people—himself among them, he implied—would be inclined to say, "A curse on both your houses." This remark seemed even to Roosevelt's strongest CIO supporters callous and insensitive. After all, it was not SWOC members who had murdered their adversaries. Lewis, increasingly convinced that FDR was an unusually devious and untrustworthy politician, found

Roosevelt's remarks inexcusable. Recalling labor's massive support for the president in the 1936 election, the UMW chief denounced the Chief Executive's bland neutrality. "It ill behooves one who has supped at labor's table . . . ," thundered the CIO leader, "to curse . . . with fine impartiality both labor and its adversaries when they become locked in deadly embrace." Lewis, a Republican in lifelong affiliation, began a steady drift away from FDR, thus adding another element of disarray to labor's tribulations.

For most labor leaders and for the masses of ordinary workers, however, Roosevelt remained the central ingredient in labor's revival and the country's hopes. Yet the reforming thrust of the New Deal, which had reached a peak with the Wagner Act and the Social Security Act of 1935, lost momentum in the later 1930s. Important legislative and political mistakes by Roosevelt and his Democratic advisors strengthened the hand of conservatives in Congress, even before the off-year 1938 elections reduced liberal strength in both houses. The La Follette Committee's investigations lost their novelty for a press and public increasingly focused on frightening international events. Conservatives in Congress, aided by bitter AFL leaders, began investigations of the allegedly pro-CIO and, some charged, pro-Communist bent of the National Labor Relations Board. While no adverse legislation resulted, the board, from its inception a bastion of industrial union sympathy, became increasingly concerned with appeasing AFL unionists, resentful employers, and congressional and press critics.

By the outbreak of war in Europe in September 1939, the labor movement was in a state of flux. True, its legions had grown enormously in the 1930s. Official AFL figures claimed over 4 million members, while CIO estimates—never as reliable as even the often-questionable AFL counts—stood at about 3.5 million. Organized labor had achieved footholds in auto, steel, rubber, and other mass production industries and had begun a remarkable new commitment to political activity. A seemingly moribund AFL had rebounded vigorously and was aggressively competing with the CIO. While problems, both those within the labor movement and in the larger society, remained to qualify labor's achievement, the New Deal years had indeed been victorious ones for organized labor.

Historian David Brody notes that by the time Hitler plunged the world into war, observant laborites remained troubled by the nature of their achievements. Despite the heroism and militancy of thousands of rank-and-file workers and despite the often brilliant and always dynamic leadership provided by Lewis and the other leaders of the industrial union movement, unionists were all too aware that circumstances outside the labor movement had been decisive in rebuilding their movement. The NRA, the Wagner Act, the La Follette Committee, and sympathetic administrations in Washington and the state capitals had been critical elements in labor's rebirth. Moreover, labor had made its greatest organizing gains at times when the economy seemed to be picking up, notably in 1933–34 and 1935–37. Whatever organized labor's sacrifices and achievements, Brody notes, the "trigger was in the larger environment."

In 1939, employment began to pick up. European nations placed large orders for war matériel and munitions. The steel mills shifted into high gear, and consumer-oriented industries followed right behind. The Roosevelt Recession was over. But at the same time, the fury and intensity of the European war, coupled with the increasingly ominous developments in Asia, threatened to draw the United States into the maelstrom. Congress beefed up military budgets and began debating peacetime conscription. No doubt, the impending war boom would strengthen the hand of the labor organizers. It might well provide the CIO with the boost necessary to complete the organization of basic industries. But it would no doubt also bring deep changes in the entire context in which labor relations occurred. If "outside" events had provided the key to resurgence in the 1930s, laborites wondered, how would their new and rebuilt unions fare in the deepening international crisis of the 1940s?

The Unions
Go to War,
1939–1945

World War II wrought decisive changes in the American working class and in the labor movement. Industrial expansion and the demands of military recruitment uprooted millions of workers and their families, initiating new patterns of living and working. As weekly earnings grew, corporate America encouraged workers to enlist in an expanding consumeristic economy, if not during the scarcity-afflicted war itself, at least when peace returned. Wartime work, however, all too often exacted heavy tolls of fatigue, increased proneness to accidents, and bewildering changes in life on the job for workers to feel secure and prosperous. Unions grew enormously, first in the defense production phase (1939–41), and then even more so in the heyday of American belligerency (1941–44). Along with enhanced membership figures came increasingly political and social influence. But for the unions the war was also a mixed blessing, for the price of growth and power was frustrating enmeshment in a tangled web of governmental regulation. And as the war ended, a tide of anti-union feeling convinced laborites that their struggle for economic security and political influence remained as problematic as ever.

DEFENSE PRODUCTION, 1939–1941

Even before the Japanese attack on Pearl Harbor on December 7, 1941, brought the United States into the war, labor struggles filled the public record. Beginning in 1939, Congress authorized a vast program of American rearmament. At the same time, Hitler's European enemies turned to American manufacturers to supply munitions and equipment. The resulting defense boom boosted employment and spurred laborites both to extend the patterns of organization achieved in the 1930s and to improve the standards of American workers. Employers continued to fight organization. Meanwhile, the federal government, especially after Hitler overran France in June 1940, intruded increasingly into collective bargaining. The period of defense mobilization, and especially the fifteen months after June 1940, rocked with labor unrest. In addition, the unique circumstances of this period heightened interunion tensions, intensifying the AFL-CIO rivalry and revealing deep splits within the CIO itself.

In 1939 and early 1940, the government began massive rearmament. After the stunning German conquest of France, the pace increased as the Roosevelt administration stepped up aid to Hitler's foes. Throughout the remainder of 1940 and 1941, the industrial heartland, the shipyards, and the new aircraft factories of California and Washington State hummed with activity. Recalled a Pennsylvania worker in a plant producing shell casings: "By mid-December [1940] we were on a seven day ten hour schedule. . . . All I did was sleep and eat." Led by the defense sector, employment rose by some 3 million workers within the first year of the buildup. By December 1941, unemployment, which had stood at over 10 million in 1939 and 8.5 million as late as June 1940, had ebbed to around 4 million. Manpower shortages began to appear in tool and die work and other skilled specialties.

Consolidation of Labor's Gains

The demand for workers in defense industry played to the labor movement's strength. With government demanding production and with employers more concerned with filling orders than with holding down costs, the time had come to complete the organizing of the industrial and transport core and to improve contracts. For the CIO, the military buildup offered the chance to attack such anti-union bastions as Ford, Republic Steel, and International Harvester. For the AFL, expanded defense and military construction benefitted the building trades unions and strengthened the Teamsters' hold on motor transport and goods handling.

While sensitive to the needs of national defense, working-class leaders believed the time had come to bring workers into the economic mainstream. In 1939, the average factory worker earned a paltry $1,250 a year. Well over 60 percent of all workers earned less than $1,000 a year. The 1940 census showed that the promise of mass affluence proclaimed in the 1920s remained grotesquely unfulfilled. In 1936, President Roosevelt had asserted that he saw "one-third of a nation ill-fed, ill-housed," and the census documented his somber vision. Over 30 percent of American dwellings lacked running water, and an even larger proportion did without indoor toilets. Nearly 60 percent lacked central heating, and over one-quarter of all dwellings had no facilities for refrigeration of food. Health care statistics revealed that working people and the unemployed were vastly more prone to sickness than were even the moderately well-off. They more frequently suffered disabling ailments, died younger, and had sicklier children. In every category—income, health care, housing, education—wage workers stood on the margins of American life, enjoying few of the glittering amenities so vividly portrayed on the movie screens.

In November 1940, the new CIO president, Philip Murray, proclaimed that the industrial federation would launch the "most vigorous, far-reaching organization drive that has ever been put on." In addition, CIO leaders sought substantial wage increases, and even normally more cautious AFL unions grew aggressive. Success in boosting wages was critical now, especially for the new unions. Few steel, auto, or rubber workers had had wage increases since 1937, as the Roosevelt Recession tempered militancy and even forced some unions to accept wage cuts. The new CIO unions remained vulnerable and unproven. But now was the opportunity, with billions of federal dollars stoking the economy, for them to demonstrate their usefulness to a generation of workers.

Through 1941 this determination to extend organization and to improve wages triggered hundreds of strikes. Led by the CIO, whose members constituted 70 percent of the total number of strikers, 2.3 million workers conducted work stoppages that year. The 4,200 strikes represented one of the highest totals in American history. During the first four months of the year, steel, auto, electrical, and agricultural implement workers struck corporations that had resisted the earlier CIO drive of 1936–37. In addition, John L. Lewis led 400,000 soft coal miners out. "Hell is breaking loose all over the place," moaned one government official.

Although lacking the lethal violence of earlier strike waves, these walkouts included some of the most decisive in the history of the labor movement. As in the 1930s, steel and auto stood in the center. The gains made by SWOC and the UAW in consequence of their victories over U.S. Steel and General Motors in 1937 remained tentative until the unions could organize other key components in these industries. Through the late 1930s, for example, Little Steel companies held out, yielding grudging step after grudging step to SWOC in legal battles and NLRB cases while continuing to promote their company unions and to resist the CIO. In 1941, however, one by one they succumbed to the union. Government pressure to avoid strikes, along with the mounting criticism emanating from the courts and the NLRB of the companies' labor policies, helped to bring them around. But it was a reinvigorated Steel Workers Organizing Committee that delivered the most telling blows to the stubborn corporations, for the massive rank-and-file support for the

SWOC locals completely discredited the claims of Little Steel that their loyal employees opposed CIO representation.

Bethlehem Steel, one of Little Steel's largest firms, bore the brunt of the labor challenge. On March 25, 1941, SWOC stunned company officials by bringing 19,000 workers out of the Bethlehem, Pennsylvania, mill to protest corporate backing of the company union. Bethlehem's officers at first used the tried and true tactics of intimidation and police harassment to quell the walkout in this company-dominated city of 75,000, but they found enthusiasm for the union too strong. Eventually, they agreed to holding NLRB representation elections, in hopes that once the excitement had passed, workers would return to their senses and reject SWOC.

Throughout the spring, however, the CIO union rolled to victory after victory in Bethlehem's scattered plants. In all, over 21,500 of the company's 28,500 employees chose SWOC, solidifying the CIO in one of Little Steel's largest firms. The others soon fell into line. Youngstown Sheet and Tube and Inland Steel accorded the union recognition without the formality of NLRB polls. Sweetest of all to the thousands of steelworkers who remembered the brutal events of 1937, however, was triumph at Tom Girdler's Republic Steel, which now rather meekly acknowledged SWOC's bargaining rights when an independent check of its records revealed that 70 percent of its 40,600 employees had joined the union.

Victories at Little Steel meant that SWOC could now confront the major producers with a solid front. Gone was the threat of company unionism. Now SWOC could move to raise wages, extend its power on the shop floor, and establish coherent contractual relationships governing the industry's chaotic wage structure. SWOC president Murray even talked about union-company partnership in defense production.

For steelworkers, however, the specific features of new contracts were less important than the sheer fact of triumph. In Bethlehem, the company had erected a toll bridge that workers entering the mill had to cross. Workers believed that years of exactations had paid for the bridge many times over; they regarded the daily toll as a humiliating reminder of the company's control of their lives. When victory over Bethlehem became certain, steelworkers surged through the city in a mass parade, sweeping over the span with its sign "One cent for Pedestrians." Art Preis, a radical journalist who marched in the parade, described the scene and recorded the strikers' sense of release: "No pennies today! Over the bridge the parade rolls in a solid stream. Ten thousand marchers and not one penny. 'Let 'em try and collect their goddam penny today!' "

Simultaneous with SWOC's triumph, the United Auto Workers at last cracked the industry's remaining anti-union stronghold, Ford. Through the late 1930s, Ford's bizarre, brutal resistance kept the union at bay. Undermined by the recession and beset with crippling internal conflicts, the UAW attempted only to keep a foothold in Ford plants while pursuing legal attacks before the NLRB and the courts. Even this cautious strategy faced violent opposition. Henry Ford, nearing eighty, relied heavily on a swaggering little Navy veteran named Harry Bennett for what passed in the chaotically run company as "labor policy." With a paramilitary force of over 3,000 men, Bennett extended Ford's repressive policies to every plant and department. Workers hated Ford's frantic work pace and its below-standard wages. But it was the degrading, violent discipline meted out by Bennett's so-called Service Department that made Ford notorious among autoworkers. Irving Bernstein describes the violent atmosphere that characterized its workplaces in the late 1930s: "Ford Service engaged in systematic intimidation. . . . 'Shaking 'em up in the aisles' was a standard practice. On occasion Servicemen would beat and even flog employees. . . . Conversation and even smiling became dangerous."

Nowhere was Ford Service more blatant and workers more bitter than at the fabled River Rouge complex. This vast facility, erected in the mid-1920s, was Henry Ford's bid to consolidate the entire auto production process—from raw materials to drivable automobiles—in one giant factory. Housing shops for raw materials processing, steelmaking, metals and glass fabricating, machine tooling, and auto assembly, the enormous plant had miles of railroad tracks, ore-boat docking stations, and giant smelters, blast furnaces, and rolling mills. As many as 95,000 workers toiled there. The Rouge was both a symbol and the harsh reality of industrial might, at once an ugly, polluting, man-driving inferno and a magnificent, awe-inspiring achievement. Mexican painter Diego Rivera, commissioned in the early 1930s to prepare murals for the Detroit Institute of Arts, captured this mixture of grandeur and horror. In his stunning frescos, magnificent machinery and awesome industrial processes combined with images of dronelike workers servicing the great smelters and furnaces to depict something of the Rouge's powerful inhuman mystique.

Yet in Rivera's work, as in the Rouge itself, the human dimension remained. Careful students of the frescos noted that the apparently robotlike workers were in fact individual in depiction, their coveralls and uniforms failing to conceal a sense of grievance and aspiration. Moreover, their combined impression was one not of helplessness in the face of such technological power but rather of strength. And so it was in the real Rouge. Recession, Bennett's minions, and the union's weakness held the Rouge workers in check, but throughout the late 1930s and into the defense production period, workers sustained a union presence, toting up the grievances and injustices.

In late 1940 and early 1941, the logjam of union activism at the Rouge broke. A newly unified UAW, armed with financial and organizational support from the CIO, won Labor Board and court cases against Ford, each one narrowing the range of anti-union tactics available. Union activists throughout the Rouge became bolder. Union buttons appeared on caps and shirts. By March, some of the most aggressively organized departments had forced Bennett into dealing on a de facto basis with union grievance committees. Membership cards began to flood into the headquarters of UAW Local 600, the Rouge local.

Unionists worried not only about Bennett's power but about racial divisions among the workers. As many as 10,000 black workers toiled at the Rouge, many in key departments such as the foundry and blast furnaces. Over the years, Ford had acquired a carefully cultivated reputation—not entirely without foundation—as being sympathetic to Negroes. A contributor to black charities and churches, Ford retained the loyalty of key groups in the black community and, through an in-plant leadership linked to black clergymen and politicians, of many black workers. In a showdown, would these black workers remain aloof, a racially defined island of hostility to the union? Even if the UAW successfully organized the Rouge, would the resulting racial tensions pose a constant threat of conflict and disunity?

In the end, the Rouge fell to the UAW with surprising ease. Union strategists cultivated the more liberal elements in the black community, and a stalwart group of black unionists emerged to bring the union message to the Rouge's black workers. By April, union stewards controlled key departments, and on April 1, when Bennett cracked down on union leaders, thousands of rolling-mill workers walked out. Joined by additional thousands in other departments, they launched a strike that the UAW leadership hastily endorsed. Mass meetings, auto caravans that blocked entry to the Rouge, and conventional picketing isolated the huge facility. By now, Ford was in complete disarray. On April 10 the company agreed to cooperate in the holding of a decisive NLRB election in May. With UAW grievance committees now operating openly and with recruitment spurred by Ford's partial capitulation, the UAW conducted a massive election drive, capped on May 19, when CIO president Philip Murray addressed 60,000 auto workers in Detroit. In the election held two days later, the UAW-CIO overwhelmed a rival AFL organization, capturing 70 percent of the 74,000 votes cast at the Rouge. An old

Polish worker voiced something of the euphoria with which auto-workers responded to their victory over this powerful, intransigent corporation: "Once in the Ford plant they called me 'dumb Pollack,' " he told a union leader, "but now with UAW they call me 'brother.' "

Throughout 1941, other CIO unions waged strikes against such corporate giants as International Harvester, Allis-Chalmers, and Weyerhaeuser. Although not all were as spectacularly successful as the UAW and SWOC achievements, all established or confirmed the CIO unions' status as permanent fixtures in basic industry. Nor were AFL affiliates idle, though most made gains in membership and wages without resort to strikes. The Teamsters extended organization in both over-the-road trucking and goods handling, while the Machinists grew in the aircraft industry. The Carpenters organized thousands of woodworkers, often in the face of ferocious conflict with the CIO International Wood-workers of America. In all, during the peak fifteen-month period of defense production (June 1940–December 1941) the unions gained about 1.5 million new members.

The period also established critical gains in wage and contract provisions. So long as open shop giants such as Ford and Little Steel held out, CIO contracts in basic industry remained brief, ambiguous documents. But with the central core now safe for the unions, employers had to extend negotiation to a wide range of previously neglected issues. For most workers, of course, wage rates were the key test of the new unions' ability to perform, and SWOC and the UAW came through, gaining ten-cent hourly increases (at a time when basic rates hovered around fifty cents) for thousands of auto- and steelworkers. The UAW's contract with Ford, negotiated in June 1941, astounded everyone by reestablishing Ford as the industry wage leader and granting the UAW sweeping union security, dues collection, and seniority benefits.

Contracts during this period also began to reflect sophisticated approaches to work rules, grievance-handling, and employee benefits. Some unionists reveled in the shop-floor struggle that characterized the earliest days of the CIO, believing that face-to-face encounters with employers kept the union militant and the leadership responsive to rank-and-file workers. Most union officers, however, and probably the vast majority of ordinary workers as well, sought stable contractual relationships governing compensation, work rules, seniority, and grievance-handling. Of course, contractual rights necessitated contractual obligations. If a matter was covered by the contract, the union could not strike over the matter during the life of the contract. Still, workers generally sought stability and regularity at the workplace. Their resentment of management practices rarely challenged the underlying legitimacy of management's right to make decisions and to carry on the production process. Rather, workers had rebelled against the capricious, arbitrary, and even chaotic means by which managers imposed their decisions. Favoritism, incomprehensible pay schedules, harsh and irrational discipline, the general sense of victimization and powerlessness—these had been the ingredients that fueled the upsurge in unionism. Workers had no desire to replace one form of chaos for another. When union leaders such as Philip Murray and Walter P. Reuther, a rising star in the UAW, spoke of union contracts that carefully governed wage rates, disciplinary procedures, work rules, promotion rosters, and seniority, they spoke the workers' language. Through their unions, industrial workers sought to bring into the factory (in David Brody's apt phrase) "the workplace rule of law." While prewar contracts remained sketchy in many of these matters, the critical organizing surge of 1940–41 laid the basis for the elaboration of union contracts in the coming years. The emerging contractual relationship, made possible by the key gains of 1940–41, eliminated, in the words of one radical organizer, "the worst evil—the total submissiveness of worker to boss." At long last, declared one rank-and-file unionist, workers were "throwing off the shackles and saying to the boss, 'Go to hell! You've had me long enough. I'm going to be a man on my own now.' "

Dissension in the Union Movement

These important achievements, however, did not bring harmony to the labor movement itself. Indeed, the period between the onset of the war in Europe and American entry found organized labor riven by new fractures even while the older ones deepened. Hostility between the AFL and CIO mounted, despite efforts on the part of some laborites and Democratic politicians to bring the two federations together. Direct rivalry escalated as affiliates of the two federations waged sharp jurisdictional conflict in the woodworking, aircraft, electrical, paper, and food processing industries. Disdainful CIO activists continually ridiculed the cautious AFL, charging its top leadership with red-baiting, toleration of corruption, coziness with employers, and general lack of vision. When AFL chieftains joined hands with corporate critics to urge sweeping changes in the National Labor Relations Board, the hostility of Lewis and other CIO spokesmen knew no bounds. AFL stalwarts in turn lashed out at the rival federation. Thus, John Burke of the Pulp Workers lamented in the summer of 1941: "The CIO is everywhere these days, spreading its poison and stirring up strife and confusion." AFL president Green promised that "we will fight against a movement which has vowed to destroy us and wipe us off the face of the earth."

But it was within the CIO itself that some of the bitterest internal conflict raged. At the center, as usual, stood John L. Lewis. Through the late 1930s, the Mine Workers' chieftain loomed as a colossus, dominating newspaper headlines and newsreels, his inimitable voice rolling over the airwaves. As the international crisis deepened, however, Lewis distanced himself from his erstwhile ally, Franklin Roosevelt. Born and reared in inland Iowa and with his sensibility shaped decisively by the provincial world of the mining regions and the ingrown milieu of the Mine Workers union, Lewis distrusted international politics. He regarded Roosevelt's efforts to awaken the American people to the threats of Naziism and Japanese militarism as war-mongering. He attacked fellow labor leaders, even CIO associates such as Sidney Hillman, who supported FDR's foreign and defense policies.

At last, in the fall of 1940, Lewis openly broke with the administration and implicitly with the rest of the labor movement. With millions of working people listening, on October 25 he took to the national air waves and dramatically announced his support for Roosevelt's Republican rival, Wendell L. Willkie, in the November presidential election. Furthermore, the powerful Mine Worker pledged that if industrial workers repudiated him by supporting Roosevelt with their votes, he would step down as CIO president. Lewis's election announcement stunned laborites and journalists alike. Over the years virtually everyone connected with the CIO preserved the memory of where he or she had been on the night of October 25. Ralph Helstein, a rising young attorney in the CIO Packinghouse Workers union, was attending a meeting in Austin, Minnesota. A score or so local unionists had gathered at the union hall to tune in to this important speech by the revered Lewis. When he revealed his abandonment of FDR, the unionists seemed stricken. They just sat there, numb and mute. At last, one stalwart activist strode to the front of the hall where Lewis's picture glowered overlooking the dais. She yanked the large photograph from the wall, marched over to a window, and tossed it out. Only then did the shocked workers break into animated discussion, incredulous at Lewis's stand and at his threat to step down from CIO leadership.

At the CIO convention, which met only days after Roosevelt's victory over Wilkie—a victory made possible by strong working-class support—Lewis honored his pledge. In an emotional speech, he turned over the reins of the CIO to his loyal lieutenant, SWOC president Philip Murray.

Over the next year, Lewis pursued an increasingly antagonistic course. Disbelieving CIO activists at last concluded that he was seeking to wreck the CIO. As Murray, Hillman, Secretary-Treasurer James B.

Carey, and other CIO officials attempted to steer the federation through the turbulent strike wave of 1941, Lewis charted his own course. Convinced that Hillman and other CIO leaders had, in effect, sacrificed the unions' independence, and thus the workers' interests, to the bourgeoning militarism of the Roosevelt administration, Lewis withdrew from CIO affairs and, in effect, forced men who had served him for years, first in the UMW and then in the CIO, to choose sides. He denounced the CIO leadership as traitors to the cause of unionism, calling them "lap dogs and rabbits." He dunned the CIO for the return of "loans" granted to the new federation in its early days by the UMW, submitting a bill to Murray for $1.6 million.

At first, Lewis enjoyed support from Communists and their sympathizers. By 1939, the Communist party was a force in the CIO, because Communists or men and women with strong pro-Communist sympathies led several important unions, maintained a strong and articulate minority presence in others (notably the UAW), and exerted vocal influence outweighing their numerical strength at CIO conventions and in state and local bodies. Although conservatives and AFL chiefs continually criticized Communist presence in the CIO, industrial unionists largely ignored these attacks, labeling them mere "red-baiting." Prior to August 23, 1939, in fact, there was little to distinguish the Communist (or pro-Soviet) position in the CIO from that of any energetic activist. Communists worked hard to expand organization, sought to strengthen workers' rights and benefits, and supported the general foreign and domestic policies of the New Deal. Lewis's early drift away from Roosevelt made pro-Soviet unionists no happier than it did those without Communist associations.

But on August 23, 1939, the Soviet Union announced that it had concluded a nonaggression pact with Germany. From being Naziism's most vehement opponent, the Soviet Union overnight had become its de facto ally. Fascism, declared Soviet foreign minister Molotov in 1940, was "a matter of taste." The war between England and France versus Germany, which began with the German invasion of Poland on September 1, 1939, was, in the official Soviet view, merely a struggle of rival imperialisms. And when the Soviets themselves seized vast chunks of Eastern Europe in 1939 and 1940 and attacked tiny Finland, it truly seemed that the rival dictatorships had joined hands to dominate Europe. Germany's occupation of Norway and Denmark, its sweep through the Low Countries, and its swift victory over France in June 1940 strengthened this dark impression. While Hitler's planes bombed Great Britain relentlessly in the fall of 1940, his eastern flank was secure as Soviet premier Stalin scrupulously fulfilled the economic terms of his pact with Hitler by delivering vast quantities of Soviet raw materials to feed the German war machine.

American Communists and their allies, including dozens of labor activists, defended Soviet behavior. For them, the workers' state, the USSR, alone could provide an unfailing source of guidance in a troubled world. And since the Anglo-German conflict was merely a war of rival imperialisms—and since, in reality, the USSR was in effect allied with the German wing of imperialism—it followed that the American military buildup was provocative and illegitimate. Hence, it became the duty of militant laborites—and Communists prided themselves on their record of militancy—to defend workers' rights regardless of the cost to the defense effort.

Thus, through 1940 and the turbulent early months of 1941, Communists and their allies lashed out at fellow unionists who believed that matters of national defense and the need to aid beleaguered Great Britain imposed legitimate limits on labor's options. At the November 1940, CIO convention, pro-Soviet unionists such as Michael Quill of the Transport Workers and Ben Gold of the Fur Workers called for unceasing militancy in the shops and mines, vilifying more moderate unionists as the stooges of the war-hungry Roosevelt administration. When Congress passed a Roosevelt-backed conscription bill in September 1940, a Communist-inspired ditty captured the venom with which pro-Soviets now viewed their erstwhile friend who had suddenly become blood-hungry: "Franklin Roosevelt / Told the People How He Felt / We Damn Near Believed What He Said / He Said: 'I hate war / And So Does Eleanor / And We won't Be Safe Til Everybody's Dead.' "

Such people, of course, seemed natural allies for John L. Lewis. And indeed, throughout late 1939, 1940, and into the summer of 1941, Communists in the CIO, who might have been exposed and vulnerable given their apparent commitment to a foreign government, found succor in Lewis's imposing strength. They supported the UMW chief without stint in the spring of 1941 as he defied the federal government in a dispute that brought his army of soft coal miners out. They welcomed his denunciations of Roosevelt and his efforts to humiliate those in the CIO, such as Sidney Hillman of the Clothing Workers, who believed that the exigencies of national defense imposed obligations on unions to maintain defense production. Lewis, in turn, shielded the Communists, considering them allies in his efforts to prevent the CIO and the American working class from being absorbed into a war-making machine under construction by the devious and cynical Roosevelt.

Critics, including some now within the CIO itself, accused Communists of fomenting labor unrest in defense industry. Certainly, government officials believed that radical agitators and Nazi provocateurs caused the strikes in the shipyards and aircraft factories. And indeed there were defense strikes aplenty in 1940 and 1941, for about 2 million workers in defense-connected industry engaged in work stoppages in the fifteen months after June 1, 1940. Some of these strikes—notably those at Allis-Chalmers, a key Milwaukee provider of electrical equipment for the Navy, and North American Aviation, the nation's largest supplier of fighter aircraft—did involve Communists operating as militant union activists.

In the North American Strike, which peaked early in June 1941, UAW leaders supported the Roosevelt administration's decision to send in federal troops to end a strike conducted by an aggressive UAW local union in which Communists played critical roles. While anti-Communists believed that strikes such as Allis-Chalmers and North American were the direct product of Communist perfidy and manipulation of innocent workers, in both cases stubborn, anti-union employers and genuinely objectional wage and working conditions undoubtedly fueled rank-and-file militancy.

Communist behavior in these strikes has remained controversial, especially in view of the rapid changes in the party line and the willingness of pro-Soviet laborites to accommodate themselves to each change. In all, the judgment of Irving Howe and Lewis Coser, sharp but fair-minded critics of the Communist party, seems most appropriate: "Communists worked hard to pursue an aggressive trade-union policy during the period of the [Nazi-Soviet] pact. . . . Whenever it seemed at all plausible, they were conspicuously eager to provoke strikes, particularly if war production were involved. . . . [At Allis-Chalmers and North American] the Communists led strikes that raised legitimate trade-union issues but in which their main purpose was clearly political."

On June 22, 1941, Hitler attacked the Soviet Union. Almost overnight, Communists and other pro-Soviets abandoned their earlier line and became ardent supporters of beefed-up military production. They embraced Great Britain, earlier castigated as an imperialistic relic but now suddenly a freedom-loving warrior, and pressed for rapid American entry into the war. With the Soviet fatherland in danger, the Communists abruptly repudiated Lewis. After June 22, they became as eager to dampen labor militancy as they had been to promote it before. Increasingly, Lewis, already on his way out of the CIO, pursued a lonely, isolated battle, while his former defenders turned ferociously upon him.

"The people of America," declared one Communist leader, "must master the military art. Military training must become an essential everyday part of our life, like the right to vote." Said the *Daily Worker*, "Any strike is bound to prove a hindrance to the war effort."

The stunning policy reversals performed by Communists in the defense production period left a legacy of antagonism toward them that persisted in the CIO. For many unionists, it seemed that Communists— and even more important, union activists who invariably supported the pro-Soviet position, regardless of their formal membership affiliations— had proven themselves cynical and irresponsible. Some critics even detected a conspiratorial apparatus at work, in which directives were sent from Moscow to be implemented through an authoritarian chain of command. Though some pro-Soviet CIO leaders, notably general counsel Lee Pressman and publicity director Len De Caux, managed to steer the narrow course between their ardently pro-Soviet sympathies and loyalty to the CIO, their critics remained uneasy so long as these men were prominent in the labor movement. In July 1941, the staunchly anti-Communist editor of the Amalgamated Clothing Workers' newspaper, *The Advance*, spelled out these themes. So long as Hitler stood, democrats and trade unionists had no choice but to cooperate with the newly belligerent Soviet Union and with Communists and their supporters in the labor movement. But, J.B.S. Hardman warned, the Soviet Union remained a bloody-handed tyranny; and American Communists and their defenders remained responsive primarily to the political needs of the USSR. "The Communist party-linemen, in the CIO and in the AFL . . . ," he predicted, "will now be loudest in denouncing 'wildcat strikes' and 'unreasonable' demands . . . in defense industries. And they will do that with the same abandon and same loyalty to their . . . masters overseas . . . as when they did just the opposite thing." Indeed, when in the fall of 1941, Lewis brought 45,000 coal miners out on strike, the *Daily Worker* labeled him among the "enemies of our class as well as of the nation."

AMERICA AT WAR

The Japanese attack on Pearl Harbor rendered many of these ideological conflicts moot, at least in the flush of early war patriotism. Leaders of the AFL and CIO quickly pledged to refrain from strikes for the duration. Aside from a handful of Trotskyists—dissident Marxist-Leninists critical of both the Stalin-led USSR and the Western capitalist democracies—laborites of all persuasions responded to Roosevelt's leadership in the military emergency. Government, which even before American belligerency had developed dispute-resolution and resource-mobilization agencies, intruded as never before into the arena of labor affairs.

The war had complex effects on the labor movement. It boosted membership, limited union activities, and caught organized labor as never before in an intricate web of bureaucratic regulation. On one level the pattern of labor relations during the war reflected the virtually unanimous American endorsement of the country's military and diplomatic goals. American workers dutifully registered for the draft, served when called, and rarely challenged governmental authority. They performed prodigious feats of production and bore considerable sacrifices in the form of deteriorated working, living, and social conditions and did so, on the whole, with remarkably good cheer. Nonetheless, even the enormous patriotic pressures of global conflict could not reverse the fundamentally contentious and conflictual nature of labor relations in the United States. The war dampened and redirected the ongoing struggle, but it did not eliminate conflict. The government's elaborate machinery established to police labor relations itself became a focal point of unrest. When the unions quickly pledged to forego the strike weapon, some employers perceived an opportunity to roll back the gains of a now-defanged labor movement. The surge of new workers into the labor force—and especially the entry of many thousands of women and black workers—reinforced long-lived tensions within the working class itself. And, especially after the most desperate phases of the war were past, wartime strikes, often unsanctioned by the unions, punctured the facade of wartime class unity.

The most important effect of the war on the working class was to integrate it more fully into the nation's dominant system of values and its politico-administrative structure. The war brought a temporary end to unemployment and, largely because of regularity of work and overtime wages, increased real weekly earnings. It brought hundreds of thousands of rural Americans, black and white, into the nation's Detroits, Mobiles, Pittsburghs, and Los Angeleses. The Selective Service System, inaugurated in 1940, drew some 36 million Americans into its net, about two-thirds of whom fell under the ordinary definition of "working-class." Government regulations eventually impinged on every phase of life. Rationing and price controls put the federal government into the grocery stores and gas stations. Conscription reached into every school and home. Security checks, military production standards, and war bond drives brought government into factories and workshops. The

Revenue Act of 1942 vastly expanded the reach of the Internal Revenue Service, increasing the number of federal income tax payers from 4 million to 40 million and introducing the withholding tax to the people.

Of course, all of these new or expanded governmental initiatives extended to the general population, not just to working people. But in each case the country's working-class population was likely to be affected for the first time. Military service, for example, brought unaccustomed patterns of discipline, hygiene, and travel into the lives of hundreds of thousands of young men from ethnic ghettoes, working-class enclaves, and isolated rural locales. The tax system, which from its inception in 1913 had impinged largely on upper-income citizens, now embraced almost literally everyone. The war brought millions into the commercial and bureaucratic channels of modern society for the first time, creating new tastes, elaborating a complex web of needs, opportunities, and obligations.

Women at War

Military and industrial needs quickly drew millions of women into the economic and social mainstream as never before. The sudden absence of sons and husbands, the fear of the dreaded telegram from the Department of War, and the annoyances and inconveniences of rationing, shortages, and disrupted family lives swept up even the most traditional housewife into the great national crusade. Millions of women responded to patriotic appeals and the goad of economic necessity to join the labor force. In one typical New Jersey family, the two eldest sons were in uniform, as was the fiance of the elder daughter. While awaiting her sweetheart's return, she worked the graveyard shift in a plant that made electrical relays. Father, a skilled electronics worker in another factory, built sonar equipment for submarines. Even mother, who had never earned a paycheck in her life, went to work at a handbag factory. The younger children collected tin cans and milkweed pods, faithfully saved their pennies for war stamps, and shouldered extra duties around the house.

While wartime employment was optional for many women, working-class wives and daughters often had little choice. They were more likely than their middle- and upper-income sisters to have gained industrial experience before the war. Since most working-class servicemen clustered in the lower ranks of the armed forces, where pay and allotments hardly approximated civilian income, soldiers' wives, sisters, and mothers needed to work outside the home.

By 1945, about 19 million of the nation's 54-million-member civilian labor force was female. In comparison, the number of males in the civilian labor force dropped from a prewar figure of 41.5 million to just under 35 million in 1945. Thus, whereas in 1940 women had constituted 25 percent of workers, in 1945 they constituted about 36 percent.

During the war and after, popular journalism and folklore created misleading images of this vast inpouring of female workers. Posters, cartoons, and advertisements sought to entice women into the factories and shops, as the relentless demands of the military machine eventually put almost 13 million Americans into uniform. A mythology about women's industrial role sprang up, carefully exploiting the physical and mental capacities of these new workers while at the same time preserving traditional sexual roles and maintaining the sexual division of labor. Thus, "Rosie the Riveter," that heroine of the aircraft fabrication plants, was perceived as a temporary worker. While keeping her alluring sexuality, she donned her coveralls, mastered unaccustomed masculine machinery, and picked up the slack left by her sweetheart's departure for the South Pacific.

The public media stressed the temporariness of women's industrial roles. Hence, while acknowledging women's valuable services, newspapers, newsreels, and magazines stressed their desire to return to hearth and home and to resume the nurturing roles of housewife and mother. Moreover, the public image of women workers reinforced the notion that women were, by nature, frail and delicate creatures, ill-suited over the long haul to the pressures of factory life. Medical opinion held that industrial conditions threatened women's reproductive functions. Shop wisdom held that women were too flighty and easily distracted to hold serious responsibility. Much comment on the factory life of women stressed the presumed sexual distraction that alluringly attired young women would bring to the assembly line. Companies instituted rigid dress codes, barring women from wearing sweaters, regulating hairdos, and imposing other humiliating rules. For a while early in the war some companies hired fashion experts to design uniforms suitable for their new labor force. Lily Daché, notes writer Richard Lingeman, "whipped up helmets and turbans for Douglas and United Aircraft" while another designer created coveralls according to elaborate specifications for Sperry Gyroscope workers. As the war ground on, however, and as the novelty of women performing "man's work" wore off, the childish and demeaning fuss over attire and fashion receded to the background.

The misleading public discussions of women's wartime employment masked certain cold realities. While some women worked to pass the time until menfolk returned from war or because of patriotic zeal, the vast majority worked out of economic necessity. Although wartime recruiting drives did bring some women who had not previously worked into the labor market, most female workers had held jobs before. With relatively well-paying jobs available in industry, women abandoned low-paid, traditionally female occupations such as waitressing, domestic service, and clerking. Once in the plants and mills, they found that the mystique of manly employment had little substance. Most jobs in modern industry required little training or detailed knowledge of machinery. Women could learn semiskilled operations and perform them every bit as expeditiously as men. True, tool-and-die work, welding, and other skilled tasks often required apprenticeships or lengthy training periods, but the failure of female workers to gain entry into these more lucrative and prestigious lines of work resulted from discrimination and lack of seniority rather than from innate inability.

Some employers paid women the backhanded compliment of holding them preferable in certain kinds of repetitive manual labor. "There isn't a thing women can't do here when we divide a job into small parts," observed a magnanimous factory superintendent. Women's small, dextrous hands and their implicitly less highly developed intellectual capacities made them candidates for boring, routine assembly work. In the airframe industry, by 1944 over 40 percent of the labor force was female. The deep thinkers there believed women valuable because their smaller and lighter bodies enabled them to crawl into narrow places for welding and riveting. In reality, however, employers and co-workers soon found that roughly the same range of aptitudes, attitudes, and performance levels prevailed as between men and women.

One area in which sharp distinctions endured concerned wages. In the 1940s, many industries observed traditional wage differentials, paying women less than men received for identical jobs. The labor movement and an increasing number of governmental directives opposed this overt discrimination, and by the end of the war the *idea* of equal pay for equal work had become prevalent. Reality, however, never caught up with conception. Employers systematically downgraded female employees. Departmental seniority segregated women in "female" lines of work and limited their opportunity to move up to higher-paying job classifications. Employers, often with the connivance of union representatives, transformed minor variations in job descriptions into justifications for substantial male-female pay differentials. Foremen and co-workers punished obstreperous women workers who presumed to invade higher-paying male preserves with sexual harassment, including outright physical abuse, snide innuendo, and ostentatious assignment of women to particularly noisome or arduous labor.

Nor did the unions step into the breach. In 1943, Auto Workers president R. J. Thomas termed the problem of substandard pay for female workers "a women's problem," a particularly obtuse comment in view of the UAW's stake in maintaining wage standards for its male members as well as for its 250,000 female dues payers. Nor was the UAW or its local unions particularly energetic about protecting its women members on the shop floor. It left uncontested grossly discriminatory company regulations that penalized women for their out-of-work behavior or that sought to govern women's attire or personal demeanor. One UAW local, the proud and militant Flint Local 559, voted not to take up grievances of any female employee "indecent in her wearing apparel or actions."

Women fought back against this condescension, discrimination, and hostility. "We are getting tired of men saying, 'Well, that's the woman's problem,' " UAW activist May McKernan declared. The Auto Workers union did eventually establish a Women's Bureau and belatedly began to press for equal pay contract enforcement and to lobby legislatively in behalf of female workers. The United Electrical Workers, with 300,000 women members, compiled an enviable record of contract gains and enforcement. Still, most trade unionists—to say nothing of employers, the press, and government officials—continued to view women as a temporary embellishment and/or burden in the male workplace, "like," in the words of one Detroit employer, "a cross between a campus queen and a Hollywood starlet."

Such attitudes rested on the fundamental misconception that women were not permanent members of the labor force. Despite over a century of industrial employment of females, males continued to perceive women workers as exotic mutants, not as co-workers in the daily struggle for economic survival and family security. Too often those who presumed to speak in behalf of women workers reinforced this perception. Thus, in 1943 the female chair of one Michigan governmental labor agency asserted that men had no cause for worry that women would remain in industry. "Women will always be women," she reassured them. As soon as the war ends "you will see women returning naturally to their homes" because, after all, "a woman's first interests are her home, her husband, and their children." Harsh reality however insured that after the war at least 30 percent of the nation's women would be permanent full-time wage earners. For these women, and for others for whom the choice of remunerative employment might provide an alternative to intolerable familial circumstances, the question was not one of working or not working. It was whether women would have high-wage, union-protected jobs or would dutifully troop back to domestic service, low-wage light industry, or nonunion retail shops.

The war years marked a milestone for women workers, despite the discrimination and harassment. The surge in employment and the beginnings of equality of treatment receded soon after the shooting stopped. Female employment, especially in manufacturing, fell sharply after the war, and the hard-scrabble working-class feminism that some activists had begun to establish receded as postwar America elevated the domestic virtues into a veritable ideology. Still, thousands of women refused to go back to home and hearth, and the drastic erosion of female employment of the 1930s ended. The graph line showing women's participation in the labor force for the twentieth century shows a steady increase through the first three decades, a noticeable leveling off between 1930 and 1940 then a sharp peak at 1944–45. The line then falls off rapidly, but the decline ends in 1946 at a level considerably above that of 1940. And then, despite the apparent national consensus that a woman's place was in the home, the rate of women's employment climbs upward again, surpassing by 1960 even the wartime peak of 36 percent. This pattern of employment has led some scholars to downplay the importance of World War II experience because they believe that it masks the overall twentieth-century trend, which has been toward ever-increasing labor force participation regardless (not because) of national emergencies. They also argue that the availability of relatively high-wage, core industrial employment for women during the war tends to disguise another overall pattern, namely that the economy's dual labor market has consistently (the aberration of the war notwithstanding) earmarked females for low-wage, nonunion, and often ephemeral employment opportunities.

Black Workers

World War II partially opened up some industrial doors for black Americans as well. At first, few government officials or business leaders saw black workers as a critical factor in meeting wartime manpower needs. Indeed, as wartime mobilization geared up through 1941, it became blatantly clear to labor activists such as A. Philip Randolph, president of the Brotherhood of Sleeping Car Porters and the nation's preeminent black unionist, that corporations would follow traditional discriminatory policies without hindrance from government. Thus, in September, a statement by North American Aviation, a leading defense contractor, that "the Negro will be considered only as janitors and in other similar capacities" was remarkable only for its bluntness. "Regardless of their training . . . ," North American declared, "we will not employ them." Nor did either federal legislation or governmental policy even address itself to discrimination in employment, despite the efforts of Randolph and a handful of liberals and unionists to awaken the Roosevelt administration.

Faced with such obduracy, in January 1941, Randolph issued a statement proclaiming that if black workers were not given equal access to employment in national defense projects, 10,000 black workers would march on Washington in protest. "We loyal Negro American Citizens Demand the Right to Work," asserted Randolph's manifesto. The appeal declared that if Negroes were to benefit from the massive public expenditures, "We Must Fight For It And Fight For It With Gloves Off."

The March on Washington movement soon enlisted black civil rights, religious, and journalistic leaders. By the spring, Randolph's conception had escalated, and his appeals now projected 100,000 militant black marchers. Eventually, Randolph used the government's apprehensions over the planned march to secure a presidential proclamation creating a Fair Employment Practices Commission (FEPC), issued on June 25, 1941, in return for cancellation of the march.

Black critics attacked this compromise. With the black community mobilized as never before and with preparations for the mass demonstration so far advanced, why call it off to appease the white power structure? The FEPC, which was to be chaired by a white southerner, would, they felt, be at best a pious fraud. Lacking Congressional funding, it would remain impoverished and timid. It was better for the black working class to rely on its own militant strength to secure industrial equality than to put its fate into the hands of a feeble federal agency, black activists charged.

And indeed FEPC proved a frail reed upon which to base the hopes of black workers. On occasion, as in a 1944–45 racially motivated strike of white bus drivers in Philadelphia, FEPC's vigorous intervention paved the way for upgrading of black workers. In racially troubled Detroit, when thousands of whites walked out rather than work with upgraded black co-workers, FEPC rulings helped UAW and black leaders to defuse the situation and gain equity for some Negro workers. In many other cases, however, FEPC proved toothless. And, as black militants argued (and as Randolph, a veteran militant himself, surely agreed), even where FEPC did achieve results, it was the pressure that an aroused black labor force and community exerted on unions, employers, and government officials that really had compelled action.

In the end, it was not goodwill, racial enlightenment, or government intervention that brought large numbers of black workers into the wartime labor force. It was the pressure of necessity. As late as the summer of 1942, blacks held only 3 percent of the country's war-related jobs. Three years later, the proportion had almost tripled, though Negroes held these jobs in numbers below their overall levels of labor force participation. In all, during the war over one million black workers, about two-thirds of them women, entered the labor market. Black employment in manufacturing, which in 1940 stood at levels considerably below predepression figures, grew by 150 percent. By the end of 1944, some 1,250,000 Negro workers, 300,000 of them female, toiled in manufacturing. Industrial employment of black workers centered on the steel and metals industries, meatpacking, Detroit-area military vehicle and aircraft production, and Gulf Coast shipbuilding. In general, black workers retained their positions at the bottom of the industrial ladder, but in areas with strong, progressive-led unions, such as the UAW in Detroit, black workers made important breakthroughs in access to higher-skill (and hence, higher-wage) classifications.

Indeed, the UAW and some other CIO organizations compiled admirable records of support for their black members. Without the presence of the Auto Workers union, Detroit's explosive racial tension might have been unmanageable. In both the shops and neighborhoods, tensions mounted almost daily as thousands of black workers encountered the resentment of other new factory workers, many of them migrants from the poor white regions of the South. In June 1943, a wave of "hate" strikes—walkouts of whites in protest over the hiring or upgrading of black workers—crested when 25,000 stopped work at a large Packard aircraft engine facility. Ku Klux Klan propaganda had circulated incessantly through the plant. Packard had resorted to racist stereotypes in an effort to resist directives to hire and promote black workers. Defying the UAW leadership, strikers milled about outside the plant, threatening black workers and vowing never to return so long as Negroes remained. The UAW, however, moved swiftly against the so-called hate strikers. President R. J. Thomas compelled the local to abandon the strike and to uphold the discharge of workers who violated the UAW's policy of nondiscrimination. The UAW also played a key role in calming race riots over housing and recreational facilities that rocked the city in 1943 and left twenty-five dead. Again and again, in the words of historians August Meier and Elliott Rudwick, "It was the [UAW-] CIO leadership, virtually alone among the city's influential whites, who came to the blacks' defense."

The experience of black workers with the labor movement, however, was far from universally positive. At least thirty-one of the AFL's affiliates, as well as most of the independent railroad brotherhoods, barred Negroes from membership. Others segregated black workers into subsidiary locals, often depriving them of full union voting and benefit rights. Although AFL conventions often piously invoked American ideals of equality, in practice even organizations which espoused egalitarian sentiments consistently deferred to the prejudices of their southern white membership and acquiesced in discriminatory wage levels and segregated facilities.

The two AFL unions most directly involved in military production, the International Association of Machinists and the Boilermakers, were among the most notoriously racist organizations in the labor movement. The IAM, which represented hundreds of thousands of aircraft workers, barred Negroes entirely, while the Boilermakers, the dominant AFL organization in a shipbuilding industry which during the war employed over 1.7 million workers, imposed relentlessly discriminatory practices on its black membership. In sharp contrast to the UAW, UE, and other CIO organizations, the AFL and its affiliates remained largely unresponsive to the unique problems of the black working class during the war.

For black workers, some of the gains of the World War II era were long-lasting and substantial. Between 1939 and the mid-1950s, the median annual income for full-time black workers rose from 45 percent of that of white workers to 57 percent. This significant increase reflected several important demographic and labor market trends. During World War II alone, over 400,000 blacks left the South, most moving from the impoverished and deteriorating southern agricultural sector to high-wage war production areas. In addition, an expanding public sector sharply increased employment of black workers by government. During the war alone, for example, the number of black federal workers leaped from under 60,000 to over 200,000. Despite lamentable racism and discrimination, government jobs provided greater equality and security and higher wages than comparable private-sector employment. Most importantly, however, the war expanded the foothold black workers had gained in the central core industries. With the victory of CIO unionism, which wartime conditions enormously enhanced, disproportionate numbers of black workers benefitted from improvements in basic wage rates and other benefits. Increasingly in industries such as vehicle production, steel and metallurgy, meatpacking, and other basic goods-producing sectors, the problems of black workers came to focus on access to skilled jobs and fighting the effects of technological unemployment. Wartime gains and the growing alliance between CIO unions and civil rights organizations, supported at least sporadically by governmental policies, insured that the nation's postwar race relations agenda would be decisively different from that prevailing since the end of Reconstruction.

The Unions at War

The war had a direct and long-lasting impact on the labor movement itself. In many respects, the international crisis brought domestic prosperity. Full employment, widespread opportunities for upgrading, extensive overtime, and relaxed employer attitudes toward costs provided a sharp contrast to the grim and grudging conditions of the depression. And as thousands of new workers moved into defense production in the central core industries, the importance of the CIO organizing thrust of the 1930s became apparent, for thousands of munitions, shipbuilding, aircraft, electrical, and vehicle workers strengthened the industrial unions. The United Steelworkers of America (as SWOC was now called), the UAW, the CIO unions in electrical goods, meatpacking, and shipbuilding, and AFL affiliates in electrical, shipping, aircraft, machine tooling, and other war-essential sectors expanded rapidly. For example, from 165,000 members in 1939, the UAW grew to 1,065,000 in 1944. By the last year of the war there were 708,000 Steelworkers, 432,000 Electrical Workers, 209,000 CIO Shipbuilding Workers, 700,000 AFL Machinists, and 225,000 members of meatpacking unions in the AFL and CIO. Teamster membership expanded from 440,000 to 650,000. In all, the unions gained approximately 5 million new members during the war, surging from under 10 million to nearly 15 million in mid-1945.

This sudden influx, however, created problems both for workers and some unions. Thousands of new industrial workers knew little of organized labor and its struggles. Often new hires automatically became dues-paying members through various union security provisions of existing contracts; on occasion, as in the shipyards, this practice resulted in the compulsory recruitment of thousands of wartime workers into AFL unions that prior to the war had had only skeletal locals in the then-declining industry. Indeed, some of the contracts arranged by the Boilermakers union and other AFL Metal Trades organizations were little more than collusive deals which cynically inflated the unions' treasuries at the expense of bewildered war workers.

Even where unions made no attempt to railroad new workers into their organizations, the tide of new hires posed problems. If an established union did not enjoy "union security"—that is, if newly hired workers were not obligated to join the union upon beginning their tasks—a suddenly expanded war factory might quickly provide the conditions necessary for the destruction of a long-established local union. A manipulative employer, seeing his labor force double or triple in a short time, might press for a representation election. With new recruits having little experience with unions and with union activists perhaps leaving for the military, a quick NRLB election might suddenly undo years of struggle and sacrifice. Moreover, veteran unionists often found the mix of inexperienced, female, youthful, and transient workers who often provided wartime manpower lacking in knowledge of unionism, collective bargaining, and industrial customs. Thousands of these workers found wartime wages a bonanza attributable to government or company largess. They often saw themselves as temporary workers and paid little attention to union affairs or to traditional work rules or practices that veteran employees regarded as critical to their own long-range well-being. New industrial recruits might be docile and acquiescent, accepting management rules and practices unquestioningly. Alternately, however, unionists found that sometimes new recruits responded explosively to perceived injustices, going out on strike or even physically confronting supervisors without regard to formalized union grievance procedures or strike-sanction regulations. Thus, as welcome as were the hordes of new union members, they also constituted an unpredictable, volatile, and, it sometimes seemed, indigestible mass.

The No-Strike Pledge (NSP) also complicated the lives of unionists. Entered into just after Pearl Harbor, the NSP was a voluntary agreement made by AFL and CIO leaders to forego work stoppages for the duration. The unions reaped immediate benefits in public acclaim and governmental goodwill. But veteran unionists and some socialist militants pointed out that for labor organizations to give up the right to strike was to deprive them of their most essential weapon. Without having to fear strikes, why would any employer *ever* negotiate in good faith? If unions could not back up their demands with the threat of strikes, why would workers join the union or pay their dues? A union without strike capability was a contradiction in terms. Even thousands of patriotic workers who in theory agreed with the NSP became bitter and resentful when they found that in specific cases involving their own wages or work rules, their own unions could not support their legitimate goals. Indeed, rank-and-file workers soon learned that their union could function as a disciplinary agent *against* its own members, as those who embarked on strikes in violation of the NSP often faced severe union sanctions.

Wartime Strikes

During the first year or so of America's participation in the war, these problems remained largely beneath the surface. In 1942, for example, the country experienced only 2,970 work stoppages, involving but 840,000 workers. The shock of Allied military setbacks, the determination to whip the Axis powers, and the novelty of wartime production combined to mask tensions in the economy. "Everyone who works for a living," declared CIO president Murray in October 1942, "has burned into his very soul the full appreciation of what this war is about." Civilization itself, he asserted, "is now being threatened by Hitler and his Nazi hordes." A few pennies in the pay envelope or a few inconveniences at the workbench seemed inconsequential in contrast.

But after 1942, as American, Soviet, and Allied forces gained the upper hand, disputes became more and more open and contentious. The No-Strike Pledge notwithstanding, in 1943 the number of strikes rose to over 3,700 and involved 1.98 million workers. The next year found over 2 million workers laying down their tools in some 5,000 strikes, the greatest number of stoppages in American history up to that point. The wave of strikes continued on a comparable level into 1945, when almost 3.5 million workers walked off the job.

Several remarkable patterns characterized these wartime strike statistics. The actual number of stoppages in 1943, for example, was not drastically higher than that of the previous year, but in another statistical category, that of "man days idle," the figure soared to triple the 1942 tally. This was because the great event of 1943 on the labor relations front was the dispute among the United Mine Workers' half-million soft coal miners, the coal operators, and, perhaps most importantly, the federal government. So although for most workers, 1943 (and especially the first half of the year) pretty much replayed the tense, quiet months of 1942, for coal miners it was a year of testing and tribulation.

By late 1943 and early 1944, however, circumstances had changed. Despite virtually universal condemnation, John L. Lewis and his coal miners had forced the government to bend its wage formulas in the 1943 walkouts. Workers, particularly in the CIO, where the Lewis mystique remained potent, began to take action to relieve pent-up frustrations and grievances. Strikes rippled through the aircraft plants, the tank and truck factories, even the weapons and munitions sector. In general, these strikes were brief, often spontaneous affairs. Sometimes workers ignored their union leadership, committed as it was to the No-Strike Pledge. A batch of unresolved grievances in a particular department, the imposition of niggling disciplinary measures in another, the failure to resolve wage-rate controversies—all of these seemingly minor problems could erupt into work stoppages in the superheated atmosphere of the late wartime shops. "If it was not one plant, it was in the other plant," recalled one UAW leader. Committed to enforcing the No-Strike Pledge on his restive co-workers, he found that company officials imposed arbitrary discipline or dragged their feet on wage adjustments because they believed the union powerless to resist without the strike weapon. As a local union president, he had to curb the workers' impatience, to act "like a fireman with a water bucket running around trying to put fires out."

Sometimes groups of workers squared off against each other. In the confused setting of wartime industry, workers in one department might resent the lighter work schedules or better shop conditions in another. Long hours, crowded housing, and the general strain of wartime working and living intensified shop-floor tension. Safety standards fell and accident rates soared during the war as employers, with military representatives egging them on, stepped up production schedules even as the shift to new military hardware disturbed routines and required unfamiliar machinery. Sexual and racial conflict erupted, as workers, deprived of the opportunity to confront the employer, sometimes turned on each other. Interunion quarrels became rampant. "Firestone had to shut down three days last week after a guard and a Negro woman became involved in an altercation," reported a Memphis CIO representative servicing a large tire factory. "During the exchange of words," he went on, " . . . the Negro called the guard a SOB, and the guard slugged her. . . . The white folks walked out in protest [over the firing of the guard], and the Negroes followed suit." All the while, the CIO man observed, a rival AFL union sought "to incite so many walkouts that even good CIO members will become disgusted."

Most of these strikes were short. Thus, although there were some 1,200 more strikes in 1944 than in 1943, the percentage of working time lost to work stoppages actually decreased. As the war entered into its final months and victory became certain, however, workers increasingly geared up for postwar confrontations. In August and September 1945, the pattern of strike activity shifted again, as unionists grew concerned over reduced overtime, lagging wage rates, and declining weekly income. Fearing a return to depression-era conditions and faced with massive cancellations of military orders, unions such as the UAW, the Steelworkers, the UE, and others in both the AFL and CIO quickly abandoned the No-Strike Pledge and sought to resume normal collective bargaining in an effort to protect the gains made under the stimulus of the pressurized wartime economy.

THE NATIONAL WAR LABOR BOARD

From the inception of the No-Strike Pledge, government advisors and labor leaders alike realized that in the absence of the strike weapon, the labor movement would need some other means of resolving disputes. Thus, in January 1942, President Roosevelt established a National War Labor Board (NWLB), a twelve-member tribunal charged with the responsibility of resolving war industry disagreements. Since the new agency consisted of four members each from business, organized labor, and the government, its establishment insured that the major unions would have, at least in this one area of government policy, equal access and an equal vote. In virtually all other aspects of wartime mobilization, the Roosevelt administration relied heavily on corporate officials. Labor leaders such as Philip Murray of the CIO and William Green of the AFL felt shut out of such key wartime agencies as the Office of War Production, the Office of War Mobilization, and the War Manpower Commission. Remarks historian Paul Koistinen, " 'Big Government' " and " 'Big Business' had virtually become one. 'Big Labor' was a pygmy by comparison." But on the NWLB, whose importance grew as the war ground on, organized labor not only had equal representation but found the "public" members of the board, and much of its technical staff, quite responsive to the dilemmas of the unions under the No-Strike Pledge.

The board functioned as part of a complex web of interaction between government, labor, and employers. For government, the NWLB provided a means for resolving labor disputes and forestalling strikes. Moreover, the board became the key factor in the government's efforts to keep the lid on wartime inflation, for invariably wage disputes were the board's most important source of cases.

For business, however, the board always remained an object of suspicion. True, like organized labor, employers had the right to name four of the NWLB's members. But whereas the labor movement's membership was embraced largely in two giant federations, "business" was an abstract term disguising thousands of diverse enterprises. No federal agency structured like the NWLB, many employers felt, could possibly provide valid representation for "business" or "employers." Moreover, business representatives believed that both the public members of the board and its technical staff shared a pro-union bias. Reluctant under the best of circumstances to turn over such critical matters as wage determination, union recognition, and management prerogatives in the workplace to government, employers charged that the pattern of board decisions strengthened the unions, distorted wage rates, and eroded managerial authority in the workplace.

Given the exigencies of wartime, most employers cooperated with the board and generally implemented it rulings. Still, when in 1944 a stubborn employer such as Sewell L. Avery of the Montgomery Ward Company defied board decisions and compelled the president to dispatch federal troops to impose its rulings, businessmen made him a hero. A widely circulated photograph of the octogenarian Avery, defiantly seated in his office chair, being evicted by steel-helmeted soldiers, symbolized for many the illegitimacy and potential for abuse of wartime governmental powers. "Hitler's thugs . . . never did a more efficient job," asserted one newspaper. Avery spoke for thousands of frustrated employers when he told the attorney-general of the United States: "I want none of your damned advice . . . to hell with the government."

Organized labor accumulated many grievances against the NWLB as well. Rank-and-file unionists found its proceedings slow and uncertain. Workers faced with harsh discipline or unfair work assignments had to endure their punishment or unpleasant or dangerous jobs for months. Employers became ingenious in divising shortcuts and loopholes; deprived of the right to strike, workers could only watch in frustration as an overworked board, which eventually disposed of over 20,000 wage dispute cases, did its time-consuming best.

Nor did even top leadership always applaud the board's actions. In July 1942, for example, the NWLB made a ruling in a critical case of wage determination involving a half-million steelworkers, and indirectly, millions of workers for whom the decision served as a pattern-setter. With full employment returning to the steel mills in 1941, the Steelworkers union submitted proposals to the Little Steel companies for substantial wage increases. Certainly, had free collective bargaining operated, the union would have held the winning hand, for the demand for steel bolstered the steelworkers' bargaining power. Moreover, the virtually guaranteed profits accruing from massive military procurement would doubtless have caused the steel companies to settle without a strike. But, of course, under the No-Strike Pledge, the Steelworkers' union could *not* strike, thus stiffening employers' resolve to resist the union's demands.

The dispute that resulted from these circumstances, of course, became the responsibility of the NWLB in the spring of 1942. Complicating the particular details of collective bargaining in the steel industry— an intricate and confusing matter in its own right—was the federal government's determination to clamp down on inflation. Fueled by the surge of emergency war production, the price level had spurted at least 15 percent between January 1941 and May 1942. The Roosevelt administration hastily hammered out an anti-inflation policy, involving agricultural subsidies, selective price controls, tax increases, and an "equality of sacrifice" campaign. But these measures required congressional action. Armed with the No-Strike Pledge, however, and with a functioning federal agency available to implement wage restraint, the government viewed the Steelworkers' matter (called the Little Steel Case) as a key aspect of the anti-inflation campaign that could be implemented immediately.

On July 16, 1942, the board announced its ruling. Steelworkers, it agreed, merited wage increases in view of the severe inflation of 1941–42. The board noted, however, that contracts in 1941 had gained steelworkers increases of almost 12 percent. Thus, the "Little Steel Formula," as the ruling became known, limited the permissible demands of the United Steel Workers to only a fraction of what unionists believed equitable. Whereas the union called for an additional increase, beyond the 1941 gains of 12 percent, the board's formula established a figure of about 5.5 as legitimate. Outraged, unionists argued that the wage gains of 1941 merely righted long-standing inequities and that steelworkers had a right to improve basic wage standards, not merely to try to catch up with inflation. They pointed out that in normal times, the union could strike in support of its wage demands. They charged that the steel companies were raking in vast profits and could easily afford the Steelworkers' demands. They lashed out at the Little Steel Formula as, in the words of the NWLB's labor members "a serious blow at the foundations of collective bargaining."

Indeed, over the next three years, laborites grew increasingly resentful over many NWLB policies and other government measures. Regulations against job-changing, for example, became ever more severe and struck at the American worker's most cherished freedom, his right to physical mobility and pursuit of new job opportunities. In the face of the sticky wage patterns that the Little Steel Formula established, workers often found that the only way they could increase their pay was to shift jobs. Especially for skilled workers, this was an attractive option in view of the prevailing labor shortages. But job-shifting soon became chronic. Some employers actually hoarded skilled labor, permitting highly paid men to sit idle so they would be on hand when new orders came in. Production suffered as turnover created chaos in some critical lines of war goods. The War Manpower Commission, prodded by the military, imposed increasingly severe restrictions on workers' mobility. In addition, NWLB rulings on various matters critical to workers— such as limitations on overtime pay, changes in work rules, and encouragement of incentive pay plans (long an object of labor's hostility)—further antagonized workers and their unions.

Local unionists bridled over the high-handed and cumbersome NWLB actions. While national leaders normally swallowed their objections in their desire to demonstrate labor's support of the war effort, rank-and-file activists were less restrained. One of the bitterest denunciations of labor's treatment came from the president of a UAW aircraft workers' local in New York. "Our policy is not to win the war at any cost," declared Tom De Lorenzo. "The policy of our Local Union is to win the war without sacrificing too many of the rights which we have at the present time." De Lorenzo went on in language that shocked government officials, journalists, and probably many laborites as well: "If I had brothers at the front who needed the 10 or 12 planes that were sacrificed [during a recent strike], I'd let them die, if necessary, to preserve our way of life or rights or whatever you want to call it."

Few working people and fewer union leaders shared such a harsh view. Although the mounting wartime strikes of 1943 and 1944 often defied board policies, in general the NWLB found organized labor cooperative in enforcing even unpopular rulings. Rank-and-filers might grumble, but union leaders increasingly found that cooperation with the board paid off for them and their unions. NWLB restrictions on wages were part of a general government policy of price and wage control, and even if the Roosevelt administration's "equality of sacrifice" program never worked as well as laborites hoped, over the second half of the war the rate of inflation did slow significantly. Moreover, in specific cases, the board found ingenious ways to raise wages or otherwise compensate workers without actually breaking the Little Steel Formula, thus blunting some of labor's most severe criticisms of the board's overall approach. So long as leaders such as William Green and Philip Murray had access to President Roosevelt and so long as the board seemed to operate in good faith to meet labor's criticisms, the support of the AFL and CIO for it remained strong, whatever the criticisms of dissidents such as De Lorenzo.

Quite apart from other factors, veteran labor leaders knew that if Congress and the public at large perceived labor as uncooperative, greedy, or unpatriotic, the government could unsheath powerful weapons of retribution. The elections of 1942 had returned a staunchly conservative congressional majority. In the summer of 1943, reflecting public hostility to coal strikes earlier that spring, Congress passed the Smith-Connally Act, an attempt to limit sharply organized labor's political and economic power. With even President Roosevelt (who vetoed the Smith-Connally bill) speaking of the need for a full-scale labor draft, men such as Murray and Green drew back from too open a criticism of the NWLB. "We may have to take it on the chin here and there for a time," UAW president R. J. Thomas admitted in 1944, "but if we can present the nation and the returning soldier with a clean record, we will gain after the war for the sacrifices we are making today."

Privately, labor leaders fulminated against the position that government policy placed them in. Even Murray, though thoroughly committed to the No-Strike Pledge, railed against the injustices of federal policy. In June 1944 he complained that government and industry alike relied on the labor movement to enforce the No-Strike Pledge; they called on union leaders "to police [the Board's] . . . damnable and most obnoxious directives." How unfair, Murray declared, it was that the dues money collected by the unions had to be used to pay the salaries of union officials who were compelled "to enforce [against the dues-paying membership] the directives of the National War Labor Board which, [in many cases] we do not believe in."

Only in unions with strong Communist representation did endorsement for the NSP remain virtually unqualified throughout the war. Communists and other pro-Soviet unionists, most of them in CIO organizations, often criticized specific NWLB and other government policies. However, they kept their remarks carefully restrained and never hinted at noncooperation. Moreover, some Communist union leaders even urged the adoption of policies from which even the most loyal partisan of the No-Strike Pledge shrank. Thus, for example, Communist national leader Earl Browder embraced incentive wage payments. Most workers viewed these "piece rate" plans as manipulative, unfair, and devisive. Thus, when Communists in the unions echoed Browder's call, non-Communist laborites were appalled.

In addition, some union leaders associated with the Communist party even urged that the No-Strike Pledge continue into the postwar period. Harry Bridges, pro-Soviet president of the International Longshoremen's and Warehousemen's Union, publicly supported national service legislation, which Murray and virtually every non-Communist denounced as virtual industrial slavery. But pro-Soviet unionists such as Bridges, Reid Robinson of the Mine, Mill, and Smelter Workers, Ben Gold of the Fur Workers, and dozens of others were eager to further the war effort and to lend every ounce of support possible to the beleaguered Red Army. Thus, they willingly, even cheerfully, ran the risk of endorsing policies and practices normally associated with odious forms of worker discipline and exploitation. Rank-and-file Communists often tried to temper the shrill admonitions emanating from top Party circles in behalf of worker discipline and unrestrained production, but the Party's wartime record undermined its influence in unions such as the UAW, where Party members had been important, and normally militant, leaders.

MAINTENANCE OF MEMBERSHIP

The NWLB's policy in one critical area did much to temper labor leaders' unhappiness. In important rulings through early 1942 the board established a "maintenance of membership" policy regarding union security. In its most definitive formulation, this meant that if a union had a contract with an employer, all newly hired workers would automatically become dues-paying members after their first fifteen days on the job had elapsed. If they did not want to join, they had to declare that intention before the fifteen-day waiver period ended. Having failed to exercise this option, the workers would be subject to discharge from employment if they did not pay their dues or otherwise remain in good standing for the life of the contract.

If unionists raged at NWLB wage policy and at having to discipline strikers, employers hated the maintenance of membership formula. Few of the unions that had emerged in the 1930s had gained any form of union security through collective bargaining; now a government board granted them virtually ironclad compulsory membership provisions. To employers, requiring union membership smacked of coercion. Employers particularly resented having to play the role of enforcer, for it fell to them to actually discharge workers who fell behind in union dues or otherwise earned the displeasure of the union. Just as labor leaders hated the role of disciplinarian that NWLB policies thrust upon them, so employers bridled at having to impose authority on workers in behalf of the detested union.

Maintenance of membership remained controversial throughout the war. Compulsory unionism seemed to many observers a violation of basic principles of individual freedom. Even some unionists disliked it, believing that it tended to make the union leadership, now secure in the flow of dues payments, unresponsive to rank-and-file workers. Still, so far as principled trade unionists were concerned, the need for maintenance of membership derived not from the insatiable demands of dues-hungry union leaders but rather from the distorted dynamics of wartime labor relations. The No-Strike Pledge and the limitations of wage policy under the Little Steel Formula made it impossible for unions to do the things they normally would do to recruit and retain members. Without the ability to contemplate strike action, unions were drastically limited in the normal functions, namely defense of workers' rights on the shop floor and improvement of conditions through collective bargaining.

Moreover, the Wagner Act itself required that unions bargain for the entire bargaining unit, not merely for union members. Under the best of times, the problem of the "free rider"—the worker who refused to join the union but who benefitted automatically with each gain achieved in collective bargaining—bedeviled labor organizations. "What is the use of paying dues when . . . [I] can have as much say so as Union members," asked one shrewd working-class calculator. The requirement of representing all workers and the loss of the strike option made some form of union security necessary. Otherwise, the hard-won gains of the 1930s might disappear overnight as new hires overwhelmed the relatively smaller number of experienced workers. We will gladly foreswear maintenance of membership, said union leaders, if we can only resort to our time-tested methods of recruitment and struggle. Deprived of these, if we are to continue as loyal partners in wartime production, we must have the time that maintenance of membership provides to educate these new workers as to the benefits of unionism.

Whatever the ethical or theoretical validity of maintenance of membership, it surely generated growth in union ranks. The rapid expansion of the great industrial unions—the UAW, USWA, UE, IAM, the Shipbuilding Workers, and others—stemmed directly from the NWLB's maintenance of membership provisions. Early in 1945, the UAW and the Textile Workers adopted convention resolutions urging that the CIO vent its criticisms of NWLB policies by rescinding the No-Strike Pledge. But President Philip Murray quickly squelched this protest, arguing that whatever the injustices of board policies, labor's gains in membership under maintenance of membership were enormous. Said Murray's lieutenant Van A. Bittner, "The no-strike pledge is the only weapon that organized labor has in this country during the war," for it protected the labor movement from the swift repression that would surely greet widespread strike action while at the same time boosting membership. Warned Murray, if the labor movement abandoned the No-Strike Pledge, it would lose maintenance of membership and bring upon itself every destructive anti-union force in the country. "The wolves are just around the corner," he admonished, "and they have got a ravenous appetite and they are ready to eat you up."

CRITICS OF WAR LABOR POLICY

Such dire prospects did not impress everyone in the labor movement, however. Members of some revolutionary grouplets saw in the pressurized atmosphere of wartime industry the opportunity to escalate labor conflict as a means of creating a revolutionary situation in the United States. After all, members of the several Trotskyist organizations argued, socialists had seized power in Russia in 1917 as a direct result of the internal crisis triggered by World War I. Since the current war itself sprang from the irrationalities of global capitalism, the escalation of wartime strikes could fatally undermine the repressive and imperialistic social order. Men and women with these views participated in many wartime strikes, hoping to encourage workers to move beyond their immediate grievances toward a broader, systemic vision of the unjust workings of capitalism. Mounting industrial unrest would also cause workers to repudiate the established labor movement, whose deep enmeshment in the bureaucratic web of government-sponsored labor relations made it incapable of serving as the legitimate voice of the working class. These Trotskyists, often enormously articulate and skilled in debate, pointed particularly accusing fingers at Communist union functionaries, for it was these putative revolutionaries who most earnestly embraced the No-Strike Pledge and most relentlessly stilled wartime dissidence.

Only one figure of consequence, however, directly challenged the government and the labor establishment in these matters. John L. Lewis surely was no Trotskyist. His mounting criticism of the NWLB, President Roosevelt, and the CIO owed more to traditional American labor voluntarism than to any radical ideology. In the spring of 1943, when Lewis's coal miners defied the government in a series of massive strikes, the wrath of Congress, the press, and the Communist party knew no bounds. One Air Force hero openly bragged of his dream of "the destruction with six fifty-caliber machine guns on an American fighter plane of John L. Lewis." The *Daily Worker* charged that Lewis "wants to throw the country into a home-front war against the President, not against Hitler." Leaders of the AFL and CIO, embarrassed at Lewis's actions, combined statements of support for the coal miners' grievances with disapproval of Lewis's behavior.

Few in the labor movement confronted the basic challenge that Lewis issued during the coal strikes. Tied to a No-Strike Pledge and beholden to federal authorities for the health of their unions, were labor leaders any longer free men, he asked implicitly. In imposing discipline on their rank-and-file members, had they not turned into henchmen in the vast government-military-industrial machine? Had the labor movement strayed so far from its traditions, he challenged, that it could not stand on its own without the likes of the slippery Franklin D. Roosevelt?

When Lewis appeared at congressional hearings in the midst of the strike, he clashed openly with glowering senators. Hurling defiance at the government, he vowed to fight in the face of repression in behalf of his ill-paid coal miners. He reminded his hostile audience that coal miners were being killed at the rate of 2,000 a year and maimed at the rate of 270 a day during the stepped-up pace of wartime production. Lewis's ability to confront even the government and eventually to wrench from an uncertain NWLB substantial wage concessions echoed through the mills and plants. Thousands of workers believed that defiance of the No-Strike Pledge and emulation of the great John L. Lewis could bring equity in place of the frustrations and disappointments of the official policies of the major labor federations.

But for all the militancy of the Trotskyists, they remained a super-minority, hardly rippling the surface except in a handful of atypical local unions. And for all Lewis's brilliant strategy and magnificent theatrics, the case of coal miners was different from that of industrial workers. The country had ample supplies of coal and alternative sources of fuel. The country could endure a cessation of coal production, but if workers stopped making shells and tanks, American soldiers would be weapon-less. In plants directly producing military goods the No-Strike Pledge had a force and plausibility, even among workers themselves, that it lacked elsewhere.

At root, most laborites realized that Lewis and his coal miners were special cases. While Lewis placed himself at the head of his militant and frustrated coal miners, he controlled the United Mine Workers union absolutely, surrounding himself with flunkies, sycophants, and bully-boys, some his own relatives. Less a modern labor union than an ancient feudal barony, the UMW could indeed explode with defiant militancy of heroic dimensions. But it was hardly a model of laborite democracy, nor was the peculiar mix of autocracy and loyalty that it embodied relevant to the factories of Detroit, Akron, San Francisco, and Birmingham.

So, despite radical critics and despite Lewis's challenge, no doubt Murray, Bittner, and the mainstream leadership of the labor movement were right. Defiance would have been suicidal. The NWLB, labor's close association with FDR, and the trade-off involving the No-Strike Pledge and maintenance of membership proved beneficial to both the AFL and the CIO. The vast expansion of membership, the growth of union trea-suries, and the political credit that a loyal and conscientious labor movement earned helped insure that there would be no repeat of the post–World War I experience.

But in a sense, Lewis and the radicals were right too. The wartime bureaucratization of labor relations did indeed further entangle unions in endless red tape and regulation. Maintenance of membership brought in thousands of union members with minimal commitment to the cause of unionism. Union leaders grew more remote from the problems of ordinary workers, now safely embraced in union security provisions. They presided over ever bigger, ever more powerful organizations, but, in the words of historian Nelson Lichtenstein, they were "also trapped . . . in a Rooseveltian political consensus that soon put them at odds with the immediate interests of their rank and file," at least in some dramatic episodes.

WARTIME BALANCE SHEET

For America's workers, the war brought a painful prosperity. With about 13 million Americans serving in the armed forces and over 9 million changing residence during the war, deracination and disruption intensified. The decline of rural life accelerated. Traditional ethnic enclaves and working-class neighborhoods, which had flourished during the heyday of immigration, weakened under the impact of wartime mobility and population shifts. The forced association of millions of people with those of different and diverse ethnic, religious, and national backgrounds may not have promoted the paradise of tolerance and democracy that some liberal enthusiasts promised, but the tense juxtapositions of the boot camps, barracks, assembly lines, and tenements did help to break down traditional ways and provincial patterns.

Commercial enterprise did its best to draw a newly prosperous working class into the national network of consumer values. Advertising skillfully defined the nation's war aims as consisting primarily of a rising, consumer-oriented prosperity. Young GI cartoonist Bill Mauldin created two quintessentially working-class American characters, Willie and Joe, to represent the American fighting man. Slogging through Italy, dodging German bullets, raiding the wine cellars of France, these two grizzled, ill-educated, yet shrewd and honorable young men epitomized the war effort, with its down-to-earth distrust of ideology and its irreverent national idiom. But what of Willie and Joe after the war, asks historian John Morton Blum. What sort of vision of the future—so necessary to any fighting man—did the nation's magazines, newspapers, and radio broadcasts hold out to its embattled soldiers?

Surely Willie and Joe would settle down after the war, Blum writes. These were not warrior princes or soldiers of fortune; they were confirmed civilians who happened to have a military task to perform. Most likely they would live "in a little white house in the suburbs." No grim tenement or phoneless shack for America's heroes. Surely each day as they returned from their (no doubt) white-collar jobs, they would find the little woman—demure, neatly coiffed—with a welcoming martini in hand. The house itself, as projected in hundreds of wartime ads, would exude an "efficient antiseptic environment created by electric appliances that cooked the meals, did the house work, . . . and left the couple free to listen to their radio." During the war manufacturers could not provide these commodities and comforts; destruction of Hitler came first. But they held out the promise that after the war America's fighting men would return not to the familiar tenements and farms but to this "decent, uninspired picture" of the good life. The war, in short, was to be the stepping-stone from Depression to Prosperity for worker and soldier, for Rosie the Riveter and GI Joe alike.

The roseate picture, of course, ignored vast realities. For all the increases in real income, working-class America relied heavily on the extra hours and full employment of the wartime boom to gain even small beachheads of savings and security. For most black Americans, the pristine suburban life was a cruel joke. For women who supported families or were married to low-wage husbands the problem of the immediate future was how to keep from being pushed out of high-wage industrial employment now that the national emergency had passed. For returning soldiers and for millions of wage workers, male and female alike, a frightening return to depression-era standards seemed more likely than did the bright future conjured up by Madison Avenue.

For those associated with the labor movement, this indeed was the problem: how to use the economic and political power that labor had gained so as to prevent a return to the bad old days. Even as Japan surrendered in September, "labor's war at home" escalated. Final victory in the Pacific ended the No-Strike Pledge. Industrial workers, frustrated over their lack of progress during the war and fearful of a sudden depression, unloosened the pent-up militancy of the war years in a wave of work stoppages. During the six-month period after September 1, 1945, more workers went out on strike for longer periods than ever before (or since) in American history. Autos, steel, meatpacking, coal mining, railroading, electrical appliances, oil refining—virtually every industrial and transport sector—roiled with industrial disputes.

For unionists and employers alike, the war had raised but not resolved basic issues. Employers believed that labor's gains, buttressed by the sympathetic NWLB, threatened to undermine business enterprise and to wrest control of decision-making from managers. Large corporations and small firms alike girded for a showdown with resolute workers. Politically, during the war the unions had established new instruments with which to translate their membership strength into political power. In opposition, anti-union forces, readied for battle, determined to build upon antilabor wartime legislation (the Smith-Connally Act) to curb the labor movement's dangerous political and economic ambitions.

As the war ended, labor leaders saw a new crisis looming. Wartime membership gains and contractual achievements could disappear overnight if labor failed to steer the narrow passage between an impatient rank and file on the one side and hostile corporate executives on the other. The normally phlegmatic Sidney Hillman painted a somber picture indeed. He reminded his colleagues that after the First World War unemployment had soared. Employers had used workers' desperate need for jobs to crush the unions that had grown during the conflict. A new round of unemployment, he warned, would provide labor's enemies with an "opportunity to break down everything that has been done in the last decade." Indeed, Hillman charged, powerful interests sought veritable "Fascist powers," so determined were they to reverse labor's gains.

In the waning months of the war, the Weavers, a quartet famous for its jaunty vocals in support of progressive causes, came out with a song that epitomized unionists' perceptions of their wartime roles. Focusing on labor's contributions, linking the efforts of industrial workers and foot soldiers, celebrating the international victory over fascism, the tune "UAW-CIO" captured labor's image of itself as champion of democracy. It went like this:

> There'll Be a Union Label in Berlin
>   When Union Boys in Uniform March in;
> And Rolling in the Ranks
>   Will be UAW Tanks
> To Roll Hitler Out and Roll the Union in.

By the fall, as strikes rippled through scores of plants and as labor's critics, heedless of wartime production achievements, brought the heavy guns of anti-union rhetoric to bear, such sentiments seemed naive. For the labor movement, despite the victory over fascism, the battle lines were reforming. Van A. Bittner, whose career as a union organizer reached back over forty years, issued a warning to his colleagues in the CIO. "We will either win this battle and have an economy of plenty, with full employment," he forecast, "or we will lose it, maybe lose many of our Unions [as well] and have conditions even worse than they were following the last war." In the shops and mills, as well as in the corporate offices and in the legislative committee rooms, preparations for the next round in the nation's labor struggles proceeded apace.

Strikes, Politics, Radicalism, 1945–1950

"Nineteen forty-eight," declares socialist Michael Harrington, "was the last year of the thirties." Indeed, the presidential election campaign of that year both confirmed and revealed the limits of organized labor's gains. The immediate postwar months, racked by strikes and bitter controversies over labor legislation, seemed a resumption of the politics of the 1930s. Increasingly, however, the issue of Communism—both on the world scene and within American institutions, including the labor movement—came to dominate public attention and to shift it from the concerns of the New Deal–Popular Front decade. Truman's triumph in 1948, followed by the CIO's retribution against affiliates that consistently hewed to the pro-Soviet line, established the boundaries of American politics for a generation. After 1948, ideological radicalism disappeared from public debate, but the labor movement committed itself to unprecedented political action that supported Democratic liberalism and carried forth the uncompleted New Deal agenda into the 1950s.

STRIKE WAVE

The end of World War II found the labor movement stronger than ever before. Its 14.5 million members composed over 35 percent of the civilian labor force, an all-time high. The central industrial and transport core was solidly union. New Deal legislation and an intimate relationship with the ruling Democratic party guarded labor's political flank. The unions' loyalty during World War II, their leaders felt, surely entitled the labor movement to an expanding role in American life.

The AFL, by far the larger of the two federations, claimed over 10 million members. Though traditionalist leaders in the construction unions still weighed heavily, the AFL had embraced industrial unionism in fact, if not always in theory. Affiliates such as the Machinists, Carpenters, and Electrical Workers now represented thousands of unskilled and semiskilled workers. With Teamsters' membership edging toward the 750,000 mark and with promising organizations in the retail, food-processing, and service trades, the AFL seemed ready for further expansion.

Although president William Green showed signs of age, a new generation of AFL leaders brought vigor and diversity to the venerable labor federation. Secretary-Treasurer George Meany had proven himself as the AFL's chief liaison with government bodies during the war. In the Teamsters, rising powers such as Dave Beck and James Hoffa combined shrewd organizing and negotiating tactics with ruthless determination to expand the IBT's membership and influence. Nor did the AFL lack broad-minded and socially concerned leaders. David Dubinsky, whose ILGW had reaffiliated with the AFL in 1940, provided a vigorous social democratic presence in federation affairs, pressing the cautious Executive Council to assert AFL views on foreign policy issues. A. Philip Randolph, the nation's preeminent black trade unionist, worked tirelessly in behalf of civil rights, both inside the labor movement and in society generally.

The CIO also exuded success. True, with about 4.5 million members it remained smaller than the older federation. But powerful unions such as the UAW and the USWA represented hundreds of thousands of workers in central core industries, bargaining with giant corporations such as General Motors and U.S. Steel. The impact of CIO negotiating, organizing, and wage policies was enormous, as UAW, USWA, and other industrial union contracts set patterns for millions of workers.

Moreover, the CIO remained innovative and well-led. In 1943, for example, the Executive Board created a Political Action Committee (PAC), a pioneering grass-roots organization to mobilize labor's electoral strength on a continuing basis. Few labor leaders in American history enjoyed the public esteem awarded to CIO president Philip Murray, who combined an appealing humility with outspoken humanitarian values. If the political views of such pro-Soviet unionists as Julius Emspak of the Electrical Workers and Harry Bridges of the CIO Longshoremen drew hostile public attention, these men were nonetheless shrewd and effective union leaders. Veterans of the UMW, such as Van Bittner, and director of organization Allen S. Haywood, provided links to the pre-CIO era of labor history, while articulate younger men, notably George Baldanzi of the Textile Workers and especially Walter Reuther of the UAW, reflected an emerging generation, fresh from the searing conflicts of the thirties.

Under John L. Lewis, the United Mine Workers continued on an independent—some said eccentric—course. Although briefly reaffiliated with the AFL (1946–47), Lewis's UMW followed its own path in the tempestuous postwar years. In part, its isolation reflected the UMW's shrinking membership in an increasingly mechanized coal-mining sector. Over the years, Lewis had cut his ties with other labor leaders, thus enhancing his vaunted independence but at the same time narrowing the scope of his influence. He deplored the bureaucratization of the labor movement. He bridled at the growth of governmental involvement in labor affairs. He openly scorned other union leaders, heaping humiliation on even some of his most trusted associates. Government leaders, including presidents Roosevelt and Truman, also felt the lash of Lewis's matchless rhetoric.

But Lewis's own control of the UMW grew increasingly authoritarian. He retreated into a small circle of old loyalists, men notable for their devotion to Lewis and their lack of imagination and even scruples. Lewis's isolation, combined with the declining importance of coal mining in the economy, limited the possibility that the lion of yesterday might again rally dissident elements in the labor movement to reshape labor history. In the late 1930s, Lewis had created organizing bodies that sought to challenge both AFL and CIO unions in expanding economic sectors. These bids to break out of the provincial world of coal mining, however, failed. In the postwar years, Lewis waged a series of dramatic confrontations with government, largely in isolation from the rest of the labor movement.

The sudden end of the war posed immediate problems for labor, business, and government. For thousands of ordinary workers, the war's end meant scrapping the No-Strike Pledge. Incidence of strikes had mounted through late 1944 and continued on through the first half of 1945, despite the efforts of union leaders to keep the lid on. The sudden cancellation of military orders and vast layoffs of war workers spurred fears of a postwar depression. Even for those workers retaining full-time employment, the ending of war-induced overtime and premium work cut take-home pay by 30 percent. Widespread tales of corporate profiteering and lavish executive compensation also spurred militancy. "A week or so before we took the strike vote," recalls one steelworker, "one of the Pittsburgh papers ran a story about a big party one of the . . . executives gave for his daughter." The members of his carpool calculated that this affair would easily cost more than the five of them earned working full time in the mills for a year. "That sort of stuff made us realize, hell, we *had* to bite the bullet . . . the bosses sure didn't give a damn for us." By November, a full-scale strike wave of unprecedented proportions had begun to roll through the economy.

Conservatives took it as an article of faith that cynical and power-hungry union bosses caused strikes. Loyal workers, so the anti-union thesis went, understood their employers' problems and realized the wastefulness of strikes. But union chiefs employed coercion and manipulation to compel obedience to strike calls. Ordinary workers had no choice but to troop out, conservatives genuinely believed, whatever their misgivings. This notion of labor union dynamics resulted in antilabor legislation that sought to separate rank-and-file workers from their leaders through requiring formal strike votes and through requirements that workers vote on employers' last offers.

Most evidence, however, contradicted this view. During the war, the Smith-Connally Act had required unions to take a strike vote at least thirty days before a walkout could begin. NLRB representatives who conducted these votes reported that frustrated and militant rank-and-file unionists pressed for strike votes, while union officials embarrassedly attempted to cool their ardor in the name of the No-Strike Pledge. The events of 1945–46 likewise revealed the erroneousness of the conservative critique of union leadership, for throughout the fall an aroused rank and file triggered strike action. Meanwhile, most union officials functioned (in C. Wright Mills' telling phrase) as "managers of discontent," hoping to develop orderly policies of reconversion in cooperation with anxious government officials and a handful of liberal corporate spokesmen.

Officials in the new Truman administration, of course, deplored strikes. Hoping to encourage labor and employers to establish long-term accord and to stem the spiral of inflation and work stoppages, President Truman issued a call in October for a labor-management conference. This high-level assembly of leading unionists and large employers would, the president hoped, arrive at solutions to all sorts of labor problems. In the short run, the president hoped, such a conference would encourage workers to stay on the job in expectation that their legitimate wage demands would receive consideration. The conference would also reassure businessmen as to the new administration's fairness in labor-management matters. If the administration could resist the mounting clamor on the part of businessmen and farmers for the removal of price controls, and thus restrain inflation, and if the conference could establish a structure for labor peace, it could achieve an orderly transition into a peacetime economy. Certainly, labor leaders politically close to the Democratic administration approved of this grand national effort to find an alternative to industrial confrontation.

But by the time the conference convened in early November, few expected success. As historian Howell J. Harris observes, "The conference took place while unprecedented numbers of workers were on strike." Indeed, deliberations in the conference committees were frequently conducted "between representatives of the corporations and the unions involved in some of the bitterest fights." The intransigence with which business attacked the administration's efforts to maintain wartime price controls convinced unionists that inflationary pressures would soon translate into soaring price levels. Thus, it only made sense for unions to seek substantial wage gains, both to keep abreast of inflation and to compensate for the lower weekly income that peacetime employment would otherwise hold out. Any hopes for the conference as an answer to the immediate problem of labor conflict ended on November 21, when 320,000 autoworkers under the leadership of UAW GM director Walter P. Reuther struck the nation's largest corporation.

Before the great strike wave of 1945–46 peaked late in the winter, hundreds of thousands of steel, rubber, meatpacking, oil-refining, and electrical appliance workers had joined the autoworkers, making 1946 the single most strike-torn year in American history. These postwar walkouts exhibited several distinctive features that set them apart from previous mass walkouts. Unlike the railroad strikes of 1877 or the 1934 strikes, these were disciplined, union-conducted work stoppages designed to improve existing contractual relations. Unlike the great steel strike of 1919–20 or the sit-down strikes of 1937, the postwar strikes posed little threat to the very existence of the unions. The specter of hundreds of thousands of mass production workers laying down their tools, manning the picket lines, and attending the countless union meetings at which strike details were relayed gave impressive testimony to the permanence and strength of the new dispensation in labor relations emerging from the 1930s.

Workers, union leaders, businessmen, and government officials all had diverse perspectives on these strikes. The enthusiasm for a showdown with management and the overwhelming support for the strikes suggested to some anticapitalist radicals that the American working class was at last ready to challenge the nation's capitalist socioeconomic order. In 1946, confrontations between workers and repressive company and public authorities escalated into virtual general strikes in Rochester, New York; Oakland, California; and Pittsburgh, adding to radicals' hopes that labor unrest might generate a broad anticapitalist movement. "The wildcat strikes, mass demonstrations, and labor holidays in 1946," asserts historian George Lipsitz, "indicated the willingness of workers to defend themselves . . . , [and displayed] the stirrings of independent political action."

But for most workers, the relatively straightforward question of wages remained the first priority. Other workplace grievances and cynicism about mainstream politics certainly played a role in working-class life after the war, but workers remained solidly indifferent or hostile to anticapitalist organizations and impressively loyal to their mainstream unions. The sharp cuts in weekly pay associated with the abrupt end of the war, however, did trigger fierce resentment and a determination to gain healthy hourly increases. Frustrated by labor relations under the No-Strike Pledge, industrial workers turned expectantly to their unions to fight for better standards and protection against inflation.

Union leaders, of course, also stressed wage demands. At the same time, however, CIO president Philip Murray and Walter Reuther, director of the GM strike for the UAW, sought broader goals. Murray hoped to develop a consistent, broad-based CIO wage policy, uniting the industrial unions in common effort to rationalize the manpower and compensation practices of core industries. Though Murray would have preferred a strike-free postwar milieu, as a veteran unionist he had no compunction about wielding the strike weapon. Throughout the war, Murray had promoted joint labor-management committees, seeing them as a means of injecting workers' representatives into basic decision-making. A student of corporatist Catholic social theory, Murray believed that once the current strikes had demonstrated the workers' power, the way would lie open for expanding union activity in every phase of industrial life.

Reuther articulated even broader goals. The thirty-eight-year-old leader believed that organized labor should lead the way toward a reshaped postwar economic and social order. "We are not going to operate as a narrow economic interest group," he pledged. He fought aggressively for GM workers' wage demands, of course, but he stressed that wage gains had to be related to general economic activity and had to coincide with the public interest. He argued forcefully that enormous corporate profits permitted wage increases of 30 percent without the need to raise prices. Higher wages would buoy mass purchasing power, thus sustaining full employment. High-volume production would reduce unit costs, ensuring steady profits, full employment, and rising prosperity. Like Murray, Reuther believed that workers' representatives should participate in decisions affecting the production process. He reached out beyond the labor movement for public support of his objectives, on one notable occasion challenging GM to open its books to public scrutiny to test its claim that it could not afford wage increases.

GM executives adamantly rejected Reuther's appeal to open the books. "We don't even let our stockholders look at the books," one official observed. Beyond resisting such scrutiny, managers of leading corporations had some goals of their own in the 1945–46 negotiations.

Many believed that during the troubled thirties and the chaotic war years efficiency and discipline had grown lax, eroded on the shop floor by arrogant laborites. Wartime cost-plus contracts had discouraged plant managers from applying rigorous standards. Too often, workers defied foremen and superintendents, so powerful had work groups and grievance committees become. To the dismay of executives, even foremen had begun to organize into unions, threatening further to compromise in-plant authority. The time had come, held such major employers as Ford, GM, Westinghouse, American Rolling Mills, and dozens of other large firms and business associations, to reassert managerial rights in the shops and factories. For businessmen, declares a careful historian of the period, the strikes and contract negotiations of 1945–46 "revolved around issues of control," with employers determined to reclaim "the right to manage."

The strikes threatened the Truman administration's entire postwar program. For the president and his advisors, public policy in the turbulent winter of 1945–46 was mainly a matter of damage control. The administration sought stable price and wage levels, hoping for an orderly transition to peacetime production. But the strikes and resulting corporate demands for price hikes to compensate for the costs of wage increases began to unravel the entire anti-inflation program. Unceasing conservative pressures for the rapid elimination of the government's remaining wartime powers of price control further undermined the administration, and through 1946 and into 1947 inflation soared.

In the end, most parties got something like what they wanted in the strike settlements and in the contracts negotiated with non-struck firms. Following the general guidelines recommended by fact-finding boards that President Truman appointed in the steel and auto strikes, most unions gained wage increases of around 20 percent. General Motors successfully resisted public pressure to open its books, and corporations soon passed along the costs of wage concessions to consumers in the form of higher prices. Employers also made important strides in reasserting their authority in the work process, compelling the UAW and other unions to include "company rights" provisions in the new contracts. By virtue of these provisions, the most notable of which appeared in the UAW's agreement with Ford, unions acknowledged important obligations to discipline members who violated the contract and conceded to management wide-ranging authority to set production standards and impose discipline in the workplace. Although the work process itself remained a battleground between workers and managers, employers felt that the 1946 contracts at least began the process of limiting and containing the extension of union power into decision-making.

Neither Murray nor Reuther realized his broader ambitions. Reuther in particular drew criticism for keeping his GM strikers out an additional three weeks after most industrial unions had settled for an average increase in basic hourly rates of 18.5 cents. Indeed, the latter stages of negotiations between Reuther and GM executives grew bitter. Company executives ridiculed Reuther's broad-minded claims and, with other unions already having settled, refused to concede even token points to the hard-pressed leader. In turn, Reuther warned his now-complacent antagonists that "you are buying bitterness in every one of your fucking plants every day." Attacked by corporate executives as a veritable revolutionary and by critics in his own union, who alleged that his ambition to become UAW president dictated his strike strategy, Reuther bowed to the inevitable in mid-March and accepted a settlement little different from those gained earlier by the Steelworkers and the United Electrical Workers.

Still, by putting himself at the head of the UAW's militant workers and by exhibiting dramatic leadership of the strike, Reuther emerged as one of the country's most forceful trade unionists. "More than any other labor leader of his time," writes historian John Barnard, "Reuther placed the unions in the vanguard of a broad social advance for all." After the strike, a story circulated around the union halls and working-class taverns. It seems that a White House meeting involving President Truman, Philip Murray, and Walter Reuther had taken place during the strike. When the UAW leader stepped out for a moment, Truman, taken aback by Reuther's brash self-confidence, took it upon himself to warn the sixty-two-year-old CIO president. " 'Phil,' " Truman allegedly counselled, " 'that young man is after your job.' " Whereupon the soft-spoken Murray replied, " 'No, Mr. President, he really is after *your* job.' "

The 1945–46 strikes revealed strength and limitations of the pattern of labor relations that had grown out of the New Deal and the war. The period 1936–45 had been one of significant, hard-won gains by organized labor. In the 1930s, a vigorous and imaginative labor movement had out-generaled a demoralized and ineptly led corporate sector. Laborites' skillful use of new government agencies in the thirties and during the war established the pattern of advance. But in the postwar strikes, corporate America showed an impressive ability to rebound from previous defeat. Led by GM, Westinghouse, and other large employers, American business fought the unions resourcefully and effectively.

In one sense, the results of the strikes, which left the New Deal–era unions powerful and intact and which provided significant wage increases for millions of workers, represented a signal victory for organized labor. Not only had the unions conducted these impressive strikes, but they had reversed the disasters of 1918–21, when employer counterattacks had decimated war-engorged unions.

But the strikes also revealed limits to the new order in labor relations. Employers grudgingly conceded that the new unions were here to stay. They accepted the need to increase pay. But they dug in firmly on matters of managerial prerogatives. The unions were a force to be reckoned with in the shops and at the bargaining table, but no union leader would share, however minimally, in the exercise of managerial rights. And, a growing number of businessmen and their allies believed, the costly strikes had created an atmosphere in which congressional critics of organized labor could make progress in their long-germinating plans to clip labor's wings and—perhaps—to scrap the hated New Deal reforms entirely.

LABOR UNDER ATTACK: THE TAFT-HARTLEY ACT

In June 1947 Congress passed the Labor-Management Relations Act of 1947, better known as the Taft-Hartley Act. This law sharply amended the Wagner Act of 1935, imposing severe restrictions on unions, strengthening managerial prerogatives, and recasting the National Labor Relations Board (NLRB). Particularly controversial features limited the right to strike and required union officers to sign anti-Communist affidavits. Another disputed provision permitted the states individually to forbid standard forms of union security. Its congressional supporters and other conservative elements hailed Taft-Hartley as a needed corrective to the support that the Wagner Act and the original NLRB had lent the labor movement. For organized labor, however, the new law signaled a sharp reversal of federal labor policy and threatened to dismantle the whole New Deal framework.

The road to Taft-Hartley had begun almost immediately upon the Supreme Court's 1937 validation of the Wagner Act. Throughout the late 1930s, employers, right-wing newspapers, and conservative legislators assailed the NLRB. The new agency, they charged, stacked the deck in favor of unions. Communists dominated its staff, they asserted. The "unfair labor practices" sections of the Wagner Act made employers sitting ducks for all sorts of union coercion. Some AFL craft unionists joined these conservative elements in seeking amendments to the Wagner Act, hoping to curb the NLRB's alleged bias in favor of the rival CIO.

Although these prewar initiatives failed, criticism of organized labor and New Deal policies remained strong. The coal strikes of early 1943 soon triggered passage of the Smith-Connally Act, which imposed drastic restrictions for the duration of the war on the political and economic activities of unions. The 1945–46 strikes further fueled anti-union sentiments, especially in the largely Republican daily press and on Capitol Hill. In the eighteen months following the Japanese surrender, over seventy antilabor bills were introduced in the House alone. Only a presidential veto in June 1946 prevented passage of the Case Bill, a sweeping revision of the Wagner Act and a major attack on a whole range of standard union practices. Even so, President Truman himself on occasion joined the anti-union chorus. In May 1946, for example, in the face of a threatened railroad strike, he proposed to draft strikers into the army and, in a bitter private tirade, lashed out at "effete union leaders," terming some of them stooges of the Soviet Union.

The congressional elections of 1946, in which supporters of the vetoed Case Bill were overwhelmingly returned to office, made the passage of restrictive labor legislation certain. For the first time since 1930, the Republican party gained control of both houses of Congress. Increasingly hostile to the unions, which had become ever more open in their identification with the Democratic party, GOP leaders resolved anew to restrict organized labor. Certain of support from a strong contingent of conservative southern Democrats, the Republicans made labor legislation a priority for the incoming Eightieth Congress.

Through 1946 and early 1947, debate over revision of the Wagner Act dominated congressional attention. Declared Congressman Fred A. Hartley of New Jersey, sponsor of the House legislation in the Eightieth Congress, "During the New Deal, labor unions were coddled, nursed, and pampered." By 1946, according to Senator Robert A. Taft of Ohio, sponsor of the Senate legislation, most employers "were practically at the mercy of labor unions." Laborites replied in kind: as the legislation neared passage in May, CIO veteran Van Bittner asserted that the impending law would bring "Fascism in its ultimate form right here in the United States."

The sponsors of the legislation that became the Taft-Hartley Act had several purposes. They hoped to reduce the frequency of strikes, to protect employers, workers, and the general public from alleged wrongdoing by unions, and to unravel some of the red tape they believed New Deal policies had generated. At root, however, lay their desire to recast federal labor policy by changing the character and functions of the NLRB. A revamped board would, in Taft's words, "restore some equality between employer and employee so that there might be free collective bargaining." Whereas the central purpose of the original Wagner Act had been the frank encouragement of employees' rights to form unions, the Taft-Hartley Act aimed to balance the interests of employers, workers, unions, and the general public by changing the NLRB from an advocate of unionism to a neutral body for whom the rights of employers to resist a union were to be equal to those of unions to gain support from employees. According to Congressman Hartley, "The Labor-Management Relations Act of 1947 wiped out, in a single enactment, the main legal prop supporting a national labor policy which had existed for twelve years."

Hartley exaggerated. The new law sharply amended the Wagner Act, building on changes in NLRB policies since the late 1930s. The Wagner Act's general endorsement of collective bargaining remained, but now unions were no more than coequal with other interested parties, namely the public and employers. Most tellingly, the new law affirmed that workers had discrete rights apart from those of unions and union leaders. For example, Taft-Hartley provided for decertification proceedings, wherein workers could oust their current union by majority vote. It expanded the rights of employers to try to turn workers against union membership, on the premise that workers should hear "both sides" —that is, the union side and the employer's side—when deciding on representation. The law also required that existing union shop contracts be subjected to special referenda, testing whether workers would remain loyal to their unions if given an opportunity to repudiate union security provisions.

Overall, Taft-Hartley furthered a legalistic conception of the relationship between workers and unions and between unions and employers, modifying the basic orientation of the original Wagner Act. And despite the desire of its sponsors to reduce bureaucracy and red tape, it could not help but render federal involvement in labor matters more detailed, complex, and litigious. Congressman Hartley believed that Taft-Hartley altered "NLRB functions from those of an advocate for organized labor to a . . . role of impartial referee . . . [and thus it] shifted the whole emphasis of government labor policies."

Organized labor objected to virtually every aspect of Taft-Hartley. A weakened NLRB, laborites predicted, would impede union organizing; employers' rights provisions would open the door to widespread intimidation of workers and would inevitably lead to endless legal proceedings. The anti-Communist affidavits, the antistrike provisions, and the attacks on union security, laborites believed, singled out organized labor as irresponsible and even unpatriotic.

Perhaps most ominous of all, believed union lawyers, was the prospect of endless bureaucratization of labor relations. CIO legal counsel

Lee Pressman, for example, warned that the new provisions, combined with important changes in the way in which the NLRB was now compelled to conduct its handling of cases, would resurrect the hated labor injunction. Moreover, he argued, Taft-Hartley's provisions would ensnare the unions in tangled legal proceedings, blunting the force of the unions' efforts and discouraging workers from exercising their right to organize. The new legislation, labor's supporters believed, would surely make the law itself—under the Wagner Act an instrument of the worker's right to organize—now a bureaucratic weapon against that right.

CIO unionists felt particularly enraged by the Taft-Hartley Act. And with good reason. Many of the "unfair union practices" outlawed in Taft-Hartley, after all, were far more aptly associated with AFL unions than with those in the CIO. The use of coercive methods of organizing, the imposition of secondary boycotts to punish employers, and the waging of incessant jurisdictional warfare, to the extent that they were legitimate problems, were devices employed largely by such AFL organizations as the Carpenters and Teamsters. Indeed, CIO organizers and firms under CIO contracts had often been victimized by them. Still, most of these practices were illegal already; the new law merely permitted employers now to compile a case in NLRB proceedings for use against a union in an organizing campaign. Each charge would have to be investigated and ruled upon, always with the possibility of protracted appeal. Thus, these unfair labor practices provisions offered opportunities for employers to string out NLRB proceedings and thereby impose great financial burdens on unions seeking representation rights and on workers seeking to exercise their right to form unions. While leaders in both federations worked vigorously to defeat, and later to repeal, Taft-Hartley, the CIO's greater vulnerability to changes in the NLRB lent a particular edge to its opposition.

Indeed, some AFL unions found Taft-Hartley advantageous to them in their rivalry with CIO affiliates. Few AFL leaders balked at signing the non-Communist affidavits, for example, thus permitting them to challenge nonsigning CIO organizations for representation rights under advantageous circumstances. And Taft-Hartley provisions often made it easier for craft unions, virtually all of which were in the AFL, to carve out distinctive units in large plants, thus eroding the force of the CIO's all-inclusive brand of industrial unionism.

Thus, while CIO leaders remained unreconciled to Taft-Hartley, AFL leaders, though still hostile to it, accommodated themselves more readily. Indeed, one economist close to the AFL found solace in Taft-Hartley's continued endorsement of collective bargaining. "Recognition of the right to organize by a conservative Congress," observed Philip A. Taft in 1948, "is an indication of the long distance we have traveled since the 1920s." Taft went on to assert that "the predictions [of disaster] of the labor unions with respect to the effects of this law have not been any more accurate than the fears of business after the enactment of the Wagner Act." But many laborites did not share this sanguine assessment: the 1947 CIO convention termed Taft-Hartley "a direct step toward Fascism" and pledged ceaseless efforts to secure repeal.

But what specifically should the labor movement do to fight Taft-Hartley? Some unionists, notably John L. Lewis, centered their opposition on the noxious anti-Communist affidavit. The UMW leader eloquently denounced this provision of the law as a violation of civil liberties; he announced that rather than sign, the UMW would foreswear utilization of NLRB services and thus repudiate a federal labor policy that had become ever more coercive and inimical to workers' interests. Other labor leaders, including many close to the Communist party and principled civil libertarians such as CIO and Steelworkers' president Philip Murray, also refused to sign the affidavit, thus also denying their organizations access to NLRB representation election proceedings.

Few unions, however, could afford to follow this line. Lewis and other nonsigners, such as James Matles, director of organization of the pro-Soviet United Electrical Workers, pledged to fight rival unions in the shops and mines without benefit of NLRB services. But most unionists felt too vulnerable to raids or employer attacks. Steelworkers' officials pressured Murray to reverse his stand: What would happen, they pled, when an AFL union sought decertification of a USWA local? Without the right to participate in an NLRB election, the Steelworkers could not prevent the loss of thousands of members. In the end, whatever their private scruples, most union leaders, including Murray, bent to this logic. Indeed, some even found that the affidavit issue redounded to the benefit of their unions once the officers had duly signed. Walter Reuther, elected president of the UAW in a narrow 1946 convention vote, launched raids against nonsigning locals in electrical, machinery, and farm equipment industries, thus expanding the Autoworkers while consolidating his own tenuous control of the union. AFL unions attacked vulnerable nonsigning CIO unions in electrical, metals, lumber, and white-collar fields, gaining thousands of new members.

Some radical laborites argued that organized labor should stage massive demonstrations to protest Taft-Hartley. Encouraged by the mass support for the 1945–46 strikes and by the outbreak of community-wide strikes in several cities in 1946, anticapitalist elements—most of which were in the CIO—urged that organized labor conduct a general strike. And scattered walkouts and demonstrations did erupt among miners, packinghouse, auto, and other industrial workers. Lewis, who single-handedly prevented the AFL Executive Council from immediate acceptance of the anti-Communist affidavit, sought at the federation's 1947 convention to shame AFL leaders into open defiance. "At least once in your lives," he lectured the Executive Council, "you should do your duty by your membership" and defy the government. AFL leaders who betrayed their members and surrendered to the forces of reaction, he declared, reminded him of the biblical passage depicting "lions led by asses." In the CIO, James Matles of the Electrical Workers led the fight for defiance at the 1947 convention, arguing that militant organizing and grass-roots activism would permit CIO unions to rekindle the fervor of the thirties while they defied an increasingly repressive government.

In the end, however, the vast majority of labor leaders wanted no part of a showdown. After all, they reasoned, Truman *had* vetoed the bill, justifying hopes that the NLRB under a friendly administration would continue to promote labor's interests, at least for the immediate future. Labor could intensify its political operations and elect a new Congress in 1948 pledged to repeal the odious law and restore the original Wagner Act. Despite the mass strikes in 1946 and the flurries of anti–Taft-Hartley protest after Congress overrode Truman's veto, veteran labor leaders simply did not believe that the American working class would support leaders who opted for the profound estrangement from the government and from American society in general that protracted defiance would have entailed.

Widespread strikes and protests, believed men such as Walter Reuther, Philip Murray, and William Green, also played into the hands of reactionaries eager to club labor into submission. It was easy for a John L. Lewis, whose dictatorial hold on his membership precluded raids on the UMW, to hurl defiance. It was to be expected that people such as James Matles, Harry Bridges of the CIO Longshoremen, and Ben Gold of the CIO Fur and Leather Workers should refuse to sign the affidavits, whatever the cost to their membership, for in this as in virtually every important issue over the past decade these men had followed the line laid out by the Communist party. But for practical leaders, however bitter at Congress for passing Taft-Hartley, reluctant compliance combined with stepped-up political action remained the only response. Though Murray often grew starkly apocalyptical when contemplating Taft-Hartley, in the end he followed this moderate course. "Although I recognize the desperation in this particular situation," he told CIO leaders in June, "I cannot even now lend comfort to an appeal which calls for

national work stoppages." "What the hell—pendulums swing," he told
them on another occasion, "and we have our cycles in life, and we [have]
got to make the best of it, using the tools at hand."

The Taft-Hartley Act and the labor movement's response to it
marked a turning point for organized labor. The law's reversal of governmental encouragement to continued growth of labor unions and its
inevitable stimulation of increasingly legalistic procedures weakened
one of labor's central supports. At the same time, labor's decision not to
defy the government revealed the limits to class-based political and ideological politics in the United States. No doubt wisely, Murray, Green,
and most other responsible labor leaders shied away from open confrontation in favor of mainstream political action. In doing so, however,
they admitted that however broad its claims to speak for the working
class in general, the labor movement could not mobilize this class as a
class. In its reluctance to stake its future on mass action, organized labor
lent plausibility to the operating premise of the Taft-Hartley Act itself—
namely, that the unions were bodies whose interests only partially coincided with those of the workers they sought to represent.

LABOR GETS POLITICAL

Union leaders believed that the best response to the challenge of
Taft-Hartley was the intensification of their fledgling political action
program. Gearing up for the 1948 elections, they believed that they
could build upon political organizations already in place and wage a
campaign that would punish those who supported Taft-Hartley, elect a
liberal Congress, and keep a friendly administration in the White
House. In the AFL, these plans required the creation of a new political
action arm and the growth of more active national direction in the traditionally decentralized federation. For the CIO, the determination to
achieve a more amenable Congress meant the abandonment of whatever
hopes dissident unionists had held for the creation of a third party. Indeed, for both organizations the politicking of the late 1940s entailed
increasing integration of labor's political operations into those of the
Democratic party. When a vocal minority of pro-Soviet leaders in the
CIO fought this strategy and supported Progressive party candidate
Henry A. Wallace for the presidency in 1948, the controversy shook the
CIO and led eventually to the expulsion from the industrial union body
of eleven affiliated unions, with a combined membership of about
900,000.

The rebirth of the labor movement in the 1930s had spurred unprecedented political action. But controversies between the AFL and

the CIO and among unions and leaders within each federation in the late 1930s and early 1940s had blunted this early thrust. It was only when the congressional elections of 1942 resulted in sweeping victories by Republicans and conservative Democrats that laborites began to move permanently into the arena of national politics. Suddenly apprehensive about Franklin Roosevelt's reelection chances and faced now with a hostile Congress, they began to build new political machinery. The AFL, with its traditions of decentralization and with some of its most influential leaders enjoying cozy relationships with the Republican party, merely urged its affiliates to step up their normal political activities. In the CIO, however, the shocking setback of 1942 spurred the formation of a new national political arm, the CIO Political Action Committee (PAC), a distinct innovation in labor politics.

Chaired by Sidney Hillman of the Amalgamated Clothing Workers, PAC sought to establish a CIO political program through every level of the industrial union federation. Upon its establishment on July 8, 1943, PAC began collecting large sums from affiliated unions for use in voter registration and political propaganda. Federal law banned unions from donating union dues money to candidates in general elections, so PAC created an elaborate structure, reaching into every local union, to solicit voluntary contributions from union members for favored candidates. PAC churned out an impressive series of pamphlets for distribution to union members and their families, graphically explaining the CIO economic and social program. It targeted appeals to women workers, union members' wives, black workers, and other minorities and groups. PAC bought time on radio stations, organized rallies, conducted door-to-door canvassing, and worked closely with local party leaders—usually Democrats—to get out the vote and to support liberal candidates.

Roosevelt's reelection in 1944 boosted PAC's reputation. Democratic leaders credited the CIO body with generating huge majorities in key industrial centers, while Republicans and conservative newspaper columnists fulminated against it as a dictatorial combination of union bossism and Communist influence. Attacks on PAC's director, Hillman, often combined red-baiting and anti-Semitism. Even sympathetic observers worried about the CIO's apparent success in marshalling hundreds of thousands of disciplined, union-oriented voters to the polls. Basking in the glow of victory, CIO leaders vowed to build an even stronger political arm.

In reality, however, 1944's success was less impressive than it first seemed. True, FDR had once again won. But his coattails proved short, with labor-endorsed candidates compiling only mediocre totals in congressional, state, and local races. Voter registration projects did help to swell the electorate, which in 1942 had declined sharply in comparison with previous off-year elections, but careful observers, including PAC's own analysts, found little evidence in 1944 that endorsements and even contributions of money and manpower played a major role in most nonpresidential contests. When in 1945 a heavily favored UAW-CIO-backed candidate lost the mayorality election in Detroit and in 1946 liberals and labor-backed congressional candidates fared poorly, these cautious assessments of PAC's potency seemed justified. Thus, while labor's pledge to avenge Taft-Hartley and to commit its political energies to keeping the White House in liberal hands meant a massive commitment of time, energy, and money, it held no guarantee of success.

PAC enthusiasts in the CIO and the staff of its AFL counterpart, Labor's League for Political Education (LLPE), created in 1947, faced a good deal of internal criticism within the respective federations. Many in the CIO, for example, saw PAC as the first step in the creation of a third party. They criticized CIO leaders for rejecting this option, for they believed that a labor party would free the unions of their dependency on the unreliable Democrats and permit them to lead an unambiguously progressive political movement. Often associated with anticapitalist groups such as the Communist party and the Socialist Workers party, these unionists believed that industrial workers and their families could provide the financial and electoral support that would bring a fundamental realignment to American politics. The existence of successful third parties and third-party-like political support groups in important industrial states such as Wisconsin, Washington, California, New York, and Michigan, and the stunning success of a social democratic labor-based party in Ontario in 1943, fueled hopes for the eventual creation of an independent labor or progressive party, one that would uphold the New Deal heritage while pressing on in such areas as civil rights, social welfare legislation, and anti-imperialist foreign policy.

Few radicals disturbed the AFL's more conventional political forums. Instead, key union leaders in the construction and transport sectors retained ties to the Republican party, thus providing LLPE with reasons for caution. Moreover, over the years AFL state and local bodies had worked out elaborate patterns of accommodation with political organizations of both parties in many cities and states, further insuring that LLPE would remain relatively careful and nonideological in its support for Democrats and liberals.

In theory, a simple arithmetic lay behind organized labor's political plans. Since there were about 15 million union members, and since these members had spouses and children of voting age, there existed an enormous reservoir of working-class voters. And since family farmers, racial minorities, and lower-income voters shared many of the same political goals with organized labor, a labor-led political movement could transform American politics.

Nor was this calculus fanciful. In 1936, for example, all observers agreed that Franklin Roosevelt had surged to reelection on a tidal wave of working-class votes and that labor support for FDR in 1940 and 1944 had been critical in his narrower successes of those years. In New York in 1936, laborites had created the American Labor party (ALP), a mechanism by which voters could cast ballots in favor of labor-endorsed candidates nominated by the major parties. Through the late 1930s and into the 1940s, the ALP line often contributed over 40 percent of the tally for the labor-endorsed (usually Democratic) candidate, indicating the existence of a powerful nucleus for a full-fledged labor party. In other states—notably Minnesota, Washington, Michigan, and Ohio—CIO-led political organizations had brought thousands of new voters into the electoral process and had mobilized powerful constituencies that had begun to challenge Republican control of state and local governments.

But veteran laborites knew too well how difficult it was to translate a theoretical laborite majority into actual political power. For example, political scientists consistently reported that working-class citizens were far less likely to register or to vote than upper-income Americans. Blue-collar turnouts rarely exceeded 50 percent. Any effective political action program would have to overcome the apathy and resignation that afflicted workers and their families. Moreover, while statisticians and ideologues might carefully delineate the levels of income and education that determined working-class status, American workers, for complex historical and demographic reasons, rarely responded to political appeals based on class. In this country, ethnic, national, and religious orientations had usually provided more accurate indicators of voting behavior than had social class per se. Nor were working people immune from ethnic, racial, and religious prejudices, despite the corrosive effect of bigotry on union struggles. With only about 35 percent of the nonagricultural labor force unionized and with these historic patterns of apathy, interclass conflict, and acquiescence in a dominant American system of social and moral values that softened class identities, labor's political operatives could hardly be complacent, whatever the galvanizing effect of Taft-Hartley.

Thus most veteran laborites rejected third-party politics. True, working within the Democratic party often involved compromise. Democratic candidates too frequently shied away from the New Deal heritage. But time and time again, events had proven that labor needed allies and that the labor movement could not mobilize working-class voters sufficiently to permit going it alone. The historic traditions of two-party politics, the vast geographic dimensions of the United States, the country's endlessly variegated ethnic and demographic makeup, and the political system's highly decentralized character all militated against third-party politics. In candid moments, some laborites admitted that it was hard enough to persuade workers to remain dues-paying supporters of their unions, much less ask them to become disciplined members of some labor party.

Quite apart from any other factor, laborites knew that as of the 1940s working people were already heavily oriented toward the Democratic party. While the party was not a labor party and while its candidates avoided appeals to class consciousness, public opinion experts regularly reported high percentages of working-class identification with the Democracy. Indeed, in the immediate post−World War II decade, American workers often voted as heavily for Democratic candidates as did British working-class citizens for the Labour party in the United Kingdom. Thus, the loyalty of American workers to the Democratic party, whatever that party's limitations as a vehicle for the kinds of progressive policies favored by labor activists, was simply a fact of life. In 1940, John L. Lewis himself had urged workers to join him in repudiating Roosevelt and the Democratic party. Their refusal to do so and their ringing endorsement of FDR held a profound lesson for labor's political operatives. As the liaison between organized labor and the Democratic party became tangled and frustrating through the late 1940s, some leftists began to think of it (in socialist commentator Mike Davis's phrase) as "a barren marriage," but in reality it was American workers, and not the labor movement, who had long before become wedded to the Democracy.

Operating within these constraints, organized labor's political operatives achieved a stunning victory in 1948. Almost miraculously, labor's candidate, President Truman, confounded the pollsters and pundits, eking out a narrow victory over his GOP rival, New York governor Thomas E. Dewey. Despite deep misgivings over Truman's electability and his performance in office, the laborites pulled out the stops for the feisty Missourian. They concentrated on key industrial states, such as California, Michigan, Indiana, West Virginia, and New York. PAC's leaders claimed that by the time the polls opened on November 2, they had created a block and precinct operation involving a million volunteers. This grass-roots politicking paid off, particularly in states such as Michigan, where PAC emerged as the dominant element in the state's Democratic party, and in other industrial and urban states, where the linkage between PAC and the Democratic organizations insured that

CIO leaders would play a key role in future deliberations. In accounting for his remarkable upset victory, Truman told the *New York Times* that "labor did it."

Laborites rejoiced. Democrats regained control of both houses of Congress, despite deep splits in the party and despite a well-financed Republican effort. Surely the reelection of Truman, combined with this seemingly ringing repudiation of the performance of the Eightieth Congress, boded well for prompt action on the hated Taft-Hartley Act. With the Democrats so obviously beholden to organized labor's efforts and to the dramatic blue-collar support for them, political operatives in both federations called confidently for quick repeal of the "slave labor law."

But despite labor's electoral and financial contributions and the Democrats' successes in 1948, the Eighty-first Congress failed to move energetically on Taft-Hartley. Although President Truman dutifully supported revision of Taft-Hartley, even under Democratic control Congress remained in conservative hands. Southern Democrats, almost uniformly hostile to the labor movement, dominated key congressional committees. While the tally sheets of labor lobbyists showed that most Democratic senators and congressmen from northern, eastern, and blue-collar districts loyally supported labor's goals, they also revealed that labor simply could not muster the strength to gain significant revision of the law.

Nor could it deliver consistently at the polls. In the 1950 Ohio senate race, in which Taft himself stood for reelection, organized labor invested heavily in the Republican's defeat only to find themselves saddled with a lackluster Democratic candidate. They were not surprised when Taft won a decisive victory, but post-election surveys of their own membership brought sobering news. Thus, reported political analyst Samuel Lubell, "Many workers seized upon Taft's candidacy to voice a protest against their own union chiefs." While loyal to their unions, Ohio workers resented what they perceived as national leaders' efforts to "dictate" to them in the sacred confines of the voting booth. By 1951, any thoughts of repeal or general revision of Taft-Hartley were dead, and unionists had to be content with sporadic efforts to secure repeal or amendment of specific secondary features of the law.

Still, labor's heavy commitment to political action in the late 1940s and early 1950s, though stimulated in good part by Taft-Hartley, was hardly a failure. For the CIO, and for an increasingly large percentage of AFL activists, political action transcended the specifics of labor legislation per se. PAC, for example, had always cast its net widely, stressing the CIO's interest in broad areas of public policy, from housing to education, civil rights, medical care, and foreign policy. CIO conventions regularly adopted resolutions on all of these matters, and PAC operatives stressed the CIO's role as leader of a broad, progressive coalition. In the 1948 Democratic convention, CIO forces had led in the adoption of the Democratic party's bold civil rights plank. CIO leaders regularly appeared before congressional committees to press for antidiscrimination legislation as well as vigorous public action in areas such as housing, national health care, federal aid for education, and welfare.

Both the AFL and the CIO spoke out frequently on overall economic policy as well, and they stressed the importance of the federal government's role in stimulating economic growth and thus in maintaining high levels of employment. While few mainstream laborites, including even those such as Walter Reuther who had roots in the socialist movement, challenged the basic premises of modern capitalism, they did unite with liberals, farm groups, and consumer and minority rights advocates to urge a particular vision of advanced capitalism. Beginning with the Employment Act of 1946 and continuing on through innumerable congressional hearings, public statements, and appearances before Democratic party groups, labor leaders such as George Meany of the AFL and Philip Murray, Emil Rieve, and Walter Reuther of the CIO urged greater governmental involvement in economic matters. A more equitable tax system, they argued, would benefit lower-income citizens and would thus expand purchasing power. Regional development projects modeled on the New Deal's massive Tennessee Valley Authority would spur economic development, provide jobs, and boost living standards in rural areas. Improvements in workmen's compensation, Social Security, education, and health care would bring greater opportunity and security to millions of lower-income Americans.

Increasingly, in fact, national labor leaders in both federations came to see the labor movement's political goals as broadly conceived support for lower- and middle-income Americans. They envied and, in their way, sought to emulate the successful Labour party in Great Britain, even then forging a comprehensive welfare state in the United Kingdom. They found that they enjoyed their greatest political successes when they functioned as an "aggregative" force, bringing together broad liberal coalitions to promote general interest legislation. Conversely, they found that their own rank-and-file members and organized labor's usual electoral and legislative allies were lukewarm at best when it came to specifically labor-oriented legislation, most notably Taft-Hartley repeal.

In recogniton of the importance of day-to-day legislative work, both labor federations and most of the larger unions developed extensive research, information, and lobbying arms. Lobbyists such as Paul

Sifton of the UAW, John Edelman of the Textile Workers, and Ted Silvey of the CIO prowled the congressional corridors, working closely with other public interest groups and friendly congressmen. George Meany, second in command of the AFL, was skilled in the techniques of legislative maneuverings, and AFL legislative director Andrew Biemiller, a former congressman himself, earned an enviable reputation as an effective and well-informed lobbyist. The CIO turned out impressive publications, offering well-informed, labor-oriented assessments of a wide range of public issues. The day of the old-fashioned labor lobbyist—a grizzled veteran whose forte was buying drinks or promising a dollop of financial support in exchange for votes on some specific enactment of interest to his union—was fast fading. Now appearing on the scene was a bevy of bright, articulate, often college-educated men (and a few women), eager to advance labor's legislative role as that of a spokesman for lower-income Americans.

Alas for the labor movement's ambitions, class identifications were so weak in the United States and workers so immune to even the strongest AFL or CIO campaigns that neither PAC nor AFL political and legislative operatives could "deliver" the labor vote. Evidence from public opinion pollsters suggested that workers, even in such politically sophisticated organizations as the UAW, paid little attention to the detailed workings of their union's political and legislative arms. Support for the Democratic party owed more to memories of FDR, the workers' ethnic identities, or plain habit than to labor's efforts. Even direct attacks on organized labor itself did not always rally working-class support for the unions' position. True, when conservative forces in some states attempted to enact anti-union legislation (so-called right-to-work laws), labor leaders could often mobilize effective campaigns. But the fight against Taft-Hartley on the grass-roots level ran into roadblocks both in Congress and on the campaign trail. Declared one Ohio labor leader ruefully in 1950, "We couldn't convince the workers [that] Taft-Hartley is a 'slave labor law.' They've been living with it for three years and nothing bad has happened to them." Labor's inability to deliver the vote even in campaigns so close to the unions' self-proclaimed vital interests eroded credibility in congressional and Democratic party circles, thus undercutting even the best research, publicity, and lobbying functionaries.

Still, unionists gained increasing expertise in generating support for liberal social and economic programs on both the state and national level. True, by the early 1950s, the New Deal agenda, insofar as it rested on direct encouragement of labor unions, had become a mere echo of the yeasty days of the thirties. But insofar as it embraced the concept of a positive government pledged to intervene in economic and social life with programs to stimulate economic growth, aid education and public services, help the disadvantaged and unemployed, and promote racial equality, the New Deal tradition remained potent even amid the frequent conservative electoral victories of the postwar decade.

Labor's political success in defending and even expanding the New Deal legacy of social and economic policy rested in good part on the dynamic expansion of the American economy. As the end of World War II approached in 1944–45, many observers feared a return to depression conditions, recalling that on the eve of the 1940 defense boom, unemployment had stood at well over 10 percent. But through the late forties and into the fifties, a surging economy provided millions of new jobs, confounding these dire apprehensions. Gross national product (GNP), which in 1940 stood at $100 billion (a figure 3% *below* that of 1929), soared to over $286 billion in 1950 and to an astounding $399 billion in 1955. Real wages jumped upward, providing enormous purchasing power for millions of lower-income citizens. Blue-collar workers, the majority of whom were now covered by union contracts, entered massively into consumer markets, buying houses in the suburbs, purchasing automobiles, and stocking their homes with appliances and conveniences.

Fortune magazine, a weekly publication serving as the business counterpart to the mass audience weeklies *Time* and *Life,* graphically celebrated American capitalism's achievements in these years. Week after week, the handsome, well-edited magazine extolled the abundance, opportunity, and progress of a free enterprise economy. The day of oppression and exploitation was past, as was the time of revolutionary upheaval. Indeed, the U.S.A., its editors proclaimed, was itself a "permanent revolution," providing ever-rising standards of living in an atmosphere of political, religious, and personal freedom, in stark contrast to the grim, authoritarian regimes of Eastern Europe and the Soviet Union, which proclaimed a socialist new order but in fact provided only repression and penury to their sullen inhabitants. *Fortune*'s brilliant labor editor, Daniel Bell, kept a careful and, on the whole, sympathetic eye on developments within the American labor movement, never failing to drive home the lesson that unions and their members gained more from a progressive, advancing American capitalism than they ever could hope to achieve under the sullied banner of revolutionary socialism.

Few laborites completely embraced this optimistic assessment of American life. If unionized workers were now beginning to achieve something approaching prosperity, millions remained unorganized, toiling in low-wage establishments with little security. The country's primitive social welfare system and inadequate educational and medical services relegated vast numbers of Americans to the margins of the country's life. Black Americans continued to suffer grinding poverty and cruel discrimination, which often degenerated into outright terrorism.

Nor should the celebrants of American capitalism forget that many of the factors that permitted the admittedly impressive performance of the economy might well be temporary. War-devastated Europe and Japan provided vast markets for American goods and services for the time being, but labor's economic experts warned that once these lands rebuilt their social and economic structures, their energetic populations would no doubt challenge American international economic supremacy. If for the nonce American capitalism rode high, union leaders resolved to take advantage of the country's prosperity by securing for their ranks the high wages, job security, and public services they needed for enjoyment of the good life promised by corporate America and its spokesmen. The New Deal, after all, had not sought revolutionary transformation—merely a better life for lower-income Americans and the promise of access to the organizational power to achieve and defend it. Increasingly, the political instruments forged in the 1940s became labor's primary vehicle for advancing their goals.

THE RADICAL PERSUASION

Not everyone in the labor movement agreed with reformist notions of labor's appropriate social and political role. Throughout American labor history, and especially since the rise of the CIO, anticapitalist radicals had sought to influence organized labor and to reach the masses of workers with various revolutionary appeals. Since the mid-1930s, the leading anticapitalist element was the Communist party, whose membership during World War II may have reached 100,000 and whose vigorous support for the war and for the alliance between the United States and the Soviet Union earned it considerable prestige in liberal and labor circles.

Since the leadership of the Communist Party of the United States (CPUSA) was closely and directly beholden to that of the Soviet Union, Communists gained a largely deserved reputation for being directed from Moscow in matters of real importance. While it is true that few Communists had any direct connection with the international Soviet apparatus and that American party leaders were free to devise their own means of implementing international Communist decisions, it is equally true that American party members did not criticize the Soviet Union or publicly dissent from important policies and decisions. The limitations of this disciplined conception of international politics became glaringly evident when Soviet foreign policy shifted drastically and when evidence of mass terror within the USSR surfaced. Thus, in the period 1939–41, when the USSR startled the world by its pact with Hitler, American Communists uncritically embraced the Soviet alliance with Germany. CPUSA members quickly echoed the Soviets' denunciation of the "imperialist" capitalist democracies, England and France, for waging war against Germany even as Hitler's blitzkrieg struck France. The sudden German attack on the USSR in June 1941 of course brought an instant reversal, not only in Soviet relations with Germany and her enemies, but in CPUSA rhetoric, which shifted overnight from cries to keep the United States out of the war to shrill calls for American belligerency. Also encouraging distrust of the CPUSA was American Communists' response to mounting evidence of widespread terror and mass victimization within Stalin's Russia. It seemed that the more solid the evidence of savagery and persecution, the more ardent American Communists became in their support for the Soviet system and the more unrestrained in their vilification of doubters and critics.

During the war, the common interests of the United States and the Soviet Union permitted American Communists to support the military effort without stint. Pro-Soviet trade unionists were the most vocal defenders of the No-Strike Pledge. Indeed, in 1943, CPUSA leader Earl Browder even dissolved the Communist party per se, changing it to the Communist Political Association. No longer, so Browder believed, would American Communists pit themselves unrelentingly against the "bourgeois" parties (i.e., the Republicans and the Democrats); rather, Communists, increasingly respected as patriotic Americans, would promote their ideals of social justice and continued friendship with the USSR through education, labor union and civil rights work, and public discussion.

Few American workers were Communists. Indeed, the CPUSA recruited so heavily from among nonproletarian elements that its membership contained many more students, accountants, dentists, and lawyers than it did workers. But during the 1930s, a number of able labor unionists who were either members of or closely sympathetic with the Communist party emerged as leading figures, especially in some of the new CIO unions. In the United Electrical Workers (UE), for example, secretary-treasurer Julius Emspak, regional director William Sentner, and director of organization James Matles were Communists, along with important staff members and local leaders. In the strategically important West Coast International Longshoremen's and Warehousemen's Union (ILWU), president Harry Bridges followed a consistently pro-Soviet orientation, and leading secondary figures openly proclaimed Party membership. In other important CIO organizations, notably the National Maritime Union (NMU), the New York City–based Transport Workers Union (TWU), and the Mine, Mill and Smelter Workers (Mine, Mill), Communists and those intimately associated with them provided the dominant leadership. In the bourgeoning UAW, Communists and other pro-Soviet activists led important locals, held key positions in the headquarters staff, and were often popular and effective rank-and-file leaders, particularly in the union's Michigan heartland.

In national CIO headquarters, publicity director Len De Caux was a Communist. The industrial union federation's brilliant legal counsel, Lee Pressman, though no longer a Party member, conferred regularly with CPUSA chiefs and coordinated activities of pro-Soviet leaders in the CIO. In all, careful observers believed that as of 1946, at least twelve of the CIO's thirty-five affiliates had a Communist or strongly pro-Soviet leadership and that Communists played significant roles in at least half a dozen other affiliates. The UE, with about a half million members, was the largest Communist-oriented CIO affiliate. Others, such as the TWU, the ILWU, the NMU, and the Mine, Mill Workers, counted fewer than 100,000 members each but were vigorously led organizations in critical sectors of the economy. Other CPUSA-oriented unions—notably organizations among public employees, office and secretarial workers, and scientific and technical employees—had little membership and less influence.

Communist presence in the CIO had always created controversy. Conservatives charged that by definition Communists were Marxist-Leninists who sought the overthrow of the U.S. government—through violence if necessary, through guile and manipulation if possible. If Communists and their supporters appeared on occasion to be "reasonable," these critics claimed, it was merely a ploy to gain advantage. Moreover, Communists were not free agents; they could not be loyal Americans. The Kremlin dictated their decisions, and the Soviet fatherland claimed their primary loyalty. Because Communists sought to destroy capitalism and embraced an atheistic ideology, businessmen, the general press, and religious groups pounced on evidence of Communist influence in labor unions. The Roman Catholic church, with millions of working-class communicants, hammered away at the evils of communism, both in the United States and worldwide. Evangelical Protestants, especially in the South and rural Middle West, also fulminated against the Red Menace and, by extension, organizations such as labor unions that allegedly harbored Communists. Since Communists were active in such progressive causes as civil rights, union organizing, and support for the unemployed, hostility toward them often spilled over to include anyone involved in these endeavors. Indeed, red-baiting—the vilification of social reformers and radicals of any stripe by calling them "Communists"—was a favorite tactic of right-wing editors, politicians, and preachers, and a chronic problem for even the most politically cautious civil rights organizer or trade unionist.

But conservatives had no monopoly on anti-Communism. Indeed, hostility toward the Communists and their defenders was more bitter, unrelenting, and intensely felt among members of liberal and socialist groups than perhaps anywhere else. While in a broad sense Communists shared similar attitudes with other leftward-oriented activists, the heritage of conflict among groups on the left was so profound that most socialists and many liberals came to see the Communists as unusually pernicious, destructive, and dishonest. Throughout the 1920s and 1930s, American Socialists, for example, had fought—sometimes literally— with Communists for influence within unions, peace organizations, student associations, civil rights bodies, and political campaigns. Communists disdained the Socialists as mere reformers, while Socialists denounced Communists as authoritarian manipulators. As Communist strength and prestige grew in the labor movement in the 1930s, Socialists watched with dismay and often led in exposing the Soviet ties of American Communists and in criticism of the policies of pro-Soviet leaders.

Very often, internal conflict among anticapitalist leftists reflected closely the bitter ideological bloodletting occurring in Europe in the turbulent depression era. In Germany, for example, Socialists and Communists had battled each other more fiercely than either had fought against Hitler in his rise to power in the early 1930s. According to official Soviet analysis, Socialists and Social Democrats were to be regarded as "social fascists"—that is, as political elements that, whatever the democratic-sounding rhetoric of their protestations, were "objectively" pro-fascist. And the Soviets had even greater contempt and hostility toward still another anticapitalist group, the followers of exiled revolutionary leader Leon Trotsky. Trotskyists, despite their ardent revolutionary advocacy and their relentless attacks on capitalism and imperialism, were, in the Stalinist formulation, "wreckers" of the Workers' State, the USSR. Since they sowed disaffection with the Communists, they divided the workers' movement and "objectively" facilitated the triumph of fascism in Europe. Indeed, in a series of bizarre purges and trials that sent literally thousands of men and women to their deaths and hundreds of thousands to slave labor camps in the Soviet Union in the mid- and late 1930s, Soviet prosecutors routinely accused the hapless victims of actively plotting along with Trotsky to assist the Nazis in overthrowing the Soviet state.

This grotesque world of international ideological politics had important reverberations in the United States. While few Americans were Communists or even Socialists, and while only a handful of people were associated with the struggling Trotskyist groups, liberals, reformers, and trade unionists followed these events closely. Indeed, in the 1930s and 1940s, many American liberals came to regard the Soviet Union as the most advanced and progressive society extant. They were impressed with the apparent cohesion and vigor of the Soviet state and contrasted images of a people struggling to build a unified socialist society with the aimlessness, drift, and despair of the depression-racked West. They hailed the USSR's apparently uncompromising resistance to fascism. They dismissed reports of brutality, slave labor camps, and mass executions as the paranoid delusions of squeamish, bourgeois reactionaries.

Since Communists in the United States always identified vocally with the rights of labor and racial minorities, many liberals came to think of Communism as little more than an extension of the American progressive tradition. "Communists," went a widely circulated aphorism, "are only liberals who mean it." Thus, in the late 1930s, when Communist party chairman Earl Browder insisted that "Communism is Twentieth-century Americanism," many influential liberals, writers, artists, and political figures nodded in agreement.

Other liberals, however, rejected this benign view of the Soviet Union and the Communist party. They viewed Communist persecution of Trotskyists, Stalin's crimes against the Russian people, and the machinations of domestic Communists with horror. They, along with their frequent allies among Socialists and Social Democrats, resented the prestige gained by the USSR and the CPUSA during the World War II alliance against Hitler. They grew indignant when their denunciations of Communist influence and (during the war) of Communist advocacy of workers' concessions in behalf of stepped-up production drew in upon them charges of red-baiting. Within the CIO, an articulate group of social democratic and liberal unionists, led by Secretary-Treasurer James B. Carey, Walter Reuther, John Brophy, and others close to liberal groups and reform-minded circles in the Roman Catholic church, spoke out against Soviet crimes even during World War II and attempted to isolate the pro-Communist elements in the CIO and the affiliated unions.

Throughout the thirties and World War II, these issues rumbled about laborite circles. During the heady days of CIO organizing, few liberals or laborites raised objections to the important roles Communist organizers played in building the new unions. During the war itself, ideological and political conflict sputtered beneath the surface, largely suppressed by CIO president Murray, himself a Catholic anti-Communist but eager to preserve CIO unity and to avoid open conflict. Only during the period of the Nazi-Soviet Pact (1939–41) did sharp disagreement erupt. Liberals and social democrats such as Reuther, Sidney Hillman, and other leaders in both the AFL and CIO decried the alliance between John L. Lewis and the pro-Soviet elements, charging that this cynical alliance of convenience strengthened Hitler, impeded necessary national defense, and jeopardized the gains American workers were making in the defense boom.

In the post–World War II atmosphere, open ideological conflict burst forth again, eventually sundering the CIO. In March 1946, Reuther narrowly won the UAW presidency. His rival, incumbent R. J. Thomas, had the vigorous support of the union's active and articulate pro-Soviet group. Later that year the CIO convention adopted a carefully phrased resolution declaring that the federation members resented and rejected interference in their affairs by outside forces, naming the Communist party specifically. Still, President Murray, who relied heavily on Lee Pressman for advice on most important CIO matters, clearly hoped that this paper pronouncement would appease the restive anti-Communists without embroiling the CIO in a disastrous bloodletting.

Events in 1947 and 1948, however, dashed Murray's hopes. Labor leaders found that the Truman administration's increasingly anti-Soviet foreign policy moves resounded within their own organizations. Soviet-directed takeovers of Eastern and Central European nations, combined with the prestige and numerical strength of Communist elements in war-torn Western European countries, spurred American reaction. In March 1947, President Truman asked Congress for American aid to Greece and Turkey, the former in the throes of a civil war pitting Communist-led guerrillas against a corrupt monarchist faction. In June, Secretary of State George Marshall called for large-scale American aid to Europe, ostensibly to rebuild its economy but, some critics believed, also to undercut Communist influence in France and Italy.

The AFL had no trouble coming to terms with the increasingly anti-Communist thrust in American foreign policy. Indeed, AFL leaders such as George Meany and David Dubinsky relied heavily on Jay Lovestone, a former Communist leader who had made a career of anti-Soviet politics, for guidance in international matters. AFL operatives were already at work in Western Europe, cooperating with anti-Communist groups to thwart what they perceived to be Soviet-inspired disruption in France and Italy. AFL leaders, in fact, urged the United States government to acknowledge the Soviet threat in Europe and eagerly embraced the government's emerging policy of containment of Soviet and Communist influence.

For the CIO, however, the American-Soviet showdown created endless agony. Official CIO policy, endorsed anew at the 1946 convention, called for continued U.S.–Soviet cooperation and for American support for anticolonialist movements around the world. In any CIO meeting, moves by people such as Carey or Jacob Potofsky (Sidney Hillman's successor as head of the Clothing Workers) to criticize Soviet behavior and to endorse American countermeasures drew sharp criticism from the strong pro-Soviet faction. Meanwhile, in such CIO affiliates as the UAW, the UE, and the Mine, Mill Workers, anti-Communist forces began a series of bitter battles with groups and leaders they charged with being, in effect, pro-Communist for control of key locals, staff positions, and even (as in the case of the UE) the union itself.

By the end of 1947, the CIO seethed with internal dispute. The ideological questions that had racked the industrial union federation for almost two years came to rest on the issue of political action strategy for the 1948 campaign. Pro-Soviet groups, clearly following the lead of the now-reconstituted CPUSA, proclaimed the need for labor to join a third-party effort, certain to be led by former vice-president Henry A. Wallace. Despite a January 1948 executive board resolution rejecting third-party politics, prominent leaders in the UE, ILWU, Mine, Mill Workers, and other pro-Soviet affiliates announced for Wallace. So did Murray's valued legal counsel, Lee Pressman, who left his position as general counsel and thus severed an association with the CIO that went back to 1936.

The pro-Wallace groups argued that the Democratic party had become increasingly insensitive to labor's needs. Almost half of congressional Democrats had joined the Republican majority to support Taft-Hartley, they pointed out. Truman's veto, they claimed, was a last-minute effort to appease the unions and did not outweigh the president's many antilabor utterances during the 1946 strike wave. The president's provocative stands on foreign policy, his crude brandishing of the nuclear monopoly enjoyed by the United States, and his support for European colonial powers in their efforts to suppress Asian and African liberation movements gave progressives no choice but to sever their ties with a Democracy that had drifted so far from the wise and generous policies of FDR.

To the complaint of the majority of CIO leaders that these third-party enthusiasts were defying CIO policy, the Wallace supporters invoked the principle of union autonomy. CIO resolutions, they argued, did not bind individual unions. If Murray and other CIO leaders believed that they could salvage the remnants of New Deal liberalism through support of the red-baiting Truman administration, that was their choice. But the CIO majority had no right to compel dissenters to follow the same (to them) disastrous path.

This disagreement was more than a difference of opinions. It reached down into the whole structure of the CIO and CIO-PAC. CIO support for Democratic candidates, and eventually for the Democratic presidential nominee (as of the spring of 1948, liberals were desperately seeking an alternative to the presumably unelectable Truman), depended on the industrial union body's local and state PAC committees and local and state industrial union councils. It was only through these often-overlapping organizations that the CIO could in fact translate pronouncements and endorsements made in the convention and at executive board meetings into concrete political action. Yet such were the vagaries of CIO history that in key areas, such as New York, Michigan, and California, state, city, and PAC organizations had become prominent forums for the unions that now endorsed Wallace.

Over the years, Communists and those close to the Party had played major leadership roles in these bodies. The CIO national leadership constantly sought to encourage, and even legislate, support for the industrial union councils and PAC organizations among often-apathetic local unions in various locales. It was natural for ideologically inspired Communists and their allies eagerly to take up the often-tedious work of these state and local committees and councils. Thus, convinced that third-party politics would result in the election of a Republican president and a reactionary congress, but faced with paralysis in key political action arms in important states, CIO leaders turned against such self-assured and intransigent pro-Soviet labor leaders as Harry Bridges in California and President Albert Fitzgerald of the UE, another prominent Wallace supporter.

The 1948 election brought to a head the question of Communist involvement in the CIO. To anti-Communist laborites, the sudden enthusiasm that pro-Soviet leaders had shown for the Wallace candidacy was merely the latest example of a long pattern of subservience to the international Soviet line. From their embrace of the Nazi-Soviet Pact to their advocacy of all sorts of antiworker plans during the war, Communists and their sympathizers in the unions had sacrificed the interests of their members to those of the Soviet Union, their critics believed. During the Pact period, they had hidden behind the majestic figure of Lewis, fomenting strikes and thus imperiling the unions. During the war, they used FDR for the win-the-war program of the CIO for their sectarian purposes. Now, despite the obvious boost that the Wallace candidacy gave the Republicans and despite the executive board's rejection of third-party politics, they had once again turned on a dime to support the Wallace campaign, despite its utter hopelessness.

Early in 1948, Michael Quill of the Transport Workers, for years a loyal supporter of the Communist party line within the CIO, broke with the Party. Soon, he regaled his CIO colleagues with intimate details of the high-handed manner in which the Party's operatives imposed the support-Wallace decision on pro-Soviet trade unionists. Veteran anti-Communists clucked with knowing approval. At last, they felt, the Party machine in the CIO was breaking down. Finally, they believed, Murray would act to rid the industrial union federation of this pernicious foreign growth.

And they were not disappointed. At the 1948 and 1949 CIO conventions, Murray and other CIO leaders lashed out again and again at the dwindling corps of pro-Soviet unionists. In the past, Communists and their allies could count on solid ranks of supporters and on their advocate, general counsel Lee Pressman, to direct the floor debate and to shape convention resolutions to steer close to the Party line. At Portland in 1948 and especially at Cleveland the next year, however, it was open season on the beleaguered Stalinists. "Are we going to be loyal to the CIO or loyal to the Communist Party?" asked Reuther. At Portland, Murray pointed to the presence of the pro-Soviet delegates in the convention's midst: "We do not want the Communist Party," he asserted, "to be pulling the strings and having them act here like Charlie McCarthy," Edgar Bergen's wise-cracking dummy. A year later, Murray committed himself fully to the anti-Communist onslaught, railing against the "sulking cowards . . . apostles of hate" who were forever "lying out of the pits of their dirty bellies" and corrupting the CIO with their pro-Soviet propaganda.

During the two years after the 1948 election, much of the CIO's attention was occupied in expelling the eleven unions with the most consistent records of pro-Soviet policies. At the 1949 convention, the CIO established procedures for hearing charges against the offending organizations and for their ultimate expulsion. CIO staff members prepared and presented elaborate, pseudolegal "cases" against the accused organizations. The CIO leadership did not attempt to prove that a given leader was in fact a member of the Communist party, but merely that he had consistently followed the line laid out by the Party. These documents went back to the period of the Nazi-Soviet Pact and on through to the debates over support for the Marshall Plan and the Wallace candidacy.

They attempted to show that leaders such as Maurice Travis of the Mine, Mill Workers, Harry Bridges of the Longshoremen, Joseph Selly of the American Communications Association, Donald Henderson of the Food and Tobacco workers, and others had parroted the pro-Soviet line on every occasion. The CIO documents attempted to show that these pro-Soviet leaders made their decisions on matters of importance to their members on the basis of the dictates of Soviet and CPUSA policy. Declared CIO researcher Paul Jacobs, the evidence was clear, for example, that "the positions actually taken by Bridges within the CIO executive board . . . never varied from those advocated by the party."

Communists and their allies formed such an unusually disciplined core within a given union that they could dominate its deliberations even while they seemed to uphold the forms of union democracy. The suddenness of their policy changes (stemming, as they did, from outside directive) was matched only by the savagery of their vilification of opponents, who might have been valued allies immediately before the Party-orchestrated assault began (as had been the case with FDR in 1939 and Lewis in 1941). Of all the criticisms of the pro-Soviet bloc within the CIO, it was this sense that its politics were not the politics of American labor but rather the subservient politics of the international Communist movement that rang truest. Ordinary notions of good faith and compromise simply did not hold when it came to dealing with the pro-Soviet groups. In 1948, the brilliant young left-wing sociologist C. Wright Mills captured the essence of the anti-Communists' bitterness: "The turns of these U.S. Stalinists from leftward to rightward, and back again, have been determined not by their judgment of the changing needs of the working people, or by pressure from these people, but by the changing needs of the ruling group in Russia."

Mills noted that the bitterest opponents of the pro-Soviet factions were often other left-wingers. These men and women believed that the Communists in their rigid adherence to Stalinist policies were actually sabotaging and sidetracking legitimate radicalism in the United States. But Mills also pinpointed the non-Communist radical's dilemma: how to defeat the Communists without playing into the hands of the right-wing red-baiters. Or, alternately: how to convince working people of the legitimacy of radicalism even while fighting the stultifying influence of the allegedly "radical" Communist party. "In its two-front war against Communist and Capitalist," remarked Mills, "the left walks an extremely difficult path."

The program of anti-Stalinist leftists in the CIO called for vigorous, democratic competition on the shop floor and in the union halls. In the UAW and a few other unions something like this process did sometimes take place. Anti-Communists sought to convince rank-and-file workers that the linkage between the pro-Soviet activists' support for the Stalin dictatorship abroad and day-to-day trade union issues was real.

On the whole, however, the ouster of the Communist-oriented elements in 1949–50 and the attacks on the expelled affiliates and their local unions usually degenerated into repression and cynicism. Sordid episodes of reckless charges, personal violence and intimidation, and collaboration on the part of anti-Communists with some of the most disreputable congressional witch-hunters and antilabor publications became rampant. In Alabama, for example, even before the CIO took action against its pro-Soviet unions, the United Steelworkers attacked a number of locals of the Mine, Mill Workers, a fellow CIO affiliate, in the mines and smelters of Bessemer and Red Mountain. In the 1930s, Mine, Mill had been a pioneer in integrating locals in this Deep South industrial belt, but after World War II some white workers charged that Mine, Mill ignored legitimate trade union issues while it promoted pro-Wallace political action. Throughout the spring of 1949 both unions staged parades and rallies. The embattled Mine, Mill leadership charged that the Steelworkers welcomed support from the Ku Klux Klan and other racist elements. On April 20, USWA toughs savagely beat Mine, Mill president Maurice Travis as he prepared for a preelection radio speech; these men claimed to have been outraged at Travis's accusation that they were "popsicle unionists," i.e., mere toadies for the employer, the powerful Tennessee Coal and Iron Company. Travis eventually lost his sight in one eye. In the key representation election on Red Mountain, Mine, Mill went down to a bitter defeat, losing its local to the Steelworkers by 463 votes out of nearly 5,000 cast. Even observers sympathetic to the Steelworkers' anti-Communist campaign in Alabama noted that the local's 2,000 black workers gave Mine, Mill virtually unanimous support.

After the outbreak of the Korean War, in June 1950, such episodes multiplied. In Montana and Connecticut, the Steelworkers found that even campaigns of virulent red-baiting could not dissuade copper miners and brass workers from demonstrating their loyalty to Mine, Mill. The UAW fought savage, sometimes bloody, contests against a small pro-Soviet union in the farm implement field. A new CIO union in the electrical industry, the International Union of Electrical Workers (IUE), waged relentless ideological and political warfare against the pro-Soviet leadership of the original UE, which walked out of the CIO in 1949.

The UE-IUE conflict soon reached appalling levels of interunion rivalry. IUE president James B. Carey made frequent use of radical-hunting congressional committees, whose activities in the past had drawn only organized labor's scorn and hatred. As the Korean War death tolls mounted, workers in Detroit and Los Angeles auto and aircraft plants sometimes took matters in their own hands, roughing up alleged radicals, refusing to work with men and women who had invoked Fifth Amendment privileges before headline-hungry congressional committees, and pressuring employers to fire workers merely accused of holding unpopular opinions.

Often, the political struggle within the unions led to suspicion of anyone with a dissenting reputation. For some unionists, since the Communist party had often been in the rhetorical forefront on matters relating to racial equality, vocal support for civil rights was enough to discredit a fellow worker. Anti-Communist radicals soon realized that government investigators, employers, and even co-workers did not make the subtle ideological distinctions that were obvious to any dedicated radical. Staunchly anti-Communist socialists and Trotskyists, many of whom supported at least the original efforts to discredit the pro-Soviet elements, found themselves barred from defense jobs, frozen out of union politics, and often hounded out of the labor movement because of their alleged "subversiveness." Thus, the labor movement had its own dispiriting version of the red scare that dominated American politics in the early 1950s, as those who sought to combine principled anti-Communism with an ongoing commitment to democratic radicalism in the unions were overwhelmed in a tide of repression that sharply narrowed the spectrum of legitimate debate in labor circles.

INTO THE FIFTIES

In retrospect, the 1948 election did indeed seem the denouement of the politics of the New Deal era. For the last time in a generation, ideological conflict played a significant role in public debate. The American electorate at once reaffirmed the reforms of the New Deal and sealed the status of the Democrats as the nation's majority party, even with FDR no longer on the ballot. Increasingly, however, anti-Communism became the lodestone of American politics, whereas in the thirties and Popular Front era the rise of labor and skepticism of the business system had claimed public attention.

The politics of the next two years thoroughly confirmed the sea change in American public life. Soviet acquisition of the atomic bomb in 1949 and the completion of the Communist revolution in China the same year, a series of spectacular espionage cases in 1949 and 1950, the strident demogoguery of Senator Joseph McCarthy beginning in February

1950, and finally the outbreak of the Korean War in June of that year all deepened the public mood of crisis and tension. The rights of labor, the battles of the unions, and the crusading sense of struggle and commitment that had permeated American life in the thirties and forties faded.

Political scientist Samuel Lubell captured something of this transformation in his important book, *The Future of American Politics.* Visiting a proud UAW local in Detroit during the 1948 campaign, he was struck by the sober, businesslike atmosphere. Where during a 1940 visit he found a union hall seething with the spirit of angry confrontation, now signs proclaiming "UAW Americanism for Us" graced the tidy desks of the local's new officers. "In 1940," Lubell observed, "the flavor of the local was one of street barricades and sit-down strikes; eight years later it was almost like a lodge hall." Lubell attributed this dramatic change to postwar prosperity undergirded by the UAW's excellent contracts. Wages had tripled since the dirty thirties. The local's members, who only a few years before had struggled on the edge of economic survival, were now home owners and car buyers themselves. "Certainly," Lubell believed, "a decade of full employment has altered organized labor's inner stresses and drive." And where once autoworkers supported FDR, in their minds a militant tribune of the common man against the powerful interests, now they turned their backs on the left-wing champion, Wallace, and quietly embraced the mainstream Democratic politics of Harry S. Truman. "The labor dynamo," judged Lubell, "has slowed down."

But Lubell drew back from the notion bruited about by some commentators that organized labor had become a "conservative" force. True, its leaders embraced the anti-Communist consensus, both at home and abroad. True, its very successes sapped the angry militancy that had generated its gains in the past. And a new cadre of leaders appeared more concerned with nuts-and-bolts issues and more willing to work within the system than their predecessors had been. One had only to contrast the rising star of the UAW and CIO, Walter Reuther, and the power-brokering boss of the Teamsters, Dave Beck, with the fading images of John L. Lewis, Harry Bridges, and the other angry men of the thirties. Still, Lubell noted, the labor movement remained a progressive force, increasingly turning its attention to mobilizing electoral and legislative support in behalf of programs benefitting broad masses of people.

With only 35 percent of the nonagricultural labor force organized, and with white-collar and public employment virtually unionless, the labor movement could not afford to rest on its past successes. The 1948 election had seemingly checked the postwar conservative tide, but veteran laborites knew that no victory was final and that struggle had always been labor's lot. As the twentieth century reached its midpoint, labor activists wondered if the skills and ideals sharpened on the picket lines and in the politically charged union halls of the thirties and forties would be relevant to the challenges of life in the prosperous, troubled, globally engaged Republic of the post–New Deal era.

5

Affluent Workers, Stable Unions: Labor in the Postwar Decades

The 1950s and 1960s were years of advance for working people and for the labor movement. An expanding economy boosted real income to record heights. Celebrants of American capitalism rhapsodized over the system's ability to create wealth and blur class lines. Organized labor rebounded from postwar political setbacks and ideological bloodletting to achieve security and influence of unprecedented proportions. Union membership continued to grow, and in the early 1960s hundreds of thousands of public employees further swelled union ranks. The unification of the AFL and CIO in 1955 and the subsequent success of the merged federation's political operations strengthened labor's influence in the Democratic party and in legislative arenas. Bold collective bargaining gains in the 1950s decisively transformed workers' life styles, both on the shop floor and in the larger society.

But this success and prosperity remained tenuous. The same indicators that charted workers' "affluence" also revealed its limitations. Income shares remained stable, suggesting the rigidity of class lines. The vaunted movement of blue-collar workers into technical and white-collar employment and into suburban life styles was less impressive and less significant than the statisticians' early reports often asserted. Economic expansion and new patterns of land use, transport, and plant location devastated traditional neighborhoods, undermined family and community life, and (in historian Frederick Siegel's words) trapped people "on a squirrel wheel of contrived consumption." Meanwhile, for all the unions' growth in membership and political clout, organized labor represented a shrinking percentage of the labor force. Conservatives fixated on widely publicized examples of union corruption to discredit a labor movement they believed had become collectivist and arrogant. Liberal critics deplored organized labor's loss of élan and discounted its often unheroic successes in collective bargaining. "The American labor movement," lamented one long-term labor supporter in 1964, "is sleepwalking along the corridors of history."

AFFLUENT WORKERS

Throughout the 1950s and early 1960s, statisticians and journalists documented the rise of a new phenomenon: an affluent working class. The figures seemed self-evident. Between 1950 and 1970, real gross national product expanded by $350 billion; real weekly earnings for production workers leapt 70 percent. Economists put over 60 percent of all American families in middle-class income brackets, seemingly making Marx's nineteenth-century predictions of the increasing immiseration of the proletariat laughable.

Indeed, wrote journalist-historian William Manchester, "the proletariat was being transformed." In the 1950s, he wrote, it was commonplace for "assembly line workers with working wives [to be] . . . driving expensive new automobiles and buying stocks." In 1940, the car-obsessed American people counted one automobile for every five citizens; in 1970 there were two. Home ownership expanded rapidly in the postwar years, embracing over 60 percent of all American families by 1960. Installment buying and credit card purchase brought a gaggle of appliances into these homes. The typical middle-class consumer, declared *Fortune* magazine in 1954, was no longer the independent businessman or the careful landlord but rather "the machinist in Detroit."

Residential patterns also suggested the virtual disappearance of the traditional working class. The country's population grew rapidly, spurting from 150 million in 1940 to over 203 million in 1970. In the decade after the war, about a million rural folk annually abandoned the farms and countryside. But the nation's cities stagnated, and some even began to lose population. The great bulk of new housing arose outside the older cities, in "the curving superblocks, garden duplexes, and red brick labyrinths and manicured lawns of suburbia," in Manchester's idyllic description. In a 1967 survey, labor leaders discovered that almost 50 percent of their membership lived in suburbs, including an astounding 75 percent of those under forty years of age. The teeming neighborhoods of the vast industrial cities, with their union halls, saloons, social clubs, and traditions of solidarity and cultural cohesion, gave way to new, transient, fragmented patterns of life.

Through the booming postwar generation, powerful trends reshaped the composition of the work force. For example, in fifty years (1900–1950) the percentage of females gainfully employed had grown by 10 percentage points, but in the two decades after 1950 alone it surged another 12, to a point where over 40 percent of all adult women held paying jobs. Particularly remarkable was the influx of married women, almost two-fifths of whom worked for wages in 1970 as compared with just over one-fifth twenty years earlier (and one-seventh in 1940).

Work itself seemed to undergo redefinition. The total number of workers in goods production remained relatively stable, despite the vast increase in the quantities of goods produced. But employment in agriculture, mining, and other extractive pursuits dropped sharply as mechanization made spectacular headway on the farms and in the mines. Meanwhile, service, clerical, and government employment surged upward, embracing 50 percent of the labor force by 1950. Agriculture and mining, the traditional work of a traditional society, had employed over one-quarter of the labor force in 1940 but in 1970 occupied but one in twenty workers.

In 1940, the U.S. Census Bureau classified about 30 percent of the work force as "white collar," meaning professional, managerial, clerical, and sales workers. By 1950, the figure had risen to 37 percent and by 1970 to 48 percent. In contrast, the 1960 census found that blue-collar employment had declined to just under 40 percent, putting it behind the white-collar category for the first time. "Increasingly," declared Manchester, "the representative wage earner became the pencil pusher working for a large, impersonal entity."

America seemed to have abolished the very idea of a working class. Ensconced in suburban comfort, performing technical and managerial tasks, affluent to the point of satiation, the American worker, most agreed, had come a long way in a short time. By the mid-1950s, the misery and conflict of the Great Depression belonged to a remote, barely believable past. In the thirties, observed *Fortune* in 1951, "bloodshed and hate stalked the streets of Gadsden, Toledo, Detroit, and Aliquippa. Looking back . . . these memories seem almost incredible."

Academic observers were endlessly fascinated by the existence of this quiescent, even complacent, working class. For a hundred years, the proletariat had loomed as an avenging force in Western society, forever erupting into protest, always threatening to storm to power in behalf of the exploited and downtrodden. How odd, really, it now was to contemplate a working class so smoothly integrated into the system, so prosperous, so lacking in the bitterness and frustration that had led workers to radical movements and system-threatening protest in the past. Social scientists and popular writers eagerly investigated this phenomenon, interviewing, administering questionnaires, occasionally putting in stints on the assembly lines and in the blue-collar taverns. The result was a series of books and articles—the *Working-Class Suburb,* the *Blue-Collar Marriage,* "Work and Its Discontents," *Automobile Workers and the American Dream*—examining these and other facets of the life of this new working class.

While acknowledging the economic gains, most of these academic observers found trouble lurking behind the prosperous facade. In the late forties, social scientists probed the reasons for mass support of the European totalitarian movements of the thirties. In their elaborate questionnaires and interviews they claimed to find disturbing patterns of authoritarianism in working-class life. Child-rearing was repressive. Attitudes toward authority were credulous. Tolerance for dissent and unorthodoxy was weak. In another study, sociologist Mirra Komarovsky concluded that work, school, and family patterns made working-class marriages bleak and bereft of emotional warmth, virtual prisons for wives of blue-collar workers.

Other investigations found that dull, unrelenting, and fragmented jobs exacted a physical and psychic toll on autoworkers, depriving them of opportunities for rich and satisfying emotional lives. Assembly line workers, whose jobs required little more than routine physical motions, passed the endless days in escapist daydreams or lapsed into despair. "When you get inside that plant," admitted one, "it's just like you are in jail." The repressed anger and frustration came to bear on the worker's stunted home and family life. In the early seventies, violent incidents erupted in auto plants. One enraged worker pulled out an M-1 rifle on arriving at his Eldon Avenue (Detroit) Axle plant job and killed three supervisors. His defense lawyers took the jury on a Dantesque tour of the dismal, clamorous plant, claiming that its daily violations of the human psyche had triggered their client's emotional breakdown. "Did you see the cement room in that plant? Working there would drive anyone crazy," one juror declared. The jury acquitted the autoworker, rendering a verdict of temporary insanity.

Even the trek to suburbia proved misleading. Working-class families settled in places such as Cicero, Illinois; West Allis, Wisconsin; and Hazel Park, Michigan—close-in suburbs, often dominated by the same sort of mills and smokestacks that dominated the parent cities. Workers' districts, whether in the great cities or in the near suburbs, were far more likely than upper-income enclaves to have their neighborhoods severed by ugly strands of railroad tracks and great gashes of interstate highways. Detroit told a tale of two suburbs. Hamtramck was a tidy Polish working-class community. Its thousands of neat, closely packed single-family dwellings, hard by the Grand Trunk tracks and threatened by the land-grabbing construction of Interstate 94 ("The Industrial Freeway"), housed many of the 30,000 autoworkers who toiled at the sprawling

Dodge Main plant that dominated the city. In contrast, just a few miles east lay the Grosse Pointes, just beyond the city limits but a million miles from its gritty realities, at the "cool end of Kercheval." Mansions glittered along the luxuriant lake shore. Single-family homes, set on lush lawns, interspersed with an occasional commercial strip featuring quality grocers, butchers, and specialty shops, housed Detroit's managers, accountants, and lawyers.

Even for workers who found themselves in the newer suburban developments—Richmond, California, near a new Ford assembly plant, for example—physical location had little influence on perceptions of life chances or hopes for the future. Studies of the schools found that even workers' hopes for their children's rise in the world were often misplaced, as the realities of social class pushed workers' offspring into dead-end vocational programs and left them ill-equipped to acquire the skills necessary for college and professional training. Even the rising standard of living, for all of its obvious benefits in comfort and convenience, was double-edged. Social commentator Daniel Bell, by no means an unsympathetic observer of the achievements of American capitalism, described the price workers paid for the material goods that increasingly defined their lives: "In our day . . . it is not physical hunger which is the driving force; there is a new hunger. The candied carrot, the desire for goods, has replaced the stick. . . . By mortgaging his future, the worker can buy a house, a car, appliances." The inevitable emptiness and dissatisfaction, Bell wrote in a classic 1951 essay, "lead not to militancy, . . . but to escapist fantasies."

The vaunted economic status of the American working class also came under skeptical scrutiny. In 1962, socialist Michael Harrington, in a brilliant and widely read book, declared that despite the postwar economic expansion "tens of millions of Americans are . . . maimed in body and spirit, existing at levels beneath those necessary for human decency." Other commentators pointed out that the economic gains of the 1950s and early 1960s had left the basic division of wealth virtually untouched. In 1970, just as in 1950, the poorest one-fifth of the population received less than 5 percent of the national income, while the uppermost one-fifth enjoyed over 40 percent. The betterment of the conditions of the poor and the working class stemmed from sheer economic expansion, which, critics argued, was uniquely dependent on a series of fragile international economic and monetary arrangements. In the 1950s and 1960s, low international prices for oil and American dominance in world monetary affairs helped to underwrite the fabulous expansion of the U.S. economy, which in turn "bought off" the potential protest of the lower classes. How long would these conditions last? How long could the United States count on resource-depleting expansion and thus escape the social and political consequences of its highly skewed system of income distribution?

Even on its own terms, the economy did not quite live up to the claims some of its more enthusiastic celebrants made for it. True, workers enjoyed higher standards of living than ever before, and true, some reports suggested that American workers, in moving out of traditionally blue-collar occupations, were becoming ever more technologically adept and ever less dependent on sheer physical exertion. But on closer examination, many of the figures depicting income and occupation told a more complex story. Thus, for example, in 1970, the United States Bureau of Labor Statistics (BLS) published figures to indicate typical American standards of living. In that year, BLS reported, it took an American family just under $7,000 to maintain a "minimum" standard of living, about $10,700 an "intermediate" standard, and about $16,000 to attain affluence. The "intermediate" budget envisioned a family of four virtually without savings, driving a four- to five-year-old car, and spending a grand total of $45 per year for entertainment. Even so, the BLS's own figures revealed that in 1970—a prosperous year overall—fully 60 percent of American workers and their families lived at or under this level of consumption. Thirty percent of all workers' families failed to get beyond the bare-bones "minimum" standard, while only 12–15 percent of working people attained the "affluent" level of $16,000. Thus, concluded social critic Andrew Levison, "eighty-five percent [of workers were] not 'typical.' " Writing in the early 1970s, Levison concluded that "it is an ironic fact that, while many commentators spoke of the affluent worker with two cars in the garage and a color TV, even today, the majority of blue-collar workers have neither."

Perhaps, though, the fact that blue-collar work was no longer typical explained this somber judgment. After all, statisticians had been noting for over a generation the rise of white-collar employment, as technical, managerial, and scientific work became ever more prominent in the labor force profile. Surely these workers, with their higher educational attainments and their creative and innovative jobs in managerial and technical work, were the workers of an emerging future. But, Levison pointed out, the traditional statistical categories masked as much as they revealed. For one thing, blue-collar employment had not *declined,* even though it was true that increasing *proportions* of the working population toiled in non-blue-collar occupations. Thus, while in 1950 BLS reported 22.4 million blue-collar workers, in 1969 it counted 26.4 million. Manual work was hardly a thing of the past.

Even more revealing, however, was the reality behind the classifier's term "white collar." In fact, the greatest growth in so-called white-collar employment was in the subcategory labelled sales and clerical work. These jobs might be "white collar" in the sense that a typist or a grocery cashier did not spot weld body joints or pour molten steel. But most clerical and sales workers, and an increasing number of office ·workers in the expanding banking, insurance, financial, and government services sectors, were wage workers whose jobs ordinarily had little creative or autonomous content. Moreover, they tended to be low-wage jobs, often requiring few skills. As a consequence, they fitted neatly into the increasing feminization of the labor market, as millions of women, large numbers of them married women who needed to work to support marginal family incomes, flooded into these so-called white-collar slots. "These women," Levison wrote in the early 1970s, "comprise 70 percent of clerical and sales workers. . . . They work as telephone operators, cashiers, salesgirls, typists, and in other low-paying, low-status jobs." In all, Levison concluded, the notion of a disappearing working class and the emergence of a new "salariat" (Daniel Bell's phrase for the putatively emerging white-collar majority) was just plain wrong. Concluded Levison in 1974, "60 percent of America is working class."

Thus, as statisticians and celebrants of the new capitalist dispensation catalogued the unprecedented affluence of the new proletariat, other observers documented its darker underside. Perhaps nowhere was the mixed nature of postwar economic growth more evident than in the case of America's black workers. The upheavals of the 1930s, the expansion of industrial unionism in the 1940s, and the migration of the black peasantry from the impoverished rural South to the booming industrial North brought significant economic gains to black workers. The growth of public employment, with its relative stability and greater equality of opportunity, provided thousands of black workers with significant opportunities, while federally mandated or underwritten transfer payments—unemployment stipends, Social Security benefits—helped to narrow the gap between the incomes of white and black workers. Thus, whereas in 1940, average family income for blacks fell below 40 percent of that of whites, by 1970 the figure had climbed to 64 percent, a rise of over 60 percent. Other figures for infant mortality, education, and life expectancy showed similar gains during this period.

Other patterns, however, cut against the grain and revealed sharp limitations to the improvement of the conditions of black workers. The migration north provided jobs, but the postwar deterioration of the great industrial cities left hundreds of thousands of blacks segregated in crumbling ghettoes, imprisoned by formal and informal codes of discrimination that relegated them to the poorest housing, the most overcrowded schools, and declining and marginal jobs. Even where black workers made significant gains, as in the auto, steel, and other mass production industries, industrial decentralization led to the closing of many large urban plants, as companies relocated in the expanding suburbs. There, housing discrimination often excluded blacks from competing for newly opening jobs. New technologies enabled employers to impose higher educational requirements, often in effect resegregating entire lines of employment. In the steel mills and smelters of Birmingham, Alabama, for example, black workers, most of whom toiled in foundry and common labor jobs, found that hard-won seniority applied only on a "department-wide" basis, thus permitting southern employers, unhindered by union contracts designed to protect white workers' standards, to keep black workers out of the higher skill gradings. Even in unions such as the UAW, where union contracts provided equal access on the basis of seniority to skilled trades, the dispersal of the auto plants, lethargic enforcement, and the poor educational background of many black workers worked relentlessly to keep Negroes in common labor grades. In 1964, Congress established the Equal Employment Opportunities Commission (EEOC), whose purpose was to help identify and correct these abuses, but this underfunded agency provided only sporadic encouragement and required long processes of litigation for redress.

The experience of black workers in one large pulp and paper mill is illustrative. In the 1940s and early 1950s, black workers in Covington, Virginia, had been at the heart of the CIO's organizing campaign. These workers, who did the heavy jobs in the wood yard and in the log-preparation areas at the large Westvaco mill, provided the key to the whole production process, for once the logs had been fed into the great mechanical and chemical cooking and digesting vats, pulp and paper-making became a relatively self-regulating process. Thus, in 1944 CIO organizers concentrated on these hardworking black men, using their militancy as a key to bringing the mill's 2,000 workers into the Paper-workers' union.

At first, the CIO's general policy of strengthening wages at the lower end of the spectrum and of reducing wage differentials between unskilled and skilled workers brought critical gains to black laborers. Soon after the war, however, the company began to automate log-handling operations. Displaced black workers sought entry into jobs within the mill itself, only to find that their union contract sanctioned the company's imposition of high educational standards that, in effect, barred most blacks, adding to the penalties that they paid for Virginia's segregated and inadequate system of public education. For years thereafter black workers fought both in the mill and in the courts to change hiring patterns. The EEOC provided important legal ammunition, and helped by the local NAACP branch, energetic, articulate black paper workers pressed claims for equal hiring practices. Since the employer's hiring patterns were endorsed by the union contract, on a number of occasions these black unionists found themselves bringing suit against their own local union as well as against the company. Through the years, basic wage rates remained strong in the mill, and unskilled workers, black and white, benefitted from the vigorous presence of an industrial union. But these harsh patterns of discrimination continued to blunt the progress of black workers and to dilute whatever feelings of enthusiasm they may have felt for the union cause.

AFL construction unions practiced even more blatant forms of discrimination. In some cases, union rules barred blacks outright from participation in apprenticeship programs. More often, informal patterns of selection weighted heavily against those without family ties or personal influence in the union, kept blacks from the higher-skill (and hence higher-pay) opportunities. Thus, although the postwar economic expansion helped create a core of relatively well-paid and union-protected black workers who were making real gains, it left untouched vast areas of discrimination that imposed sharp limits on black progress.

In the late 1960s and early 1970s, America's journalists and social critics began to rediscover the grievances of working people and the limitations to the postwar affluence. Barbara Garson and Elinor Langer depicted the dull, routinized monotony afflicting autoworkers, telephone operators, cannery workers, and hospital employees. In 1970 wildcat strikes among a youngish work force at a spanking new, super-efficient Gerneral Motors plant in Lordstown, Ohio, brought a flock of reporters and rated a *Playboy* interview for the leaders. The racist presidential campaigns of Alabama governor George Wallace in 1964 and 1968 gained the support of thousands of blue-collar workers in solidly unionized Wisconsin, Indiana, and Michigan, leading some observers to wonder aloud if the liberal politics of the working class was not a thing of the past. When hard-hatted construction workers assaulted a group of long-haired antiwar demonstrators in New York City in May of 1970, the notion that workers had suddenly become a malignant, authoritarian force grew. In 1971, TV producer Norman Lear introduced the inimitable Archie Bunker to the viewing public, thus sharpening the stereotype of modern workingman—ignorant, bigoted, a grotesque yahoo of the loading dock, saved from being sinister only through his ludicrousness and ineptitude.

These popular perceptions of working-class people, however, were finally as misleading as was the popular image of the affluent worker in the 1950s. At the turn of the century, journalist Hutchins Hapgood had attempted to get inside the world of working people once and for all. What was on the worker's mind, he asked? Who spoke for the worker? What was the essential reality—the violent strike, the endless days of unrelenting toil, the haunting insecurity? After drinking in the workers' saloons, visiting their homes, and talking with workers and their wives, Hapgood threw up his hands. "The world of labor is so big . . . ," he eventually concluded, "it has so many aspects, so many threads, that no man can possibly stand at the center of it."

Hapgood's modesty might have stood the social observers of the fifties and sixties in good stead. As throughout its history, the American working class of the postwar generation could not be compressed into neat statistical categories or tidy sociological or journalistic capsules. Observers such as Garson saw only a world of alienation and trivialization in America's shops and factories, but even at the height of concern over the so-called declining work ethic, surveys showed that most workers expressed satisfaction with their jobs. Even those who fretted most about the alienation and despair of working Americans acknowledged that in the end, most workers put down roots, harbored aspirations for their children, and had little interest in intellectuals' dreams of social transformation. Nor did the resentment that occasionally erupted in short-term support for mean-spirited political movements carry very far, especially as political analysts found that upper-income voters were often more prone to vote for Wallace and his ilk than were workers.

American workers in the 1960s, no less than those in the 1920s, were proud of their contributions, eager for improvement in their material standards, and anxious to acquire and exploit opportunities for advancement for themselves and their families. Sensitive to the harshness and fragmentation of much of the work they did in an increasingly mechanized economy, they focused their emotional lives outside the workplace. Relentlessly bombarded by the gaudy consumerism of mass media, they provided less support than had their predecessors for dissident political and social movements. For most workers, traditional ethnic identities receded and social and political life based on the cohesive urban neighborhood dissolved in the individuating life-style of the suburban tract. Did the postwar trends ultimately pay off for workers in opportunities for personal enrichment and social mobility? Or were they a dead end, offering only a bogus consumerism and limited lives now bereft of traditional class and cultural resources? With all the surveys, reportage, polemics, and scrutiny that an expanding academic and journalistic industry churned out in the affluent decades, few commentators ventured final answers to these central, yet elusive, questions.

THE UNIONS: COLLECTIVE BARGAINING

The fifties and sixties were years of achievement and frustration for the labor movement. The unions made critical breakthroughs in collective bargaining and important strides in organizing new categories of workers. The merger of the AFL and CIO in 1955 seemingly ended twenty years of internecine conflict and the newly united AFL-CIO honed labor's already impressive political operations. The extension of Democratic congressional majorities through the Eisenhower years of the 1950s and the return of liberal Democratic administrations to the White House in the 1960s owed much to labor's energy and resources. Organized labor survived the passing of the veteran leadership—Green and Murray died within days of each other in 1952—and grew accustomed to operating at the center of power, its endorsements and its support for legislation eagerly sought by candidates and policymakers.

As usual, however, the labor movement had more than its share of critics and opponents. Revelations of chronic corruption in several unions, notably the huge International Brotherhood of Teamsters (IBT), led to harsh regulatory legislation and tarnished labor's public reputation. Even unblemished unions came under criticism for having become stodgy and bureaucratic, ever more remote from the concerns of a younger membership. Conservatives sought further legislative curbs on labor's political and organizing activities. The pages of the nation's leading general audience magazine, the *Reader's Digest*, subjected the labor movement to a steady barrage of criticism, while the National Right-to-Work Committee blasted the labor movement as authoritarian and collectivist. Meanwhile, even friends of labor's general purposes chastised its leadership for failing to recapture the vigor and social purpose of the 1930s. Thus, according to one activist, "The trade unions have become an appendage of the corporations." "Almost universally," he charged, "the democratic foundations of the trade unions have been undermined."

Yet few people, whatever their overall assessment of organized labor, denigrated its effectiveness in the post–World War II decade in the collective bargaining arena. Basic wage rates for production workers, as established in successive "rounds" of negotiations between the industrial unions and major employers, rose by about 45 percent in the late 1940s, another 56 percent in the fifties, and an additional 44 percent in the 1960s. Even with substantial inflation, the growth in real earnings was a remarkable 41 percent. Pioneering auto industry contracts starting in the late 1940s included such income-protecting devices as periodic cost-of-living adjustments (COLA) and automatic annual increases to compensate workers for rising productivity (the annual improvement factor, or AIF). The postwar gospel of high wages and expanding mass purchasing power reigned supreme.

For leaders such as Reuther and Murray, however, rising wages left important needs of modern workers untouched. Over the years, mass production industries had developed hiring and layoff policies geared largely to the industries' short-term needs. What of the worker facing mortgage payments, installment loan demands, and college expenses for his children? Did not he or she have as much need for long-term financial planning as the largest corporation? Even before World War II, Murray and other unionists had argued for some sort of guaranteed annual wage, a method of insuring workers a certain amount of work time (and hence of income) in a given year. This would protect workers from unemployment and would force employers to follow more rational and more humane schedules of labor use. It might help, especially if workers' representatives were brought into the actual production process itself, to free American industry from its cursed boom-and-bust patterns. Murray and Reuther advocated worker-management planning as sorely needed in America's complex economy. Employers fiercely resisted such notions, attacking union-generated proposals as merely another means of fattening paychecks, imposing wasteful labor practices, and putting union bureaucrats into sacred areas of decision-making.

Eventually, some unions, led by the UAW in its 1955 contracts with Ford, did achieve a sharply modified form of annual income. The union and the auto companies agreed to a complex formula through which autoworkers would gain benefits from a fund established by the company to supplement state unemployment benefits. These supplementary unemployment benefits (SUB), when added to government payments, originally provided for about 65 percent of normal weekly pay. Over the years, the UAW bargained successfully to increase SUB benefits to replace as much as 95 percent of lost weekly income, thus providing something approaching a guaranteed annual wage. But the UAW's plans were unique, for few employers enjoyed the auto industry's huge profit margins. And even so, the UAW-negotiated plans provided benefits only so long as the SUB funds remained solvent. In neither the UAW plans nor in any of the few that emulated them in other industries did the unions gain any sort of entry into the realm of managerial prerogatives relating to planning of production.

So-called fringe benefits also provided a frontier for postwar collective bargaining. Such matters as pensions, health care provisions, group insurance, and vacations with pay were more than mere "extras" to supplement pay packets. The unions' successes in these areas in the late 1940s and 1950s established a distinctively American approach to workers' rights and benefits, one that contrasted sharply to the approaches of other industrial countries. The peculiar "mix" of benefits, combining as they typically did negotiated pension or insurance benefits with government programs such as Social Security, broke both with past American practices and with the patterns established in most other industrial societies, where the state typically played a much larger role than in the United States.

One traditional model of benefits provision, potentially both the most radical and most conservative, viewed the unions as independent, self-contained providers for their own members. The craft and construction unions, whose members normally did not toil for one particular employer but rather for a variety of individual contractors, provided health, pension, and death benefits derived from the high initiation fees and dues they charged. Some labor organizations even established their own banks and insurance companies. Unions in the printing trades erected retirement homes and hospitals for aging and ailing craftsmen. In some countries, notably Israel, this approach to workers' needs served as the basis for the creation of a worker-centered complex of social and economic institutions, cooperatives, and investment funds, a sort of parallel society strengthening the labor movement's power and independence. In American unions, however, apart from innovative social insurance and cooperative housing projects maintained by the garment workers' unions, union-provided benefits reinforced the AFL's tradition of narrowly conceived business unionism.

Before the 1950s, union-derived benefits played little role in the lives of the vast majority of industrial workers, apart from the innovative programs of the needles trades unions. Since organized labor had virtually no presence in steel, auto, electrical, metallurgy, rubber, and other mass production industries before 1935, employer largess provided any benefits that workers enjoyed. Early in the twentieth century, some mass production employers launched "employee welfare" programs. Some provided visiting nurses or company-paid doctors. Others built and maintained housing. Still others established profit-sharing and stock-purchase plans. The electrical products industry, for example, prided itself on its concern for its employees. Westinghouse maintained a scholarship fund for workers' children. In the wake of World War I—era strikes, Westinghouse and General Electric began retirement programs, housing projects, group insurance, and stock ownership plans. These moves helped to discourage workers from seeking union representation and to encourage them to identify with the company's well-being. Since most of these benefits terminated when an employee left the company, welfare capitalism helped reduce labor turnover. "By increasing the employee's dependence on the company," observes a careful student of Westinghouse and General Electric, these programs "would also presumably inspire loyal behavior in the event of a crisis," such as an organizing campaign or strike.

In the 1930s, government programs, such as unemployment insurance and Social Security, brought certain minimal benefits to broad masses of workers, irrespective of the employers. After World War II, industrial unionists resolved to establish a system of worker benefits through collective bargaining, at once supplementing these new government initiatives and going beyond them. Unions had made some headway during the war when collective bargaining, unable to affect basic wage rates because of War Labor Board wage formulas, often focused on nonwage benefits. After the war the industrial unions mounted major campaigns to establish health care, pension, insurance, and other benefits, now entirely free from employer discretion. Most large employers, while no longer particularly interested in welfare work themselves, resisted these initiatives, realizing that "fringe" benefits would open up vast new areas for bargaining. Moreover, they argued, by implication basic federal labor law did not require them to bargain on "nonwage" issues other than working conditions. Employers also cautioned that enormous pension and insurance funds would generate irresistible opportunities for corruption and misuse.

Despite these objections, however, unions made rapid progress in postwar bargaining. In 1947, the United Mine Workers gained sweeping medical and insurance benefits. In 1949, the Supreme Court ruled that such nonwage matters were indeed legitimately subjects for collective bargaining, thus undercutting much of corporate America's resistance. The 1949 Steelworkers' contract, hammered out after a lengthy strike, gained pension and insurance funds free from employer control. In 1949 and 1950, the UAW made similar gains, again after long work stoppages. Fringe benefits, as nonwage provisions came to be termed, soon proved a significant area of collective bargaining, and labor analysts traced a rapid increase in the percentage of employee compensation taken up by health, insurance, and pension initiatives. Together with the social welfare legislation of the 1930s, as supplemented periodically by postwar improvements, these contract breakthroughs brought a degree of security and thus a kind of freedom to millions of workers and their families. Along with the impressive wage gains of the postwar era, they undergirded the American working class's fierce commitment to social stability and its ever-deepening distaste for system-threatening political or social radicalism.

The gaining of modest pension and insurance rights left many problems unresolved and created new ones. Early pensions were minimal. Millions of workers remained without any pension rights. Many plans were tied to Social Security benefits, conceived as supplements to these government old-age stipends. Thus, even conservative employers, ordinarily hostile to governmental expenditures, often supported legislation to fatten Social Security payments, for as they increased, employers' pension obligations shrank (or at least grew less rapidly). Workers and union experts worried about the problem of "vesting." They thought of pension gains as really deferred income on the part of workers and thus felt that individual workers should have rights to the accumulated pension funds even if they retired early or changed jobs. Gradually, major contracts in auto and steel, which often served as pacesetters, extended vesting rights, although actuarial principles and employers' desire to have access to pension funds for investment purposes rendered most pension plans detailed, complex, and subject to chronic revision.

The problem of control of investment funds generated by union pensions remained troublesome. In general, the funds established in the contracts negotiated by the UAW, USWA, and other unions in mass production industries posed few problems, for the relatively small number of companies engaged in most of these fields permitted centralized accounting and actuarial policies. Typically, UAW and USWA contracts left decisions on how pension funds should be invested to corporate managers, while guaranteeing benefits for the workers. This arrangement helped to insure prudent investment practices, for, obligated as they were to provide stipulated benefits, employers were not likely to invest fecklessly. But as some critics pointed out, these arrangements also took the use of worker-generated funds—money that might have been used for cooperative housing projects, worker-managed industry, or other forms of innovative social investment—out of the hands of workers and put them into the hands of the banking establishment. With maximization of income as the money manager's exclusive goal, union pension dollars in effect endorsed and buttressed the priorities of finance capitalism. Too often, union funds were being used for investment in nonunion firms or for financing of racially segregated housing facilities. One diligent investigator learned that money from a union pension fund had helped to finance construction of the headquarters of the National Right to Work Committee, an aggressive foe of organized labor.

The alternative of union-controlled funds, however, generated even more serious problems. In its pioneering 1947 contract, the UMW gained control over the medical and retirement funds to be created by royalties on each ton of coal mined. The union established excellent hospitals throughout the Appalachian mining regions, but union mismanagement of the fund soon dried up benefits and forced some of the hospitals to close. At one point, UMW-employed medical authorities joined coal company doctors in legal cases against petitioning miners afflicted with silicosis, for both sides had an interest in denying these "black lung" claims so as to minimize liability for treatment. Moreover, both John L. Lewis, who retired as UMW president in 1960, and his corrupt successor, Tony Boyle, shamelessly used the carrot and stick of pension rights to reward supporters and punish dissidents within the union.

The pension funds established by the International Brotherhood of Teamsters in the 1950s generated even greater problems. Controlled in effect by IBT president James Hoffa, the Central and Southern States Pension Fund accumulated hundreds of millions of dollars, which Hoffa used for a wide variety of investments, many of them speculative ventures in ill-conceived real estate and entertainment complexes. Teamster money, far from being available for the kinds of social projects identified with organized labor, flowed to hotels, night clubs, and casinos, helping to underwrite the grotesque world of Las Vegas. The fund's dealings with all sorts of shadowy figures, many seemingly connected with organized crime, made the IBT and Hoffa himself the target of endless governmental probes and helped make the very name "Teamsters" anathema to labor activists and union critics alike.

Reliance on union-negotiated pension, health, and disability plans also worked to further the already-severe segmentation of the American labor force. In countries such as West Germany and Sweden, high levels of public benefits helped to maintain a certain unity among all workers. Generosity of benefits depended only marginally on the size or market strength of one's employer. In the United States, however, divisions between those workers toiling in large, prosperous corporations with powerful unions and those employed by marginal, competitive firms deepened. Even vigorous unions such as the ILGW, which could organize only a fraction of the workers in the highly competitive, unstable sector of clothing manufacturing, negotiated benefits far below the levels achieved by the UAW and the Steelworkers.

The more successful unions continually sought the expansion of public benefits, in part so that they could concentrate more effectively on improving wage rates and shop-floor conditions. The growing gap between favored workers in central core industries and those toiling in the country's service, light manufacturing, and casual labor markets widened, however. Political consequences flowed from this division, for union leaders found that workers protected by strong contracts with good benefits were often indifferent to political action in behalf of expanded public programs. Observes one careful student, the unions' "very success in the area of social policy . . . seems to have divided American Workers into a hierarchy of relatively privileged and relatively under-privileged, in which organized labor comes to be perceived . . . as a special interest group."

Despite these limitations, on the whole organized labor's postwar record in nonwage aspects of collective bargaining was impressive. Not only did union contracts provide increasingly important health care, insurance, vacation, and pension benefits, but they set a standard for employers everywhere. Given the modest levels of social insurance and medical care underwritten by government in the United States, union-negotiated benefits spurred private employers, many of whom sought to prevent the union virus from infecting their employees, to follow suit. By the 1970s, though such matters as unemployment compensation, health insurance, and other nonwage benefits in the United States lagged behind the levels of state-provided services of comparable countries, the main features of the "mix" of negotiated and state-underwritten benefits were in place. Declared labor writer Thomas Brooks, "There . . . [are] few frontiers left to explore in this area." The unions' role in developing this system, both through collective bargaining and through political and legislative work, was central. By the early 1970s, pensions, health insurance, and the like had become so commonplace that millions of Americans took these hard-won benefits for granted. Few remembered the generations of militancy that paved the way for the UMW's 1947 health plan, the sacrifices of striking steelworkers in 1949 that gained the first substantial pension plan, or the strikes and shrewd bargaining of the UAW in 1949 and 1950 that created auto industry pensions.

One result of these new developments in collective bargaining was to compel unions to develop their own staffs of experts. Lawyers, accountants, economists, health and safety experts, and investment analysts joined union payrolls, giving organized labor the same sort of bureaucratic cast that characterized other large-scale enterprises in a paper-shuffling society. Even those contractual matters closest to the shop floor—provisions defining the content and pace of work, pay differentials, seniority, management's disciplinary rights, and grievance procedures—developed complex bureaucratic dimensions. Contracts themselves expanded from the simple one-page documents of the 1930s to enormous volumes, specifying every possible contingency. Companies such as U.S. Steel, the Aluminum Company of America, Ford, and dozens of others systematically analyzed their thousands of jobs, developing rigid production standards and job descriptions. A 1947 Aluminum Company study, for example, came up with 56,000 separate job ratings, each one of which carried specific qualifications, performance expectations, and pay rates. All of these matters appeared eventually in collective bargaining contracts, as employers relentlessly sought to expand productivity through technological change and the reorganization of work, and as workers sought to protect wage standards, seniority rights, and established work rules.

At the heart of the postwar system of collective bargaining lay the union contract's increasingly elaborate provisions governing work rules, discipline, and disposition of workers' grievances. Indeed, it was in the matter of grievances that the modern union daily reaffirmed its vital role in its members' lives. Modern collective bargaining typically took place in highly publicized national arenas, with contract provisions relating to wages and fringe benefits being determined each year or, more frequently, every two or three years. The centralized character of this bargaining and the long duration of basic contracts led some critics to conclude that the system that had developed from the 1930s onward encouraged a passive relationship between the rank-and-file member and his or her union. True, the worker voted on the contract negotiated by the union's top officers, and rejection of these agreements was by no means rare. Still, with everything important settled at the top and with contracts of two, three, and in some cases five years' duration, there seemed little opportunity for day-to-day involvement in the affairs of the union.

But by definition, matters relating to work rules, discipline, job assignment, and grievances had to remain on the level of the local plant and local union. It was here that managers and workers struggled to define the content and character of the work performed. Even with the relatively amicable system of collective bargaining that developed in most core industries in the forties and fifties, the shop floor remained (in Richard Edwards' phrase) "contested terrain." As elaborate as contracts might become, they could never describe the multiplicity of jobs and the diverse possibilities that real life in the workplace entailed. Managers always sought greater flexibility in assigning work; workers struggled to retain hard-won rights and privileges. Each used the language of the contract to its advantage. Unionists, from grievancemen and local officers in the plant's most basic production units to international union leaders, paid close attention to the workers' daily experiences in the shops. In addition to the formal patterns of union-company bargaining and grievance-handling, informal groups, consisting of workers in a particular department or possessed of a particular skill or specialty, pressured company and union alike to safeguard distinctive work practices.

While it was true that in theory no-strike clauses in standard contracts limited the changes either management or workers could make, in practice each side maneuvered endlessly to broaden its autonomy. During periods of unemployment, for example, managers encroached on traditional (and often contractually protected) work rules and assignment policies in the name of economic survival. Conversely, cohesive work groups, articulate committeemen, and zealous local unions fought management by conducting strategic work stoppages, slowdowns, and "work-to-rule" campaigns. Union leaders, frustrated perhaps by management's efforts to bend the contract to its advantage, would quietly encourage a theoretically illegal wildcat strike, all the while innocently denying that the union itself was responsible. In the auto industry, key matters, such as the speed of the assembly line, remained outside the purview of the contract and hence susceptible to strike action. In steel, the giant industry and the USWA fought ceaselessly over work rules, with the Steelworkers engaging in a four-month strike in 1959 that was triggered primarily by the industry's effort to secure key changes in job assignment practices.

Typically, grievance procedures provided binding arbitration in the event of deadlock. The establishment of arbitration in collective bargaining contracts, a development stimulated by the no-strike policy prevailing during World War II, was a major victory for the industrial unions. It gave workers a final recourse other than the strike, a particularly valuable weapon in view of the fact that many grievances over work rules and production standards involved small groups of workers. Without an arbitration provision, an obdurate employer could in effect present a union with a divisive dilemma: either accept management's policies or call a strike in behalf of a few workers. With arbitration the union could file a grievance, prepare its case, and, if upheld, eventually gain justice in an award that could include back pay or other compensation for the afflicted employee without the need to conduct costly and perhaps divisive work stoppage. Managers initially resented arbitration, so fearful were they of subjecting their decision-making processes and personnel policies to outside scrutiny.

The presence of a grievance procedure topped with binding arbitration created (in David Brody's words) a "workplace rule of law." Matters that an employer wanted to prevent from being arbitrable were left out of contracts and thus were strikable. But for the vast majority of issues relating to job content, wage differentials, promotions, seniority, and other aspects of daily shop-floor life, contractual provisions specified practices and procedures. Aggrieved workers, in most cases, were required to follow management's orders while their grievances were being resolved. Final resolution, either through the in-plant grievance procedure or through outside arbitration, defined the worker's rights, compensating him or her for injustices suffered in the interim. In theory at least, and according to the most detailed study, for the vast majority of workers most of the time in practice, the grievance-arbitration process did provide a reasonable means of resolving problems, one that workers, union leaders, and managers preferred to the fabled shop-floor conflict of the 1930s and 1940s.

Critics, however, pointed to serious flaws and abuses. As historian David Brody observed, "If workers disputed a management action, it remained in effect until altered through the grievance [or arbitration] procedure." However, if management disciplined a worker, the alleged transgressor "was subject to immediate discipline, and was considered guilty until proven innocent." The arbitration system, though containing important protections for workers and unions, helped to remove workers' complaints from direct action on the shop floor to the remote realm of lawyers and experts.

During the heyday of the CIO, union leaders such as Murray and Reuther and rank-and-file militants, some with agendas of fundamental challenge to American capitalism, hoped for basic breakthroughs in the management of America's factories and shops. Some "brass-knuckles" militants sought direct control of the production process and unrelenting challenge to supervisors and managers at the point of production. For national leaders such as Murray and Reuther, extension of union influence in a given company's planning, scheduling, and production methods would gradually reshape and democratize America's hierarchical business structure. The system that developed after World War II to embrace worker-manager conflict over questions of work, pace, scheduling, seniority, and the like followed neither scenario. Strong unions, their internal politics heavily influenced by still-potent work groups, confronted a still-authoritarian corporate managerial structure. Organized labor was no closer to the centers of managerial decision-making in 1960 than it had been in 1945. Detailed contracts, however, limited managerial prerogatives while the two parties continued to struggle for advantage both on the factory floor and in the arbitrator's chambers.

Some disillusioned workers and activists believed that this system degenerated into company-union collaboration at the expense of workers. "Most of the women I talked to," a reporter investigating the West Coast tuna canning industry observed, "knew they were being used by the company and sold out by their union." However, careful observers of a wide range of American industrial experiences in the postwar era found that despite the constraints imposed by complex contractual relationships, workers and unions retained a good deal of leeway. Informal shop practices, skillful union bargaining, and the ever-present threat of slowdowns, work-to-rule campaigns, and wildcat strikes gave workers a real, if sometimes informal, voice in shop-floor control. To be sure, in weak or apathetic unions, or in industries with transient labor forces, the struggles of workers to retain control over the pace and content of work amounted to a kind of only marginally effective guerrilla warfare, often conducted in defiance of complacent union representatives. But in autos, steel, rubber, and other solidly organized mass production industries, British scholars Steven Tolliday and Jonathan Zeitlin conclude, "sophisticated union leaders . . . were always careful to remain in touch with the mood of the rank and file and sought to incorporate demands over workplace issues . . . into their bargaining strategy." The greatest impediment to effective union presence in these matters, they observe, was the view of the great majority of workers that the union's primary function was that of achieving monetary gains.

Tolliday and Zeitlin conclude that "the contractual system of collective bargaining which emerged from the Second World War placed substantial constraints on management's freedom to deploy labor and impose arbitrary discipline." Nevertheless, managers' determination to retain key prerogatives, the unions' tendency toward centralized decision-making, and workers' customary priority on economic gains imposed sharp limits on efforts to contest management initiatives. Through the sixties and into the seventies, as throughout the industrial history of the country, the workplace remained a battleground. Worker resistance and union strength restricted management prerogatives. At the same time, however, the various weapons of workers' defense did not—nor were they intended to—challenge fundamental management control.

All in all, the achievement of the workplace rule of law, together with the breakthroughs in non-wage areas of collective bargaining, represented the labor movement in its finest hour. What historian Ronald Schatz wrote of the unions' establishment of seniority rights might well be applied to the broad range of collective bargaining innovations achieved by this postwar generation of unionists: "This was the greatest accomplishment of the union movement of the 1930s and '40s [and early '50s], the achievement which justifies [the labor movement's] . . . claim to stand beside abolitionism, civil rights, and women's rights as one of the great movements for freedom and dignity in American history."

MERGER

Despite its successes in collective bargaining, the labor movement of the 1950s and 1960s often seemed poised on the edge of crisis. In 1952, for example, the Republican party swept to victory, electing the first GOP president since 1933 and gaining majorities in both houses of Congress. For the first time in a generation, organized labor was without a friend in the White House. The deaths of CIO president Philip Murray on November 12 and AFL chief William Green two weeks later drove home the sense that the old order of the 1930s was fast fading. Internal conflict within the CIO over Murray's successor led to speculation that the Steelworkers union, under its new leader, David McDonald, might disaffiliate, a move sure to plunge the industrial union body into turmoil. Meanwhile leaders in both labor federations chewed over the grim results of the election, which showed that perhaps 40 percent of blue-collar voters had ignored the unions' advice and cast their ballots for Ike.

The multiple shocks of November 1952 paved the way for eventual merger of the warring federations. The new AFL leader, former secretary-treasurer George Meany, though deeply rooted in the craft unions, had worked with CIO functionaries who served with him on various World War II labor boards and committees. As president of the New York State Federation of Labor (1934–39) he had criticized ancient AFL prejudices against mass production workers and had grasped the importance of political action, a stand that put him closer to the CIO than to many of the traditionalist leaders in the AFL.

Fifty-eight years old at the time of his accession to the presidency, Meany nonetheless was something of a Young Turk in his openness to newer methods of organizing and political action and in his acceptance of industrial unionism. A big, jowly, gruff-voiced man, he seemed to editorialists and political cartoonists the very epitome of the labor boss, autocratic and disdainful of the more romantic traditions of laborite activism. "It may interest you to know," he once told a reporter, "that I . . . never went on a strike in my life, never ran a strike, never ordered anyone else to go on strike and never had anything to do with a picket line." Meany repeatedly voiced his enthusiasm for free enterprise and prided himself on the vigor and consistency of his intense anti-Communism. As a cigar-chomping, president-baiting, power-wielding union chief, Meany provided ample copy for reporters and broadcasters, few of whom wasted opportunities to contrast his acceptance of American capitalism with the radical tradition of labor's past.

Yet Meany was no tame lackey of the capitalist class. He worked vigorously for extension of social welfare legislation, presided over the expansion and perfection of labor's political apparatus, and acted as an able spokesman in behalf of lower-income Americans in a thousand hearings, speeches, and press conferences. True, he was something of a labor bureaucrat. His earlier career had been spent in a Bronx Plumbers' local so effectively organized that its members never had to resort to strikes to gain their demands. His experiences as a state federation functionary removed him from some of the hurly-burly of collective bargaining and some of the drama of the picket line, but they also gave him a shrewd understanding of the legislative process and of the importance of political and legislative affairs for working people.

The new CIO president, Walter Reuther, posed a sharp contrast to Meany. Barely forty-five at the time of his election, Reuther had made his career on the picket lines of Detroit, first as a young union activist in the 1930s and later as head of the UAW's General Motors Department in the critical 1945–46 strike. Like Meany, Reuther came from union stock. His upbringing in Wheeling, West Virginia, however, stressed the broad social goals of the labor movement. His father, Valentine Reuther, imbued his sons with visions of labor's martyred struggles so forcefully that three of the boys—Walter, Victor, and Roy—committed themselves to lives in the labor movement. In the 1920s and 1930s, the Reuthers were active socialists. Walter and Victor spent 1934 in the Soviet Union, working in a Russian automobile factory and observing the Workers' State at first hand. Although originally sympathetic to the Soviet experiment, however, all three soon became vocal anti-Communists, and Walter rose to power in the UAW in good part by virtue of his skillful campaign against Stalinist influence in the union.

While Walter Reuther never disdained the importance of fattened pay packets, he aimed to lead organized labor beyond the specifics of economic gains to a broad, progressive role in society at large. Now regarding socialism per se as unattainable in the American environment, Reuther nonetheless retained close ties with democratic socialists at home and abroad. Labor's struggles, he believed, were linked intimately with those of black Americans and with the plight of the poor and powerless everywhere. He believed earnestly that working people, under the leadership of dedicated men such as himself, could broaden the definition of democracy by extending it from the narrow confines of the ballot box and the legislative arena to the workplace and the corporate boardroom. In contrast to Meany, Reuther cultivated social reformers, progressive politicians, and intellectuals.

Reuther, who had worked as a tool-and-die maker in the auto shops of Detroit and Gorki, belied many of the stereotypes of labor leaders so cherished by the press. In personal habits, he was abstemious. The blowzy comradeliness of smoke-filled union halls and blue-collar taverns made him uncomfortable. Although respected and even revered by sympathetic labor journalists and intellectuals, he often seemed mechanical and remote to the rank and file, a leader to be trusted and loyally supported but not one to inspire that final drop of affection sometimes granted less able, but more accessible, leaders.

The accession of Meany and Reuther and the stunning 1952 election defeats spurred talk of a merger of the AFL and CIO. Two decades of personal rivalries, jurisdictional conflict, and angry rhetoric divided the two bodies. Until the CIO ousted its pro-Soviet affiliates in 1949–50, AFL leaders regarded the industrial union federation as a hotbed of disloyalty. In turn, CIO unionists ridiculed the older federation for its unhappy record on civil rights, its cynical tolerance for corruption among some affiliates, and its cozy relationships with employers. Proud of their idealistic heritage, CIO people disdained the fusty, unimaginative, and, to them, sordid world of the AFL.

Unfortunately for these men and women, however, by the early 1950s the AFL was a good deal healthier than the CIO. True, the industrial union body embraced several of the nation's most vigorous and dynamic labor unions, notably the huge UAW and USWA. But with the exception of a handful of vigorous and ably-led affiliates in clothing, textiles, and communications, most of the other CIO unions remained small, struggling, and often dependent on financial subsidies from the CIO. Moreover, the death of Murray had exposed bitter division between the two leading CIO affiliates. USWA president McDonald detested Reuther and constantly leaked hints to the press that the Steelworkers might pull out of the CIO, perhaps to affiliate with the AFL, perhaps to join with Lewis's Mine Workers in a third labor federation. For his part, Reuther grew quickly weary of the petty world of the CIO's internal politics, investing most of his time in the dynamic UAW, of which he remained president.

For all of the mutual hostilities, the actual road to merger proved relatively smooth. In 1953, the two federations agreed to a No-Raiding

Pact. CIO legal counsel Arthur J. Goldberg led in the drafting of a new constitution. For a time, the problem of a name for the merged body proved troublesome; "Congress of American Labor" was popular until a reporter pointed out that its acronym was "COAL," which too vividly evoked the specter of John L. Lewis. In the end, leaders in both federations gradually approved a new constitution which retained the names of both bodies and which preserved the basic structure of the labor movement.

Individual affiliates remained the basic units, with the powers and prerogatives of the national headquarters dependent on an executive council composed of leaders of these affiliates. At the insistence of CIO leaders, the new labor federation housed an Industrial Union Department (IUD) to serve as a stimulus to expansion of organization and as the embodiment of the CIO's central purposes. The new constitution departed from traditional AFL practice in giving the executive council important powers to impose sanctions on unions that failed to observe a new code of ethical practices. CIO officials, however, were disappointed that the new constitution contained only general commitment to racial equality and did not arm the executive council with power to punish affiliates that clung to discriminatory practices. Among other things, the new constitution permitted the AFL to drop at last the scarifying rhetoric that had remained a part of its constitution from its founding in the turbulent 1880s. No longer did labor's major oganization declare that "a struggle is going on . . . between the oppressors and the oppressed . . . which grows in intensity from year to year."

The merger, consummated at a joint convention in December 1955, aroused hopes and fears. Editorialists and businessmen worried that the ending of labor's lengthy civil war would revitalize the movement and send labor's legions into the unorganized shops and factories. The new AFL-CIO, critics charged, constituted a virtual labor monopoly. Labor's powerful political operations, now consolidated in the giant federation, would no doubt grow bolder.

For Reuther, the merger permitted organized labor to marshal its forces both politically and organizationally. "We've got to change the basic character of the whole labor movement," he told his fellow CIO officers. George Meany would, of course, be president of the AFL-CIO; Reuther hoped to keep the CIO spirit alive through his leadership of the IUD. And at age forty-eight he could contemplate Meany's departure from the scene perhaps just a few years down the road, leaving him as the logical successor. He believed that the now-united labor movement could soon "launch a comprehensive, effective organizational crusade to carry the message of unionism to the dark places of the South" and into other anti-union strongholds. He was convinced that a united labor movement could "organize from two to four million new workers" within two years of the merger and that "we can build small unions into powerful unions and we can move forward and do a more effective job on the legislative and political fronts."

The fears of critics and the hopes of laborites both proved excessive. The merged federation did depart from business as usual in the area of ethical practices, but the results proved discouraging. In 1957, after extensive hearings and debates, the AFL-CIO executive council expelled the huge and powerful Teamsters union because of the complicity of its leaders in corrupt dealings. This unprecedented exercise in central authority briefly promised an entirely new relationship between national AFL-CIO headquarters and the affiliates.

The Teamsters, however, took their expulsion in stride and flourished outside the AFL-CIO. Free now from AFL-CIO jurisdictional boundaries, the IBT organized aggressively, becoming by the mid-1960s America's largest labor organization. Its reputation for strong-armed tactics, involvement with organized crime, and disdain for labor's traditions of social idealism grew, but so did its membership and treasury as the IBT extended its sway promiscuously by recruiting clerks, industrial and agricultural workers, and eventually even policemen and college professors. As if to mock the goody-goodies of the AFL-CIO and the high-minded tut-tutting of disapproving editorialists, Teamster organizers in the sixties passed out badges bearing the omnipresent happy face: "Smile," read the inscription, "the Teamsters are Here!"

Unfortunately for Reuther's dreams, the AFL-CIO proper failed to mount equally effective organizing campaigns in most areas. Union membership grew, to be sure, but growth remained slow and failed to keep pace with the expansion of the work force. True, organizations such as the Retail Clerks and the Service Employees made important gains, particularly the enlisting of thousands of new female workers. The Communications Workers of America, an ably-led former CIO affiliate, extended its organization of telephone operators and repairmen and began moving into related fields, recruiting important groups of white-collar and technical employees. Nonetheless, Reuther's hope for $15 million for an AFL-CIO—directed organizing campaign, funded by an assessment of a dollar a member, never materialized. Meany believed that mass campaigns were not effective; workers sought out unions, he believed, when they felt the need to. The circumstances that permitted mass organization in the 1930s and 1940s were past. No longer did a friendly administration in Washington back up the unions. No longer did a pro-labor NLRB facilitate recruitment. Nonunion employers shrewdly matched union-negotiated contract gains to preclude organization. With the central industrial core organized, remaining plants were most often small and scattered, making them costly to organize and service. As an AFL-bred leader, Meany had always been skeptical of centralized organizing, citing as proof the failure of the CIO's massively financed and miserably ineffective campaign to unionize the South after World War II ("Operation Dixie"). Organizing responsibilities, he believed, rested primarily with the affiliates and depended on careful, low-keyed strategic probes along paths of least resistance. Reuther and his CIO partisans, Meany believed, were foolish to dream of reviving the heroic drives of the thirties and launching a new era of mass organization. Reuther constantly pressed in Executive Council for the commitment of AFL-CIO resources: "We have got to find a way to zip open those money bags [and] . . . to get these resources dedicated to an organizational crusade," he once declared. But Meany would have none of it, and his quickly demonstrated ability to dominate the Executive Council left Reuther frustrated and resentful.

PUBLIC EMPLOYEE UNIONISM

The labor movement did surge forward in one key area, expanding rapidly in membership and influence in the public sector. Aggressive organizing by such unions as the American Federation of State, County, and Municipal Employees (AFSCME), the American Federation of Teachers (AFT), and other unions of firefighters, policemen, nurses, civil servants, and postal employees capitalized on the "proletarianization" of public employment to swell union membership among government workers from under 400,000 in 1955 to over 4 million by the early 1970s.

As remarkable as the sheer growth was the dramatic change in character among these unions. AFSCME, long a genteel lobbying agent for small groups of technical and professional workers, led the surge, and by 1973 counted 500,000 members. It now functioned as a sort of "gray-collar" industrial union, recruiting thousands of custodians, sanitation men, laborers, and clerical workers. Jerry Wurf, who wrested the presidency in 1965 from the union's original elitist leadership, combined a streetwise aggressiveness with determination to bring "power to the public worker." AFSCME and other public employee unions helped to change the whole vocabulary of public employment. "Public servants," a phrase smacking of the old gentility, became "government workers," more descriptive of the people who toiled at grimy social services offices and on the city road maintenance crews and garbage trucks. "I am *not* a public servant," snarled one belligerent unionist to a nonplussed journalist.

By the early 1970s, AFSCME had become one of the AFL-CIO's largest affiliates. Some important organizations of public employees, however, remained outside the mainstream labor movement. The National Education Association (NEA), for years a buttoned-down, administrator-dominated professional outfit, began to function as a bona fide labor union. Soon, it claimed over a million members in bargaining units and held contracts with hundreds of school districts. The AFT, affiliated with the AFL since 1919, grew less dramatically than the NEA, but by 1973 it counted a quarter-million members, most of them concentrated in the nation's large cities. Like the NEA, the AFT abandoned its no-strike traditions, and soon work stoppages by teachers had become as much a part of the annual fall ritual for parents and children as the trip to the shoe store and the first football game. The rise of militant teacher unionism shocked those who continued to regard the nation's classrooms as sacrosanct refuges from sordid reality. With a mixture of fascination and alarm, journalist Paul Braun heard one enthusiastic young AFT organizer declare that "the American Federation of Teachers is determined to control the public schools of the United States. And someday," the activist added, "we will." According to Braun, the AFT bred tough-as-nails attitudes in their organizers. "All A.F.T. organizers growl," he reported.

Behind the surge in public employee unionism lay dramatic changes in the scope and content of public workers' jobs. Government employment between 1947 and 1967 increased from 5.5 million to 11.6 million, with about 85 percent of that growth occurring on the state and local level. In 1970, public workers constituted about 18 percent of the nation's labor force. Rapid recruitment brought thousands of black and female workers into the public sector. These workers often encountered long-entrenched patterns of racial and sexual discrimination with resultant lack of job security, making them particularly receptive to the union appeal. Moreover, the surge of public employment and of union activism coincided with the racial and sexual revolutions of the 1960s, putting public employee unions near the center of important social crises in the turbulent decade. At times, public employee unions found themselves ranged against minority spokespeople. In New York City's Ocean Hill–Brownsville school district, militant black community leaders challenged hard-won AFT job security rights, triggering a long walkout in 1968. More usually, however, the unions served as a critical channel for the aspirations for economic gain and equality of treatment on the part of women and minorities.

Changing job structures also added to the union appeal. Whereas public employment had once enjoyed a certain elitist reputation for gentility and security, by the 1960s it had become as much an arena of disputation and conflict as the assembly line or loading dock. Hard-pressed governments, seeking to hold the line on taxes, imposed new productivity standards or burdened employees with additional tasks rather than hire new people. The U.S. Postal Service, compelled by law to show a profit, embarked on a relentless program of job-cutting, mechanization, and cost-slashing. "With their ranks reduced," notes a careful observer of this process, letter carriers "found their routes lengthened, their traditional work patterns disrupted . . . , and their actual work observed by time study specialists and monitored by devices in their vehicles." School teachers, who at one time may have been content with trading adequate compensation for the security and prestige of their profession, rebelled against low pay scales at a time when their classrooms were becoming front-line battlefields in the racial and social warfare of the sixties. An earlier generation may have viewed a postal job, work in a government office, or a slot on the high school faculty as a mark of status and privilege, but the young, diverse labor force of the sixties, many of them products of union households, soon applied the lesson contained in the old mine workers' song to themselves: "Union miners stand together / Heed no operator's tale / Keep your hand upon the dollar / And your eye upon the scale."

Strikes among public employees, for years virtually unheard of, punctuated the late 1960s. In 1966 alone, for example, teachers staged thirty-three walkouts, as compared with a total of twenty-six for the entire previous decade. By the early 1970s, scores of teachers' strikes annually delayed school openings. Nor were teachers the only militants. In 1967, some 250 public employee strikes erupted, quintupling the previous one-year record. Most of these disputes were traditional labor battles, with unions seeking wage increases and fairer promotion, seniority, and discipline procedures, or attempting to resist the efforts of school boards and government agencies to increase workloads and intensify productivity standards. Some walkouts, however, such as the uprising of Memphis sanitation men in 1968 and of Charleston hospital workers in 1969, poignantly asserted the most elementary demands for basic human rights in the workplace and in the community. "I am a man" was the eloquent clarion of Memphis' ill-paid and chronically maltreated black garbage collectors.

The most massive public workers' strike of this period was the wildcat conducted by 180,000 postal workers and letter carriers in the summer of 1970. Defying the federal government, urban postal workers, about two-thirds of them black, struck in protest over their poor pay schedules and in resistance to the Postal Service's headlong rush to step up productivity even while it slashed payrolls. For several tense summer days, National Guard units tried to deliver the mail in key cities until the unions, faced with the might of the federal government, were forced to accept a contract that improved pay scales while giving the Postal Service a virtual green light in its campaign of mechanization and productivity.

In a sense, the upsurge of public employee unionism validated Meany's argument that unions grew when workers were ready for them, making heavily financed recruitment drives irrelevant. Moreover, his point that favorable governmental attitudes were critical to union success also had justification, for President John F. Kennedy's Executive Order 10988, issued in January 1962, had declared encouragement of union representation among federal employees to be government policy. No doubt, this pronouncement stimulated the enormous increase in union membership in AFGE and the postal workers' unions throughout the sixties. Meany's perspective, often ridiculed as overly cautious and unheroic, was based on a home truth: unions flourished best in favorable environments.

Still, Reuther's stress on struggle, sacrifice, and commitment also applied to the public sector. In the decisive breakthrough by the New York City teachers' union in 1962, for example, Reuther's IUD provided critical strike support for the AFT. Whatever the impact of Kennedy's order for federal workers, AFSCME and other public-sector unions often had to fight entrenched political machines and to tap the wellsprings of idealism to gain recognition for state, county, local, and school board workers. AFSCME's organization of sanitation, custodial, and other unskilled workers, many of them minorities, owed nothing to Meanyite complacency. In Memphis, throughout the winter and spring of 1968, a small cadre of activists kept the union spark alive among the garbage men, mounting demonstrations and protests that linked the aspirations of these hard-working trash collectors with the civil rights movement and brought Martin Luther King, Jr., to the Tennessee city for his tragic visit. And when an innovative and aggressive hospital workers' union sought recognition and union standards for hundreds of Charleston service workers, most of them black women with little education, it was Reuther's UAW that provided financial support, and Reuther, not Meany, who linked arms with them on their multiracial picket line.

The period from the early 1950s through the early 1960s was one of success and achievement for the labor movement. Even if postwar prosperity was less satisfying and less widespread than the celebrants believed, the rising American standard of living was the envy of other people. Even if collective bargaining's achievements left millions of workers untouched and helped to deepen divisions within the working class, nonunion employers nonetheless found themselves forced to approximate the wages and benefits won by the unions. While the hopes of labor activists generated by the merger of the AFL and the CIO proved unrealistic, the rapid expansion of public employee unionism launched a new pattern of labor growth. With organized labor's political operations becoming ever more sophisticated and effective and with Democratic presidents once again occupying the White House in the 1960s, organized labor, despite its many critics, seemed well-situated for the challenges of a new decade.

6

Race, War, Politics: Unions in the 1960s

The social conflict that rocked the country throughout the 1960s had profound impact on the labor movement. Used to positions at the forefront of social change, labor leaders found themselves attacked by radical activists and student demonstrators as part of the establishment. Despite labor's general support for the mainstream civil rights movement, critics exposed the unions' spotty records of performance among their own ranks. Organized labor's ritualistic support for the anti-Communist fixation of American foreign policy, while reaping advantage within the counsels of government itself, alienated large sections of the labor movement from the increasingly passionate opposition to the war in Vietnam. Labor's bid to regain control of the national liberal agenda through its unstinting support for Hubert Humphrey's 1968 presidential candidacy narrowly failed, thus closing out on a sour note a decade that had opened rich with possibilities.

THE LABOR MOVEMENT IN THE SIXTIES

Despite the breakthrough in public employee unionism, in the 1960s organized labor receded from the forefront of social change and public controversy. The mass demonstrations of the civil rights crusade, the escalating antiwar movement, and the stirrings of a new women's consciousness claimed the spotlight and defined this generation's commitment to social justice. A "New Left" emerged, grounded in the politics of peace, race, and ecology, scorning the labor-centered sectarian ideological conflict of the past. Dissident students shut down great universities in protest over the war in Vietnam and the sins of the WASP power structure. One city after another exploded with racial tension and social rebellion. The politics of protest often turned inward, as young people discovered the consciousness-expanding properties of hallucinogens. Some attempted to create a "counter culture," to undermine the profit-seeking, goods-consuming, power-mongering system of their parents and political leaders. In the summer of 1968, the streets of Chicago erupted in savage confrontation as the city's police clubbed antiwar activists at the Democratic national convention. It became fashionable to quote William Butler Yeats' lines: "Things fall apart; the centre cannot hold; / Mere anarchy is loosed upon the world. . . ." In a time of flower children, burning ghettoes, and open contempt for traditional American values and aspirations, no wonder the world of the wage worker and the trade unionist seemed remote and even irrelevant.

Even so, some labor struggles did capture attention. The long crusade of California farmworkers, led by the charismatic Cesar Chavez, pitted impoverished Filippino and Chicano grapepickers against powerful agribusiness combines, arousing the sympathies of young people and liberals throughout the sixties. A mass boycott of table grapes permitted people who had grown disillusioned with the labor movement per se to renew their sense of identification with the underdog. Clothing and textile workers' unions could occasionally arouse public sympathy over the low pay and poor conditions prevailing in the cotton mills and garment shops, especially when high-handed employers overplayed their hand against the weak and powerless. In general, however, the concerns of organized labor and of working people generally slipped out of focus, as the marches, demonstrations, and upheavals associated with civil rights, urban rebellion, and the war in Vietnam held center stage.

It was not that American workers had suddenly become quiescent. In the sixties, as usual, the levels of strikes in the United States remained well above those of most comparable countries. Although the relative prosperity of the fifties and sixties had led most observers to regard American workers as safely integrated into the social and political system, the strike weapon remained potent. During the Korean War of the early 1950s, for example, workers fought aggressively for wage increases and expansion of nonwage benefits at a time of sharp inflation. In 1952 the number of strikes in the country for the first time surpassed the 5,000 mark, and the 3.54 million strikers exceeded the number of any previous year save 1946. The steel industry remained a chronic arena of industrial conflict, with national strikes in 1946, 1949, and 1952. In 1959, United States Steel triggered a 116-day walkout by its insistence on drastic changes in traditional work rules. In the early 1960s strike incidence declined, but toward the end of the decade and into the early 1970s it spurted upward again. Industrial workers staged several large-scale walkouts, notably involving a coalition of unions in 1969 against General Electric and 400,000 autoworkers against General Motors in 1970. Public employee strikes, capped by the huge postal walkout of 1970, continued to erupt. In 1968, for the first time in fifteen years, the number of work stoppages topped 5,000, and for the five-year period 1967–71 every index of militancy—number of strikes, percentage of work time lost, number of workers on strike—showed sharp increases over the figures of the early 1960s.

Rank-and-file dissidence led some activists and reporters to speculate that the stream of workers' protest would become part of the generational revolt of the sixties and early seventies. Rank-and-file rejections of contracts negotiated by union leaders rose. Unauthorized strikes broke out in record numbers. Journalists and veteran unionists alike reported that a younger work force seemed to be repudiating the acquisitive values of their fathers. Issues relating to health and safety, freedom from overtime, discipline in the shops, and general quality of life in the workplace underlay a generation gap in the plants and union halls. A 1968 NBC documentary analyzed the "blue-collar blues," depicting long-haired young workers in a California Pinto plant expressing their hostility toward company and union alike. Employers complained that younger workers ignored work schedules and disciplinary measures to take time off as the spirit moved them. Reports of widespread alcoholism and drug abuse on the assembly line attracted media attention. Absenteeism rose.

The violent social conflict of the late 1960s and early 1970s brought virtually every major American institution under attack. The unions were no exception. For those who still harbored hopes that the working class could be on the cutting edge of social transformation, the established unions were obstacles rather than vehicles. "The unions," declared radical critic Jeremy Brecher, "are no longer capable of dealing with the new situation." Much of the criticism of organized labor that gathered force through the 1960s and into the 1970s focused on two central areas: organized labor's support for the Vietnam War and the unions' insensitivity to the aspirations of black Americans.

LABOR AND VIETNAM

The labor movement's enmeshment in U.S. foreign policy operations dated back to the early cold war period. From the late 1940s onward, functionaries from the AFL and the CIO had collaborated, sometimes openly, sometimes clandestinely, with the government, first in Western Europe and Japan and eventually around the globe. In 1946 and 1947, for example, AFL operatives in Europe bolstered anti-Communist labor organizations on the docks and warehouses of France and Italy, sometimes relying on underworld elements to combat Communist unions. Throughout the period of American occupation in Germany and Japan, both AFL and CIO operatives, sometimes hired by the government, sometimes paid by the labor movement, collaborated with anti-Communist groups and increasingly followed priorities laid down by the Department of State. As the American government grew bolder in engineering the overthrow of left-wing regimes in the Middle East and Latin America in the 1950s, it often found organizations established under the auspices of the AFL (and, later, the AFL-CIO) useful conduits for financial transactions and the placement of agents. American-manipulated coups in Guatemala in 1954 and British Guiana in 1963–64 relied in part on the faithful cooperation of organized labor.

Few critics faulted American labor for being anti-Communist as such. Virtually none of those who charged AFL-CIO president George Meany and his chief foreign policy advisor Jay Lovestone with complicity in these affairs held any brief for the Soviet Union. Many explicitly disavowed any association with the near-moribund CPUSA and carefully distanced themselves from organizations in which Communists had been active. They did argue, however, that the labor movement's anti-Communism, forged as it was in the specific circumstances of the 1930s and 1940s, had become a sterile formula. Perhaps once the United States government had played a positive role in thwarting Soviet ambitions, though even here, critics of American policies argued that the United States itself held major responsibility for the onset of the cold war. But now American leaders viewed any struggle on the part of the exploited masses to gain social justice as a part of a Communist conspiracy. Consequently, historians such as Ronald Radosh and Henry Berger contended, the United States supported right-wing dictators, whatever their excesses against their own people, as bulwarks against Communism. Even where the United States claimed to endorse reform, it followed the priorities of ruling elites and threw its weight against the aspirations of the broad masses.

The AFL-CIO's eager support for U.S. policy in Southeast Asia through the 1950s and 1960s gave substance to these charges. Between 1960 and 1968, the AFL-CIO served as the conduit for $20 million in funds supplied by the Agency for International Development, an arm of the Department of State, for support of non-Communist unions in Vietnam. Remarks Meany's biographer Joseph Goulden, "The AFL-CIO sent a steady flow of consultants and study groups to Vietnam." The East Coast Longshoremen's union worked directly with U.S. military authorities to resolve waterfront labor problems in Vietnam and to keep American military equipment flowing into Southeast Asia. Most important, however, was the AFL-CIO's unwavering public endorsement of U.S. policy, even when the American government found itself backing a series of military dictators, corruptionists, and petty warlords in its determination to defeat nationalist-Communist forces. In 1954, Meany had berated the Eisenhower administration for failure to prevent Communist success in North Vietnam, warning that the Geneva agreement that ended French occupation of Indo-China "has merely served to whet the appetite of the Communist conspiracy for further conquest." Ten years later, as Lyndon Johnson's administration launched direct American military participation in the protracted war, the AFL-CIO Executive Council unconditionally backed his efforts. In 1965 it adopted a resolution that pledged support for "all measures the Administration might deem necessary to halt Communist aggression and secure a just and lasting peace."

Meany, Lovestone, and the AFL-CIO Executive Council supported American policy in Southeast Asia without reservation. At the 1967 AFL-CIO convention, an antiwar resolution went down to a 2,000 to 6 defeat. "Suppose we stepped out of Vietnam. What would happen? Two million people would go into slavery immediately," declared Meany. The Communists, if victorious in Vietnam, would not stop there. "I would rather fight the Communists in South Vietnam than fight them down here in the Chesapeake Bay," he told the Executive Council. He ridiculed the antiwar movement, clashed ferociously with dovish politicians and intellectuals, and reiterated AFL-CIO's blank check support for the Johnson administration.

Labor's critics believed that Meany's pronouncements and the AFL-CIO's open collaboration with the Department of State and the military effort shamed the labor movement. Senator Fulbright charged that the AFL-CIO had been "bought" by the Johnson administration, a charge that Meany, pointing to a decades-long record of fervent anti-Communism, effectively refuted. John Kenneth Galbraith, new head of the Americans for Democratic Action, a liberal group with impeccable anti-Communist credentials, lashed out at the AFL-CIO establishment. Labor's leadership, he charged in 1967, was "aged, contented, and deeply somnambulant," and he accused it of being even more reactionary on foreign policy than the Republican party. Critics argued that in embracing this bloody war, whose growing casualties included disproportionate numbers of young working-class Americans, Meany had betrayed his constituency and had lost touch with the rank and file. Meany's supporters, however, pointed to polls which showed blue-collar America solidly behind the American military effort and deeply estranged from antiwar excesses. It was the long-haired, pot-smoking, flag-desecrating "peace" movement, they held, that gave comfort to the enemy and was out of touch with the real America.

By the late 1960s, elements in the labor movement itself began to repudiate the war. The UAW led the opposition, although, as Meany and Lovestone were quick to point out, Autoworkers' president Reuther had voted in 1965 in favor of the basic AFL-CIO carte blanche resolution of support for Johnson's policies. In 1968 Meany, relying on distorted information supplied directly to him by the Federal Bureau of Investigation, accused antiwar labor spokesmen of being dupes of the CPUSA and of the Soviet Union. Emil Mazey, Reuther's close associate and secretary-treasurer of the UAW, accused Meany of "character assassination" and "suppression of dissent." In July 1968, in good part as a consequence of disagreements on foreign policy, the UAW left the AFL-CIO. In 1972, Meany and the majority on the AFL-CIO Executive Council broke with twenty years of labor politics by refusing to endorse the Democratic presidential candidate, rejecting George McGovern largely because of his antiwar stand and despite his consistent pro-labor record as a senator. As union activists in the affiliates and at the state and local level mobilized in behalf of McGovern's hopeless candidacy, the rupture in the labor movement seemed irrevocable.

For critics, Meany and Lovestone epitomized the extent to which organized labor had become entangled in the power structure. Unresponsive to rank-and-file workers, accustomed to issuing top-down directives and to treating politics as mere power brokering, the men who dominated the AFL-CIO were so integrated into the foreign policy apparatus that they had lost any semblance of an independent voice. Lovestone, a shadowy figure in labor circles for a half century, dominated an essentially provincial labor leadership with his encyclopedic, but highly skewed, knowledge of the ins and outs of Marxian sectarianism. As for Meany himself, naturally the plumber's son from the Bronx enjoyed the prestige that association with the nation's foreign policy elite lent him. What better indication that organized labor, once outcast and victimized, had arrived at the seat of power than that presidents, generals, and foreign leaders courted and cajoled its leading spokesman?

Meany and Lovestone rarely deigned to answer their critics directly. They regarded academic leaders of the antiwar crusade as "intellectual jitterbugs." They believed that foes of the Vietnam War failed to understand the power of a Communist avalanche that had engulfed half the world and was threatening much of the rest. Students, professors, and peace activists might underestimate the Communists, but the labor movement had fought in the front lines during the struggles against Stalinism in the 1930s and the 1940s. Labor opposed tyranny and injustice everywhere; convention resolutions regularly condemned right-wing dictatorship in Spain, Portugal, and Latin America. But Communism posed the greatest menace. It was in the "Workers' State," the USSR, that honest trade unionists and democratic socialists were most brutally silenced. The slave labor camps bulged with workers and socialists. Wherever Communism triumphed, workers bore the brunt of the inevitable suffering. Count the dead in the USSR and in Communist China, challenged labor intellectuals who defended the Meany record; find a country where a Communist tyranny once established had been overthrown by a democratic uprising. American labor, said commentators such as philosopher Sidney Hook and civil rights hero Bayard Rustin, had nothing to apologize for in its support of a non-Communist government in Vietnam. By the time the antiwar enthusiasts realized the implications of Communist victory, they declared, it would be too late for the people of Southeast Asia.

BLACK WORKERS, WHITE UNIONS

Questions of race and civil rights also led to the disaffection of liberals and radicals from the labor movement. Through the 1950s and into the 1960s, the AFL-CIO failed to compel some of its affiliates to stop discriminatory and segregationist practices. True, by the early sixties only a few small unions clung to formal disabilities against blacks, but critics charged President Meany and his cohorts with a double standard: the AFL-CIO dealt swiftly with any affiliate charged with Communist influence, and it sometimes acted vigorously when charges of corruption arose. But constitutional bars to black membership, de facto patterns of exclusion from favored jobs, and maintenance of segregated locals and lines of seniority drew only endless palaver and pious declarations of good intentions. And in 1959, when A. Philip Randolph of the Brotherhood of Sleeping Car Porters, the only black member of the twenty-seven-man executive council, raised these matters forcefully at the AFL-CIO convention, Meany ridiculed him: "Who the hell appointed you as the guardian of all the Negroes in America?" the AFL-CIO president challenged, in a pointed allusion to the porters' miniscule membership.

Actually, although outraged at Meany's outburst, a new generation of militant black activists in effect raised the same question. By the early 1960s, they pointed out, black workers constituted at least a quarter of the AFL-CIO membership. The UAW and the Steelworkers had hundreds of thousands of black members, and the fast-growing government employees' unions were enrolling hundreds of blacks monthly. Yet aside from Randolph, who presided over an organization that was now as limited in influence as it was rich in tradition, no blacks sat in labor's highest councils. Nor were black spokesmen to be found on the executive boards of even unions (such as the UAW) that enjoyed liberal reputations. In 1960, a group of black activists established the Negro American Labor Council (NALC), designed to press the interests of black workers and to criticize the labor movement's shortcomings in racial matters. Originally, Randolph chaired the council, striving to have Meany recognize it as a legitimate pressure group within the AFL-CIO. Soon, however, militants began to use the council as a forum for sharp criticism of AFL-CIO leaders. Randolph, who had worked for over forty years for the integration of black workers into the labor movement, resigned the presidency of NALC in 1966. Under its new leader, Cleveland Robinson, the body continued to criticize the unions and the AFL-CIO, but it soon began to unravel as some black activists, irate over the established unions' compromises with racial injustice and inequality, threatened to break with the AFL-CIO entirely and to use NALC as a separate organization for black unionists.

Although NALC did not prove a permanent channel for the aspirations of black unionists, its very existence in the 1960s reflected the restiveness of a new generation of black workers. The leadership of most of the major unions rested in the hands of white men, most of whom had risen to power in the turbulent thirties and the exciting days of World War II. To leaders such as Meany, Reuther, David McDonald of the Steelworkers, David Dubinsky of the Ladies' Garment Workers, and their colleagues, success in the searing conflicts of the 1930s and 1940s had earned them their current esteem and power. They knew poverty and injustice at first hand and had spent their lives achieving security, opportunity, and rising material standards for American workers. On the other hand, these were patriotic men who defined their lives as much in terms of their struggles against fascism and Communism, the central issues of their generation, as in terms of labor versus capital. They were proud that the unions had arrived, that organized labor's representatives were consulted by government officials, and that they themselves enjoyed the respect of corporate leaders and newspaper editorialists. For men of the generation of the depression and World War II, men who had fought successfully to bring the labor movement from defeat and despair to triumph and repute, the American system worked, whatever its flaws and temporary injustices.

Even the most sensitive among them simply did not understand the rage and desperation that swept through black America. In the 1950s, organized labor had been a loyal ally of the standard civil rights movement. Labor lobbyists had played important roles in the passage of the first civil rights legislation since Reconstruction, the Civil Rights Acts of 1957 and 1960. Before the merger, both federations had hailed the seminal 1954 Supreme Court decision barring segregation in the public schools; indeed, CIO lawyers had filed a supporting brief in the case. Convention platforms invariably endorsed racial equality. Laborites collaborated with civil rights groups in dozens of campaigns to elect liberal candidates and to limit the gains of Eisenhower Republicanism. Organized labor's key victories in 1958 state referenda in Ohio and California, defeating so-called "right-to-work" proposals, owed much to black voters.

In the sixties, organized labor continued on this course. Lobbyists and political operatives supported the pathbreaking civil rights legislation of 1964 and 1965, with the AFL-CIO even throwing its weight behind the controversial Title VII of the 1964 enactment, a measure which, among other things, outlawed discrimination in union constitutions and practices. Unions such as the UAW worked closely with civil rights leaders, notably Martin Luther King, Jr. Labor operatives in the South plugged away at voter registration, laying some of the groundwork for rising black political consciousness that underlay the great marches and demonstrations that eventually forced passage of the 1965 Voting Rights Act. At the stupendous August 1963 March on Washington, which drew over 250,000 civil rights supporters to the Lincoln Memorial, delegations from hundreds of union locals swelled the crowd. Orange and black UAW placards bearing the slogan "Jobs and Freedom for Every American" bobbed above the heads of shirt-sleeved marchers, and UAW president Walter Reuther shared the podium with Roy Wilkins, John Lewis, James Forman, and the incomparable Dr. King.

But beneath the surface of labor support for the civil rights movement ran a disquieting tide. The established labor leadership often failed to grasp the urgency and intensity of blacks' demands. In 1961, for example, the tenacious Randolph, as loyal to organized labor as he was insistent upon racial justice, was formally censured by the AFL-CIO Executive Council for making public statements critical of certain powerful union leaders. Noting that even labor leaders ostentatious in support of civil rights had failed to back Randolph, one prominent black militant angrily asked, "Where was David Dubinsky, where was Walter Reuther, . . . where was Jim Carey? Where were all those liberals on the Council?" In censuring the lone black on the Executive Council, charged Richard Parrish of NALC, Meany and his supporters had made a "show of power to demonstrate to Negro union members that they represent nothing when it comes to setting policies . . . even though they pay dues."

Throughout the sixties, critics hammered away at the unions' foot-dragging and lack of progress in pivotal areas such as black representation in leadership positions and access of black workers to skilled jobs. In the UAW, a 1968 survey revealed, only seventy-five of over a thousand union staff positions were held by blacks, who then made up about 33 percent of the union's membership. A 1967 survey showed that among the craft and construction unions in general, despite years of pressure and litigation, black employment remained miniscule. Thus, blacks constituted but 1.6 percent of the membership of the Electrical Workers, 1.7 percent of Ironworkers, 0.2 percent of Plumbers, and 0.2 percent of Sheetmetal Workers. By the early seventies, these numbers had improved only marginally. Notes legal historian William Gould, by 1972 "black trade union leaders were denouncing Meany for his reluctance" to force affiliates to abandon traditional discriminatory practices and were condemning "AFL-CIO smugness about the labor movement's limited efforts toward undoing the past." Carefully documented charges of racial discrimination in the corruption-riven East Coast longshoremen's union, in the Teamsters, and among locals in the American Federation of Musicians surprised few, for none of these organizations had ever proclaimed racial justice as a priority.

But exposure of racism and discrimination among industrial unions was more disturbing. Thus, studies in the Steelworkers and Rubber Workers' contracts revealed patterns of seniority and transfer rights that thwarted blacks' efforts to gain access to the higher skill ratings in many plants. Even where formal contract provisions appeared to guarantee equality, some locals refused to process grievances for black workers seeking job upgrading. Black workers resorted to Title VII of the 1964 Civil Rights Act, suing both employers and unions for complicity in systems of de facto discrimination. In 1962, NAACP labor secretary Herbert Hill authored a scathing attack, charging the venerable International Ladies' Garment Workers Union (ILGW), one of the nation's oldest and proudest industrial unions, with racism and discrimination. The ILGW, noted Hill, enjoyed a historic reputation for liberalism. But now, charged Hill, "there are two faces to the ILGWU." There was a public image of equality, rising standards, and support for worthy causes. "But," he declared, "there is another face to the ILGWU, one that is the daily reality for the Negro and Puerto Rican members of the union." A rigid bureaucracy, he asserted, dominated the union. As the original generations of Jewish and Italian immigrant workers passed on, a new Negro and Latino proletariat replaced them in the shops. But few minority members ever found their way into union offices; few black or Puerto Rican workers ever gained access to skilled jobs and elite locals. Union rules and regulations systematically barred the masses of newer workers from running for office while their dues provided hefty salaries and pleasant perquisites for the aging immigrant-generation leadership. ILGW spokesmen, led by the union's able publicist Gus Tyler, angrily rebutted these charges. Through the mid-sixties the debate between Hill and Tyler spilled over into the pages of several liberal and radical publications, further discrediting organized labor in the eyes of many readers.

Perhaps most disconcerting to liberal defenders of the labor movement, however, was the racial tension in the United Automobile Workers. The prestige of the UAW among American liberals of the 1950s and 1960s was unique; under Reuther, the autoworkers provided a solid bedrock of progressive unionism around which liberals rallied throughout the somber 1950s. Here was a mass industrial union that had achieved splendid contracts for hundreds of thousands of auto and other industrial workers. In 1946 Walter Reuther had defeated a Communist-supported incumbent in an open convention. The UAW's internal operations exuded probity. A public review board subjected actions of the leadership to periodic scrutiny, thus providing an independent forum for union members with grievances against the leadership team.

The UAW's progressive politics also stood out. In public testimony, lobbying, and political activity on a whole range of issues from tax reform to national health insurance, the Autoworkers led innumerable liberal campaigns. And from the start, the UAW and its able leadership had embraced and collaborated with the postwar civil rights movement. Indeed, when on occasion southern UAW locals balked at obeying the antisegregation provisions of the union's constitution, the top leadership swiftly intervened, lifting charters, putting locals under central control, and compelling compliance with union policy.

But the absence of black representation on the UAW executive board angered black workers and troubled the union's friends. Repeatedly, Reuther and his associates rejected arguments in favor of separate black representation, holding that a special black seat on the board would amount to "racism in reverse." The UAW's 300,000 or so black workers were scattered throughout several of its administrative regions. Since racial consciousness among the rank and file in effect precluded election of a black regional director by a white majority, critics felt that, without a special provision for a black representative, the UAW's largest minority remained voiceless. Moreover, some black activists believed that Reuther systematically undercut and exiled the UAW's most active and articulate black leaders, relegating men such as Horace Sheffield II of Detroit and Willoughby Abner of Chicago to the back benches and boondocks. In 1962, when the UAW finally did provide for a black seat on the executive board, the all-powerful Reuther caucus passed over these vigorous spokesmen.

Even more disturbing was the situation in the UAW's shops and plants. Notes Gould, at the very time of the 1963 March on Washington, at which Reuther shared the podium with King, "hardly any black UAW members were to be found in the high-paying and prestigious skilled-trade jobs." That this situation resulted less from overt discrimination on the part of the union than from the demographics of employment in the industry and the discriminatory practices of the automakers did not prevent critics from contrasting Reuther's fervent speeches in Washington with his apparent lack of vigor in Detroit.

In the late 1960s, black militancy burst forth in the auto plants and on the city streets. As was the case in the twenties, thirties, and forties, Detroit once again became (in labor writer B. J. Widick's phrase) "a city of race and class violence." By the late 1960s, black workers had become majorities in many inner-city plants, especially those belonging to the financially beset Chrysler Corporation. In the huge Dodge Main complex, in the heart of Hamtramck, for example, at least half of the 30,000 workers in 1968 were blacks, as were 80 percent of those who toiled in Chrysler's large Eldon Avenue gear and axle plant. Moreover, the work force in auto, and particularly in Chrysler plants, was young. White workers took retirement on UAW pensions or moved to the new plants and new neighborhoods in the suburbs, their places in the inner-city facilities filled by young black men (and some women). As of 1968, for example, over a third of the UAW's Chrysler membership was under thirty, and over half had fewer than five years' seniority.

By the late sixties, an explosive combination of racial consciousness, deteriorating working conditions, and hostility toward a white power structure—as represented both by supervisors and white union officials—convulsed the UAW in and around Detroit. Chrysler, in serious economic trouble, permitted work and safety conditions to deteriorate. Harassed foremen, under pressure from their superiors, barked out orders. The young black men in the plants, many of them imbued with racial pride born of the civil rights movement, seethed with resentment over the raw racism they encountered, especially from older supervisors. In 1967, Detroit blazed into open rebellion, with the police murdering black suspects and angry blacks torching dozens of city blocks. Special Detroit police teams roamed the ghetto neighborhoods, gunning down suspected criminals and infuriating an already-bitter black populace. Both inside the plants and in the neighborhoods, Detroit seemed ready once again to erupt.

Black radicals sneered at the UAW, "their" union. The same racism that permeated the auto companies, they charged, afflicted the Reuther regime. In plant after plant, groups of black workers, encouraged by student intellectuals at Wayne State University and by a handful of revolutionary organizers, created black workers' councils. The largest and most active arose in the Dodge Main plant and was called the Dodge Revolutionary Union Movement, or DRUM. Other councils sprang up at the Rouge (Ford Revolutionary Union Movement, or FRUM), Eldon Avenue Gear and Axle (ELRUM), and elsewhere. Their mimeographed publications bristled with the violent language of Third World liberation movements; they embraced a racially charged Marxist-Leninism, often of a wild and romantic cast, but sometimes informed by the penetrating anti-imperialist idiom of Caribbean Marxist C.L.R. James. DRUM activists harangued fellow workers, called meetings, and provoked wildcat strikes in protest over harsh working conditions and shop-floor injustices. Although these activists attacked the corporate establishment, they reserved their bitterest denunciations for the UAW leadership, from Reuther on down. "I finally got the news / How my dues was bein' used," ran the refrain of one song sung by members of the League of Revolutionary Black Workers, the umbrella organization.

Black activists and their allies heaped contempt on Reuther and his lieutenants. Charles Denby, a sympathetic Marxist observer of the black workers' uprising in the UAW, wrote that Reuther's ostentatious support for black hospital workers in Charleston and his advocacy of voting rights in Alabama "has not fooled black workers. . . . When they see him marching on a picket line in Charleston or Selma . . . , they know that he hasn't been on a picket line with his own UAW workers for so many years he's forgotten what it's like. Reuther," charged Denby, "is always glad to integrate anything—outside of his own union." Even more embarrassing was the specter of UAW staff members breaking the picket lines of DRUM-instigated wildcat strikes.

The DRUM phenomenon subsided rather quickly. Black militants lost local union elections repeatedly throughout 1968 and 1969. Some UAW leaders, notably secretary-treasurer Emil Mazey, hammered away at the small cadre of dissident black workers, branding them a "handful of fanatics who are nothing but black fascists, using the same tactics of coercion and intimidation that Hitler . . . used." Others, notably executive board member Douglas Fraser, recognized the legitimacy of the grievances of black workers and knew, as a long-time Chrysler worker and union official, at first hand of the abysmal conditions in the inner-city plants. While Fraser disavowed extremism, he urged his fellow leaders to "work on unity with DRUM" and to take seriously the grievances of the newly aroused black work force. Over the next several years, a number of large Detroit-area UAW locals elected black officers, while the international union sharply increased the number of black staff members on its payroll.

Whether these changes brought permanent improvements on the shop floor was moot. The revolutionary union movement used vivid language and bold tactics to gain publicity, but it most likely embraced only a few hundred hard-core activists at its peak, just as UAW leaders always maintained. Turnover among young workers, combined with widespread auto industry unemployment in the early seventies, no doubt flushed many activists out of the plants. Reuther's death in an airplane accident in May 1970 removed one visible target of militant anger; it was much harder to rally antagonism against his successor, the somber, low-keyed Leonard Woodcock. Improvements in the UAW's agreements with the car companies for minority entry into the skilled trades helped to mitigate some black grievances, while the winding down of the Vietnam War, the deflation of the civil rights movement, and the general national impatience with the radical rhetoric that seemed so threatening and half-persuasive in the late sixties isolated the handful of remaining militants.

The UAW's racial problems were unique only in intensity and spectacle. The proud autoworkers' union reflected the tensions and ambiguities of the entire labor movement as it sought to deal with America's racial dilemmas. In a sense, organized labor became the victim of its own rhetoric and achievements. Intoning the rights of working people and the sanctity of social justice, organized labor proclaimed a higher standard and a more exacting criterion of judgment than most other institutions. When labor failed, or even when its leaders simply indulged in the give-and-take normal to politics, the contrast with its high-minded declarations stood out boldly. Were the George Meanys, the Walter Reuthers, and the David Dubinskys more obtuse than other citizens? Did the contrast between their earnest professions of equality and their compromises with injustice expose them as particularly hypocritical? For angry black workers, self-assured radicals, and dissident young people for whom the war in Vietnam underlined the racism and hypocrisy of American institutions in general, the answer was clearly yes. Others, impressed with the distance labor had travelled in matters pertaining to race and troubled by the strident self-righteousness of the unions' critics in the late 1960s, remained more hopeful.

Union activists Brendan and Patricia Cayo Sexton, for example, put organized labor's racial dilemmas in perspective in a 1971 commentary. They noted that despite often-justified criticism of the unions' racial performance, "blacks have won more influence in unions than in any other social institution." The reader who mentally surveyed the power structure of big business, the mainstream churches, the armed forces, or the nation's universities immediately saw the Sextons' point. "Even in the carpenters' union," they noted, which was "among the most exclusionist, black membership is about 2 percent of the total—higher than the black proportion in most Northern college faculties." Newspapers, they observed, continually exposed the racial failures of organized labor, but even the papers' own craft unions—certainly no paragons of racial justice—were more thoroughly integrated than the editorial staffs of the *New York Times* and other major dailies. In short, however legitimate the complaints of minority spokespeople and their allies against organized labor's performance in this critical area, there was an element of class bias in the singling out of the country's *most* integrated major institution for special condemnation.

THE POLITICAL DIMENSION: VICTORY AND DEFEAT, 1955–1968

The election of 1968 marked the end of the New Deal dispensation. In a year of countercultural excess, racial upheaval, assassination, street violence, and mounting Vietnam casualty lists, organized labor marshalled its political forces in one final bid to sustain the politics of New Deal liberalism. Labor had its ideal choice, Vice-President Hubert H. Humphrey, whose candidacy in normal times would surely have represented the triumphal culmination of organized labor's quarter-century of political action in defense of the New Deal tradition. Nineteen-sixty-eight, however, was not a normal year. With the war and the dissident candidacies of Eugene McCarthy and (until his murder in June) Robert F. Kennedy, alienating normally Democratic voters, and with Alabama governor George Wallace bringing his racist appeal to the blue-collar districts, Humphrey and his labor backers faced powerful challenges from the right and the left, as well as from the fiercely competitive Nixon Republican party.

In 1948 Harry S. Truman had faced a similarly divided party and an equally efficient Republican challenge. His upset victory kept an administration friendly to labor in the White House and helped to sustain the essential features of New Deal reforms. Despite the even-more wrenching divisions in the Democracy in 1968 and despite a conventional wisdom that as early as Labor Day proclaimed Nixon the hands-down winner, labor's operatives surged into the battle, fighting off the Wallace menace on the right and seeking to mobilize the traditional New Deal–

Democratic constituency against the hated Nixon. And they almost pulled it off. When the ballots were counted, Humphrey and his labor allies fell 500,000 short in an electorate of over 72 million. Nixon won with 43.4 percent of the vote, as compared with Humphrey's 42.7 percent. Many Nixon supporters conceded that had the election been held a week later, their man would have lost. Some observers believed that Nixon's narrow triumph was an aberration and that the New Deal–labor coalition would soon return to center stage. More astute observers, however, saw in 1968 the final gasp of the traditional Democratic coalition and noted that the labor movement, long a champion of a broad range of liberal and public-minded programs, was gaining a reputation, even among some of its nominal allies, as merely another "special interest." With a Nixon administration in place to set the nation's priorities and with generational, racial, educational, and status divisions fracturing the Democracy, the future did not look bright for the heirs of the New Deal.

Labor Rides High, 1955–1966

Although the 1955 merger between the AFL and the CIO disappointed those who expected new organizing drives and a general renewal of the spirit of the thirties, the merger did pay off quickly in the area of political action. The AFL-CIO's political arm, the Committee for Political Education (COPE), soon combined the efficiency and idealism of CIO-PAC and the broad grass-roots coverage of its AFL counterpart, Labor's League for Political Education. As usual, labor faced difficult problems of organizing and mobilizing its members. Ethnic diversity, the weak perceptions of class identity, a hostile mass media, and the deeply personalistic nature of presidential politics hampered COPE's efforts. Still, it soon became a potent force in key industrial states and in the Democratic party. Conservatives began to fear and respect COPE's ability to mobilize labor voters and its ability to provide funding for Democratic candidates on every level. Although the extraordinarily popular General Dwight Eisenhower cut heavily into the so-called labor vote in his two spectacularly successful presidential campaigns in 1952 and 1956, Democrats regained control of Congress in 1954, kept it despite the Eisenhower landslide in 1956, and increased their numbers in the 1958 elections. Indeed, aside from the presidential races, the most notable political phenomenon of the decade was the tenacity of Democratic majorities in the states and the growing numbers of liberal congressmen, senators, governors, and state legislators. And many observers credited COPE with the lion's share of this impressive success.

"The skill and potency of this machine," wrote one conservative analyst, has "given organized labor its position as the most politically powerful economic bloc in America."

In the mid-1960s, organized labor's political operations reached a culmination of efficiency and influence. Operatives from the AFL-CIO and from the international unions and state and local federations worked tirelessly for John F. Kennedy in his narrow 1960 victory over Richard Nixon. The trend toward liberal supremacy in the party continued. Long-time Republican states such as Indiana, Wisconsin, Michigan, Ohio, and Maine sent labor-backed senators and congressmen to Washington and elected liberal Democratic governors and legislators. In the elections of 1962, for example, Democratic congressional majorities held firm, despite the historically strong pattern of presidential party loss in off-year elections. The AFL-CIO's energetic support for Lyndon Johnson in 1964, spurred by laborites' fear of the deeply conservative candidacy of Republican Barry Goldwater, paid off with a landslide Democratic victory, both in the presidential election and in the composition of the new Congress. Throughout the 1950s and 1960s, COPE, politically oriented unions such as the UAW, the Steelworkers, the Machinists, and the garment and textile unions, and state and local labor bodies became ever more directly integrated into the structure of Democratic party politics. In some areas, such as Wayne County and the state of Michigan, labor played the dominant role in the party, with the UAW supplying the manpower, finances, and votes to overturn decades of Republican control. In other states, such as Ohio, Illinois, and Pennsylvania, powerful labor organizations worked closely with strong Democratic urban machines and growing blocs of minority voters. In large, diverse states such as New York and California, shifting cross-currents of interunion rivalry, machine and ethnic politics, and fragmented demographic patterns blunted the direct impact of labor's political efforts. Nonetheless, even in these critical states, active labor operatives played major roles in the Democratic party, strengthening its more liberal tendencies.

So deeply enmeshed was organized labor in the structure of the Democratic party that some observers by the mid-1960s argued that America was on the verge of social democracy. In most Western European countries, and in the industrialized British commonwealth nations such as Canada, Australia, and New Zealand, the labor movement played a direct role in political life, aligning itself formally with socialist parties. In England, for example, the Trades Union Congress (TUC), the equivalent of the AFL-CIO, participated formally in the Labour party; the TUC directly financed Labour party candidates and its people sat, as union spokesmen, on the party's directing boards. Similar situations prevailed in Germany, Sweden, Norway, and other Western nations. Throughout the twentieth century, the United States had been the exception. "Why is there no socialism in America?" went the perennial question. But with labor's critical financial and vote-generating role earning for union leaders ever greater influence in party councils, shrewd observers such as socialist Michael Harrington and political scientist David Greenstone perceived the possibilities of a labor-led Democracy becoming a de facto social democratic party. It would not proclaim the formal socialist rhetoric of its European counterparts, of course, but its commitment to popular control of economic decision-making and egalitarian social policies made it an American equivalent, they believed.

Few day-to-day labor politicos indulged in these speculations. They were content with plugging away in behalf of progressive candidates and legislative liberalism. On the national level at least, the fifties had required a holding action. With a Republican administration stressing fiscal restraint and hostility toward the Roosevelt-Truman legacy of governmental activism, labor lobbyists worked closely with congressional liberals. When the economy periodically plunged into sharp recession, labor's economists called for larger government expenditures, job creation and training programs, and enhanced funding for the unemployed. Labor-supported liberals succeeded in expanding the scope and amount of Social Security benefits and attempted to keep such long-range liberal goals as national health insurance and mass construction of low-income housing on the public agenda. Labor spokesmen testified frequently in congressional hearings, attacking the administration's plans to turn over tidal oil reserves to the states, opposing its efforts to privatize the Tennessee Valley Authority, and flailing away at Eisenhower's economic policies. Labor people did yeoman work on the civil rights laws of 1957 and 1960, criticized the lack of presidential leadership in the school desegregation battles of the later 1950s, and collaborated regularly with liberal groups such as the Americans for Democratic Action, the NAACP, and the Farmers Union.

The electoral victories of the Kennedy-Johnson years paved the way for more positive legislative action. The AFL-CIO dissented from the tax cut proposals introduced by Kennedy, arguing that the administration's plan awarded little to lower-income citizens while skewing tax breaks to corporations. Laborites would have preferred to stimulate economic growth—the goal of the Kennedy program—by increasing expenditures on the country's deteriorating public parks, schools, highways, and other facilities. Kennedy, however, ignored this New Dealish approach, and, certain of labor's ultimate approval, wooed conservative support for stimulation of economic growth through encouraging private consumption and reducing corporate and upper-income taxes. Ever the realists, labor lobbyists swallowed the administration's economic policies, while working to keep such proposals as area redevelopment, aid to public schools, national health insurance, public housing, and the like on the agenda. AFL-CIO operatives applauded Kennedy's introduction of significant civil rights legislation in the summer of 1963 and collaborated with administration aides and mainstream civil rights groups both to secure its passage and to persuade black militants to moderate their demands and tone down their modes of protest and activism.

Johnson's overwhelming victory in 1964 carried scores of labor-supported liberals into Congress. Through the first half of 1965, the Democratic majorities passed a dozen key administration bills. Legislation attacking air and water pollution, expanding federal aid for education, establishing a massive scholarship program for college students, and providing funds for programs aimed at elimination of poverty made seasoned observers recall the fabled "hundred days" of the first Roosevelt term. AFL-CIO operatives particularly welcomed legislation that provided important health care benefits for the elderly and indigent, for it represented the first significant congressional defeat of a powerful medical lobby that had thwarted labor-led national health initiatives for over thirty years. Although Johnson's congressional career in the 1940s and early 1950s was steeped in the anti-union world of the Texas Democratic party, laborites collaborated eagerly with administration aides and hailed Johnson's "Great Society" as the culmination of the New Deal's uncompleted agenda. Much of labor's legislative energy was devoted to passage of broadly conceived legislation designed to help lower-income and minority citizens. Indeed, laborites often placed these public welfare and civil rights proposals ahead of more specific pro-union measures on their priority list. This "aggregative" approach to legislation won for labor's people the plaudits of liberals everywhere. It was during this period, notes David Brody, that "labor came into its own as a legislative force" and became, increasingly, a "champion of the general welfare" and a dynamic leader of the diverse liberal coalition.

Thus, in the middle of the sixties, the labor movement appeared to have arrived at the center of power and influence. Although the proportion of the labor force enrolled in unions had begun to shrink from the high point of 35 percent (despite the gains among public employees) and although critics often accused the AFL-CIO of lethargy and lack of idealism, the political and legislative arms had proved powerful indeed.

Conservative critics envied and sought to emulate its success: archrival Senator Barry Goldwater of Arizona declared that in getting ready for a reelection bid, "I just get out COPE's book on how to do it and use it." With an incumbent Democratic president, massive majorities in both houses of Congress, "a slew of Republican electoral corpses," and a string of legislative victories, COPE, the AFL-CIO, the larger-than-life George Meany seemed to be riding high.

The Election of 1968: The Last Hurrah

Before long, however, labor's political efforts were back on the defensive. The salad days of 1964–65 soon proved an aberration rather than a norm. Even with labor's great successes in the 1964 elections and in legislative maneuvering in 1965, the AFL-CIO failed to gain its long-sought repeal of a particularly noxious provision of the Taft-Hartley Act (Section 14B) that permitted states to outlaw standard forms of union security. Time and time again, laborites had sought revisions of Taft-Hartley. After the labor-led liberal victory in 1958, for example, AFL-CIO lobbyists had pressed for revision in Taft-Hartley. But labor legislation became bogged down in controversies over widely publicized charges of corruption and abridgement of democratic rights of union members. The resulting legislation, the Landrum-Griffin Act of 1959, left untouched the main features of Taft-Hartley and imposed stiff requirements of disclosure and standards of conduct that tightened the web of legalistic complexity already choking the labor movement.

The massive Democratic majorities of 1964–65 led Meany and his lieutenants to believe that at last they could gain repeal of the union-security provision in Taft-Hartley. Once again, however, they found that even two-to-one Democratic majorities were inadequate. Organized labor, it seemed, could be brilliantly successful when it came to "aggregative," or general interest, legislation, but when it came to legislation to benefit organized labor specifically, as in the proposed repeal of Section 14B, its allies got cold feet and found all sorts of excuses for backing off. In 1965–66, for example, Republicans and Southern Democrats successfully thwarted labor's efforts with a senatorial filibuster. Most observers believed that had the Johnson administration wanted to, it could have broken the conservative talkfest. "The president," declares a careful student of labor politics, "remained unconvinced that labor leaders wielded sufficient electoral influence to force him to go to great lengths in their behalf," however much he and his party relied on the labor movement for political and legislative legwork.

Even worse, however, was the Johnson administration's plummeting popularity and the daily-deepening fissures in the Democratic party and within the liberal coalition. Democrats lost forty seats in the 1966 elections, thus ending the "Great Society" phase of the LBJ presidency. As the bloody war in Vietnam ground on, organized labor began to pay a heavy price for its long and virtually unquestioning support of the government's definition of an effective anti-Communist foreign policy. One by one, liberal groups and voting blocs distanced themselves from the administration. The college campuses, through the sixties a focal point of idealist social commentary and action that had played a critical role in the civil rights movement, erupted in dissent. The Americans for Democratic Action, long allied with organized labor as an anchor of the party's liberal wing, condemned the war. In February 1967, Dr. King spoke out against the administration's Vietnam adventure. The AFL-CIO alone, if often seemed, stuck with Johnson. Administration spokesmen, only yesterday the heroes of liberal legislation and civil rights crusades, became pariahs to their own constituents as they grimly prosecuted the war. "Hey, hey, LBJ / How many kids did you kill today?" chanted massed protesters. When Johnson stepped down in the face of almost certain electoral defeat and permitted his loyal vice-president, Hubert Humphrey, to carry the administration torch in the 1968 campaign, many ignored the garrulous Humphrey's three decades of effective liberalism. Labor leaders embraced him as the ideal candidate, both progressive and anti-Communist, but antiwar protesters and disaffected young people vowed to "Dump the Hump."

Indeed, the almost incredible events surrounding the 1968 election found organized labor isolated from many of its usual allies in the liberal community and beset from both the right and the left. The anti-war candidacies of Minnesota senator Eugene McCarthy and of Robert F. Kennedy throughout the spring energized anti-administration dissidents in a dozen primary elections. The murder of Dr. King on April 4 and of Senator Kennedy two months later, along with the violent outbursts of outraged blacks after King's death, cast a frightening pall over the entire electoral process. Every day the toll of young Americans dead in Asia mounted. The August Democratic convention became an orgy of organized mayhem, as the berserk Chicago police, true to their traditions of violent repression, assaulted antiwar demonstrators and soon wielded their clubs indiscriminately. The swift unfolding of these multiple calamities shocked the country and plunged the Democracy into chaos. By the time Humphrey had given his grotesquely cheerful acceptance speech, crushing defeat seemed inevitable.

As if these violent events were not enough to ravage the Democratic party, third-party candidate George C. Wallace mounted a noisy campaign from the right. In 1964, Wallace had used thinly veiled racist appeals to challenge then-incumbent President Johnson in several Democratic primaries. No real threat to Johnson's hold on the party, Wallace nonetheless ran shockingly well in northern industrial states, gaining a third of the vote in Indiana, 40 percent in Maryland, and large numbers of ballots in Wisconsin and Michigan. Pundits quickly guessed that Wallace's success rested on blue-collar resentment over the liberal policies and civil rights enthusiasm of union leaders and mainstream Democrats. Although careful analysis often called the distinctively blue-collar element in Wallace's support into question, the news media latched onto the phenomenon of "white backlash" and of the blue-collar alienation. And indeed, the ethnic and working-class precincts of Milwaukee, Indianapolis, Baltimore, and Detroit showed visible signs of uneasiness over black militancy. Perhaps the southern governor had struck a responsive chord in his shrill denunciations of "pointy-headed liberals" and his demogogic calls for "law and order."

In 1968, Wallace supporters took the third-party route. They formed the American Independent Party, nominated Wallace and General Curtis Le May, and attacked both major parties, gaining a national audience for their racially focused message. They capitalized as well on widespread patriotic resentment over the occasionally bizarre or excessive rhetoric of the antiwar movement.

The Wallace phenomenon challenged organized labor on two levels. In the first place, to the extent that blue-collar voters deserted their normal Democratic allegiance to cast ballots for Wallace, the chances of the Republican candidate, Richard M. Nixon, would grow. Even more important, however, would be the effect of a blue-collar Wallace tide on the internal dynamics of the labor movement and its political operations. For forty years, working people had led in the struggle for progressive legislation. Union leaders identified completely with the New Deal-Great Society traditions. Moreover, they knew that a rising proportion of organized labor's actual and potential membership consisted of blacks and other minorities. That Wallace's gubernatorial record was anti-union, that he was an ignorant demagogue, that, if elected, he would jeopardize important elements of the post–World War II labor-liberal achievement, was less important than the fact that his very candidacy sought to detach working people from their liberal, New Dealish moorings and enlist them in a retrograde political movement.

Thus, in the two months before election day, COPE and the rest of the labor establishment pulled out all the stops. Training their heaviest fire on Wallace, they innundated working-class areas with literature exposing his antilabor record as governor. They depicted Alabama as a state rife with poverty, injustice, and ignorance, pointing out that under

Wallace it ranked near the bottom of the list in virtually every category of economic and social progress.

A team of British reporters observed the labor effort carefully, expecting at first that labor's normally cautious spokesmen would shy away from the race issue and concentrate on Wallace's poor gubernatorial record on economic issues. They ended up giving labor operatives high marks for forthrightness, however. The conventional wisdom, they noted, was that "affluent" white workers disliked blacks and would vent their racism by voting for Wallace. "The only social forces, it had become fashionable to say," wrote Lewis Chester, Godfrey Hodgson, and Bruce Page, "which could move the blue-collar vote now were appeals to racial prejudice, jealousy, and frustration." But, they added, "at every level . . . the leadership of labor decided to test these pessimistic and indeed insulting assumptions" by exposing Wallace's racism and by proclaiming anew labor's commitment to racial justice.

Through September and October, labor operatives redoubled their efforts in behalf of Humphrey. Thousands of union volunteers manned telephone banks, distributed literature, and canvassed neighborhoods. Early in the campaign, Humphrey, saddled with the Johnson war and unable (or unwilling) to disavow it, seemed confused and uncertain. But by mid-October, ever the cheerful campaigner, he had hit his stride. Polls showed him narrowing Nixon's once-commanding lead and revealed that support for Wallace was evaporating each day. By election night, most experts held the election too close to predict.

For a brief moment, as the returns flooded in, it appeared that Humphrey might be on the verge of an upset victory that would rank with the miracle of 1948. If so, organized labor would have surmounted overwhelming odds, and its role in the election would earn for its leaders unparalleled respect and influence. A Humphrey presidency would help labor's liberal agenda—sketched out in the Roosevelt years, defended in the inhospitable fifties, and partially realized in the flush of Johnson's victory—once again to occupy the center of American politics.

But Humphrey lost, trailing Nixon by less than one percentage point in the popular vote. Wallace captured 13 percent of the vote, most of it concentrated in the South, where he picked up his full total of forty-six electoral votes. Paper-thin Republican victories in Illinois, California, New Jersey, and Ohio accounted for 109 of Nixon's 301 electoral votes. Labor's efforts helped to carry Michigan, Pennsylvania, New York, and Maryland for Humphrey, but in the end the Democratic party's disarray, the perceived bankruptcy of the Johnson-Humphrey administration's policies in Southeast Asia, and Nixon's ability to rise from the ashes of previous defeats brought the presidency to the GOP.

Nixon had always been one of labor's chief nemeses, dating from his red-baiting campaigns for the U.S. Congress and Senate in 1946 and 1950. By a narrow margin, now, the labor movement would have a bitter antagonist in the White House. A Humphrey victory, whatever the cleavages within the Democracy, would doubtless have given laborites a significant voice in establishing priorities for political action in the 1970s. Though Nixon had effectively cultivated some elements of the labor movement—hard core conservative construction unions, for example, and a huge Teamsters' union by now almost completely isolated from and disdainful of the AFL-CIO—it was clear that the desperate campaign of Hubert Humphrey and his laborite allies was the last fading echo of the politics of the New Deal era.

As the seventies dawned, political scientists speculated on the meaning of the wrenching events of the late sixties. Some spoke of the breakup of the so-called fifth American party system, the political alignment that had prevailed since the days of FDR. Others wrote of an emerging Republican majority, bringing the more affluent elements of the working class together with newly Republican bastions in the South and West. Still others saw seemingly random, discontinuous patterns of victory and defeat, divided government, absence of mandate or direction. Few on the liberal side of things drew much comfort or sustenance from the cataclysms of the late sixties.

Democratic socialist Michael Harrington, however, sketched out a scenario that drew the possibilities of liberal-radical resurgence from the defeats of the sixties. In *Toward a Democratic Left* and other writings, Harrington noted that some liberals, environmentalists, and peace activists had given up on organized labor. The labor movement, they sneered, was but a junior partner in corporate capitalism; its politics were the politics of an outmoded productionist ethic of wasteful growth and mindless consumption. Its leadership was aging, white, and complacent at a time when blacks, other minorities, women, and an alienated, well-educated younger generation were surging to the fore in other areas of life. And, noted Harrington, to the extent that George Meany, the AFL-CIO, and other mainstream labor chieftains continued to support the Vietnam War, to drag their feet in desegregating the remaining exclusionist unions, and to remain hostile to environmental reform, the labor movement deserved much of this disdain.

But, he argued, the labor movement was not dead. "In fact," he asserted, "it may well be stirring to new life." Twenty million Americans belonged to unions. Whatever the defections and apathies of union voters, they still supplied the basic mass support for liberal candidates and progressive policies. True, unions such as the Teamsters and Mine

Workers in the late sixties were steeped in corruption and dominated by repressive and undemocratic misleaders. Even so, the vast majority of unions were honest and democratic. Without organized labor, Harrington cautioned, even the best intentioned social movements lacked the resources, manpower, and economic standing to sustain themselves. Sympathetic to impatient blacks, Harrington nonetheless reminded his readers that workers and their unions had a legitimate stake in defending hard-won seniority rights. Applauding the efforts of environmentalists, the socialist reminded them that for workers, unemployment remained a constant threat and that plans for conservation and cleanup had to take into account the legitimate fears of working people.

Above all, however, Harrington asserted the possibilities for reknitting a new version of the New Deal liberal coalition. He saw signs that new leadership in some unions, the rise of public employee unionism with its large numbers of female, black, and well-educated recruits, and the activities of insurgent groups in unions such as the Teamsters, Mine Workers, and Steelworkers could purge the labor movement of some of its more hidebound practices and policies. Already, he noted in 1968, important labor organizations were breaking with the AFL-CIO's disastrous Vietnam policy and reestablishing organized labor's independence in the area of foreign policy. In short, Harrington's scenario— hardly a prediction, in view of the many difficulties and obstacles— posited possibilities of revived progressivism, aroused by the experience of life under Nixon, in the seventies. And organized labor—battered but unbowed, chastened but still potent—stood at its center.

In 1968, partisans of the Republican governor of California, Ronald W. Reagan, had a different scenario. They believed that the era of the New Deal had passed. Goldwater's 1964 crusade had pointed the way of the future, though Goldwater himself did not have the personal qualities to carry his ultra conservative program effectively to the people. Their favorite, Governor Reagan, had travelled the path from New Dealism to conservatism. Indeed, in the 1940s he had been a labor leader, president of the Screen Actors Guild, AFL. Their quiet campaign to gain for him the 1968 nomination ran up against the Nixon steamroller, but even with a Nixon reelection in 1972, their man would remain popular and viable. After all, he would be only 65 in 1976. So as laborites tried to adjust to Nixon's presence in the White House, Governor Reagan and his allies bided their time. How ironic, some no doubt mused, if the first union leader to be elected president turned out to be a Republican.

7

Epilogue: Into the Eighties

In the spring of 1984, a full-page appeal appeared in the *New York Times* and other national publications. Sponsored by the Ad Hoc Committee for an American Solidarity Movement, the statement declared that "American unions are under attack." Supporters included scores of academics, artists, scientists, activists, and political figures. The ideological spectrum ran from unrepentant former members of the CPUSA to anti-Communist stalwarts of long standing. Folk singers, economists, novelists, poets, women's rights advocates, black activists, clergy, historians—all agreed that "for the first time in half a century there is a real possibility of the de-unionization of America." Labor was not always in the right, the statement readily acknowledged, but "criticisms must now take second place to our expression of solidarity in Ronald Reagan's increasingly anti-union America."

Indeed, the mid-eighties found the labor movement besieged and uncertain. Doleful statistics charted the shrinking percentage of workers belonging to unions. They documented chronic unemployment, failed organizing campaigns, decertifications of established unions, and widespread public disapproval of organized labor. In the 1984 election, labor's political power appeared to have vanished. Economists and social critics relegated unions to the margins of public life. Warned one academic expert in 1984, "there is . . . a chance that the United States may become the Western world's only union-free country." Worst of all perhaps were the words of Irving Kristol, issued even before the present crisis: "Trade unionism," he declared in 1970, "has become that most dangerous of social phenomena: a boring topic."

Evidence of labor's disarray was easy to find. The percentage of the labor force enrolled in unions had dropped from 35 in 1954 to under 20 by 1984; 80 percent of that decline had occurred since 1960. Small unions were decimated, while giants such as the United Steel Workers, the United Automobile Workers, and the Teamsters lost hundreds of thousands of members in the recession of the early eighties. On the organizing front, unions were faring poorly in NLRB elections. Once victorious in at least 70 percent of these contests, labor organizations by the late 1970s had begun to lose more than half of them. Even powerful unions submitted to "concession bargaining," trading wage increases, work-rule changes, and fringe benefits for jobs. "Two-tier" systems of compensation began to appear, with new employees being hired at less than union scale. Even after the economic recovery of 1983–84, unemployment remained at over 7 percent, ravaging traditional working-class communities and urban ghettoes with particular force.

Nor was labor able to recoup politically what it was losing in the shops and picket lines. AFL-CIO support for the Democratic party continued, but a changed political landscape caused many politicians to distance themselves from such traditional elements in the New Deal coalition as the unions. In 1976 and 1980, laborites eschewed concerted political efforts during the early stages of presidential years, only to find themselves saddled with a candidate for whom they had little attachment. But in 1984 they threw their weight behind long-term ally Walter Mondale before the primary season, with the result that the Minnesotan was pilloried as a tool of special interests. The defeats of both Carter in 1980 and Mondale four years later revealed widespread rank-and-file defection from the Democrats, especially among younger workers, and suggested the sharp limits to labor's vaunted political clout. The unions continued to be the most important financial supporters and suppliers of campaign workers for the Democrats, but "key Democratic elected officials," observed journalist Thomas Edsall, "treated the leadership of the AFL-CIO with disdain" in party deliberations and public encounters.

Organized labor's decline could be seen most poignantly in the deterioration of life in the great industrial arc from New York State to Minnesota that had nurtured the basic industries and given birth to the CIO. Many forces sapped this once-vibrant area. An aging infrastructure; inadequate reinvestment; spirited Japanese and, increasingly, Third World competition in autos, appliances, basic steel, and other core industrial products; corporate flight to the American South and, even more alarming, to low-wage Asian and Latin American countries— these problems combined to devastate states such as Pennsylvania, Ohio, Illinois, and Michigan. The whole region reeled under the shock of "de-industrialization."

Labor lawyer Thomas Geoghegan pictured the scene on Chicago's once-vital South Side. The unemployed steelworkers "seem dazed, sleepwalking. . . . They are too old to retrain or move to Houston."

Once-thriving neighborhoods were now populated with "truck drivers whose terminals have closed, steelworkers living on government cheese, old men sipping Cokes in bars at noon, young men drifting back from Houston to enroll in community colleges" to become male nurses and computer programmers. In Detroit throughout the recessionary early 1980s, news vendors imported stacks of Sunbelt papers so that the region's quarter million laid-off autoworkers could search the want ads of the *Dallas Morning News*, the *Denver Post*, and the *Houston Chronicle*.

True, the economy did produce jobs, 2 million new ones most years. Indeed, some observers welcomed the decline of smokestack industry and the rise of high-technology enterprise, which, it was said, brought more rewarding tasks and made for more flexible and innovative work environments. With the number of fast-food workers and private security guards surpassing the number of auto- and steelworkers, however, and with computerization of offices often leading to more fragmented and minutely supervised toil, the roseate view of high-tech enthusiasts such as Alvin Toffler were hard to credit. "A service economy [which the United States was fast becoming]," noted economic writer Bob Kuttner, "needs engineers and executives at one extreme—and millions of secretaries, fast-food workers, sales clerks, computer operators, and janitors at the other." These new employment patterns, Kuttner feared, would destroy the "middle"—the high-wage production worker—sector of the labor market. Thus, "it becomes increasingly difficult to maintain the United States as a middle-class society."

The feminization of the labor force also brought dilemmas to traditional unionists. To be sure, for over a century women had actively participated in the labor movement. Mass organization of telephone workers, teachers, and other public employees had increased the proportion of women among union members to 30 percent. Still, the high concentration of women workers in the expanding job sectors spelled difficulty for a labor movement rarely effective in its recruitment of women. Organized labor had never done well in the clerical, secretarial, insurance, banking, and white-collar fields where most of the new female entrants into labor markets toiled. Certainly, in the seventies and eighties women workers bridled at pay inequities and sexual harassment, but there was no guarantee that working women's grievances would lead them into the unions.

For labor organizers and officials, nothing better explained their inability to extend organization than the degeneration of the country's system of labor law. Since the mid-1960s employers had grown even bolder in flouting the National Labor Relations Act in often-successful efforts to stop organizing campaigns. Laborites watched helplessly as union activists were victimized: indeed, one 1980 study demonstrated that one union supporter in every twenty was fired in organizing campaigns. The law provided penalties, but these were weak and ineffective. NLRB backlogs and the complex legal procedures encouraged by the labor law made sanctions against determined employers of little use in assuring vulnerable workers that their rights were real. Acknowledging the structural, demographic, and internal problems faced by the unions, laborites nonetheless pointed to the contrasting experience of neighboring Canada. In the mid-1960s, both countries had had similar proportions of their workers enrolled in unions. Since then, however, despite common economic problems, union membership in Canada had surged to over 40 percent while it dipped to under 20 percent in the United States. It seemed clear that labor law reforms in Canada, which expedited representation elections and discouraged employer violations of workers' rights, accounted for this remarkable divergence.

Ronald Reagan's accession to power in 1981 exacerbated all of labor's problems. Appointment of conservatives to the NLRB swung that agency sharply to the right. The new secretary of labor and the new director of the Occupational Health and Safety Administration—both critical posts for unionists—showed little sympathy for labor's views. The president himself stunned laborites with his crude characterization of welfare recipients and with his disdain for the problems of the jobless in "South Succotash." Yet the president remained popular, no matter how sharp the recession of the early eighties nor how ill-informed and even callous his comments. When the administration crushed an ill-advised strike of federally employed air traffic controllers in the summer of 1981, unionists concluded that the administration's harsh retribution against strikes was designed to send a message to workers and employers everywhere.

Yet labor's critics, duly noting all these tribulations, pointed fingers at the unions themselves. Radicals accused entrenched union leaderships of lack of responsiveness to the black, Hispanic, and female workers who increasingly occupied the low-wage rungs most in need of vigorous union organizing. Neoconservatives and neoliberals decried labor's attachment to the politics of the New Deal era, with their stress on regulation of business, government intervention in the economy, and interference in the creative magic of free markets. Observed one commentator, "The association of unionism with industrial decline is no accident; unions stand accused of having rendered American industry uncompetitive through exorbitant wage demands and rigid work rules."

Granted all of these problems, did the state of the unions make much difference? Certainly, in the up-scale, quiche-eating America of the 1980s, the union hall and the picket line often seemed relics of a distant past. Perhaps in the eighties, as it had seemed at the end of the 1920s, labor's day was over, and the unions, while no doubt continuing in marginal sectors, would gradually fade from the scene, no longer central economic, social, and political institutions in a high-tech future.

It was, of course, to this very possibility that the signatories to the American Solidarity Movement manifesto addressed themselves. For some, of course, support for unions was an article of faith, a bedrock commitment. Unions no more needed justification than did motherhood or the Golden Rule. Union membership on the job was like citizenship at the polling place—a means of participating in the central activities of a democratic society.

By the mid-1980s such reflexive pro-unionism, however, had become rare. For many, defense of unions had to rest on more empirically valid grounds; union membership had to pay off at the bottom line, both for the individual worker and for society as a whole. If indeed unions extracted wage advantages for a minority at the expense of the non-union majority, the argument ran, good riddance to them. If in fact unions impeded productivity and encouraged inefficiency, they could no longer be tolerated in a competitive world economy. If unions were special interests, seeking the narrow concerns of their members, they deserved the thrashing they had received in the 1984 election.

Fortunately for those who continued to reserve for organized labor a central role in a democratic society, journalists and scholars provided some heartening reinforcement. Studies of post-Watergate changes in the political system, labor's relationship to inflation, and worker productivity refocused attention on the more positive features of American unions. For scholars and writers such as Richard B. Freeman, James L. Medoff, Robert Kuttner, and Thomas B. Edsall, in a society genuinely committed to egalitarianism and productive economic growth, organized labor belonged at the center, not on the fringes, of American life. That their studies of economics, politics, and social organization were based solidly on detailed empirical investigations held out hope of a rekindling of interest in labor's role in the so-called postindustrial order.

Thus, Thomas B. Edsall in a careful 1984 study analyzed the political consequences of labor's recent decline. "In the late 1970s and early 1980s," he concludes, "the collapse of labor's legislative power facilitated the adoption of a set of economic policies highly beneficial to the corporate sector and to the affluent." Labor's decline, he argued, had implications far beyond the fate of the unions themselves and their members, for "without a strong labor movement, there is no broad-based institution in American society equipped to represent the interests of those in the working and lower-middle classes in the formulation of economic policy." As of 1984 approximately 48 percent of all Americans had incomes below $20,000. Yet with a labor movement crippled and defensive, who would speak for these inarticulate masses in the political arena? With half the electorate almost voiceless, corporate and business dominance of American politics would go unchallenged.

In another study, economists Richard B. Freeman and James L. Medoff examined the economic and productivity implications of unionism. Far from contributing to a gap among categories of workers, they found, unions have historically been an egalitarian force. Rising union wage rates have buoyed those of nonunion workers in regional labor markets. Black workers have made their strongest and most enduring gains in association with egalitarian union wage scales. Union wages (in a point also stressed by economics analyst Robert Kuttner) have bridged the gap between the low-wage "secondary" labor markets characteristic of clerical and service workers and the high-salaried world of American professional and executive compensation. Indeed, argued some business analysts, it was the astronomical levels of executive compensation in America's corporations that revealed the real inequities in the business world. White-collar workers, themselves resistant to the union appeal, often piggyback on union gains, receiving from management comparable wages and benefits to prevent office staffs from getting ideas about organizing.

Freeman and Medoff also addressed the problem of efficiency and productivity. Detailed studies of workplaces indicated that, despite horror stories of "featherbedding" and job protection, strong unions were positively associated with managerial innovation and technological improvement. They found union-protected workers less resistant to innovation in the workplace, for they had less to fear than nonunion workers that change would eliminate their jobs. Moreover, as employers began to see the value of flexible job assignments, increased worker initiative, and greater workplace autonomy, they often found the lack of a union detrimental to these innovations, though few acknowledged this point. Workers did respond to positive changes in the workplace, to be sure, but nonunion workers were far more likely than their organized counterparts to perceive changes as potentially job-threatening and hence to withdraw cooperation, or to sabotage experiments. In the end, authoritarian workplaces, however benign their facades, proved less productive of efficiency than democratic workplaces. And workplace democracy, argued labor's partisans, was meaningless without independent worker representation—in other words, unions. Thus, argued Freeman and Medoff, a society genuinely concerned about increasing productivity would encourage, and not disparage, a strong labor movement.

Granted the social value and democratic character of trade unions, was there any sign as the eighties reached their midpoint of a revival of labor's élan? The AFL-CIO's Executive Council met in February 1985, amid gloomy election post mortems. Reflecting on President Reagan's overwhelming reelection, one staff member muttered that "the union busters are in hog heaven now." In a rare admission of perplexity, labor's general staff invited academic and industrial relations experts to share their prescriptions for recovery. In general, these analysts noted, organized labor had such a bad image among unorganized workers and the general public that it might be wise to downplay union membership. Perhaps the unions could establish auxiliary bodies, associations of workers nominally unattached to the unions, for representation at non-union workplaces. Organized labor should stress issues of wage equality and workplace democracy, perhaps toning down the rhetoric of confrontation and militancy.

Some laborites merely shrugged and awaited the morrow. It seemed, said Machinists' president William Wipisinger, that each generation of workers had to learn its lesson the hard way. After all, reflected some historically minded labor partisans, the great John L. Lewis himself had believed in the existence of cycles in the affairs of men, periods of defeat and periods of resurgence. And to be sure, parallels to the dark depression days, if not exact, were not hard to come by. But where, as the executive council deliberated in the Florida sunshine in the winter of 1985, was John L. Lewis?

Bibliographical Essay

The following bibliographical essay notes the published works that I relied most heavily upon in writing this book. It includes no archival sources or unpublished materials, such as dissertations and conference papers. Even so, it is far from comprehensive. For additional bibliography, consult Maurice F. Neufeld, Daniel J. Leab, and Dorothy Swanson, *American Working-Class History: A Representative Bibliography* (1983), and the following essays: David Brody, "The Old Labor History and the New: In Search of an American Working Class," *Labor History* 20 (1979): 111–26; David Montgomery, "To Study the People: The American Working Class," ibid. 21 (1980): 485–512; and Jonathan Grossman and William T. Moye, "Labor History in the 1970s: A Question of Identity," in Thomas A. Kochan et al., eds., *Industrial Relations Research in the 1970s: Review and Appraisal* (1982), 283–307.

GENERAL THEMES

The best of the general histories of American labor is Foster Rhea Dulles and Melvyn Dubofsky, *Labor in America*, 4th rev. ed. (1984). Joseph G. Rayback, *A History of American Labor* (1959, 1966), is dated and episodic in coverage. Thomas Brooks, *Toil and Trouble: A History of American Labor* (1964, 1971), suffers from similar problems but contains illuminating material on the 1960s. Philip A. Taft, *Organized Labor in American History* (1964), is packed with information but is narrow in focus and interpretive thrust. David A. Gordon, Richard Edwards, and Michael Reich, *Segmented Work, Divided Workers: The Historical Transformation of Labor in the United States* (1982), provides a breathtakingly conceptualized reinterpretation of American labor history. Harry A. Millis and Royal E. Montgomery, *The Economics of Labor*; vol. 3, *Organized Labor* (1945), remains a mine of useful information about unions and labor history. Books by Richard O. Boyer and Herbert M. Morais (*Labor's Untold Story*, 1955, 1980), Jeremy Brecher (*Strike!* 1972), and Sidney Lens (*The Labor Wars: From the Molly Maguires to the Sitdowns*, 1973) are long on consciousness-raising excitement but lack subtlety. Two excellent pictorial histories should also be consulted: Raymond Boryczka and Lorin Lee Cary, *No Strength without Union: An Illustrated History of Ohio*

Workers, 1803–1980 (1982) and Steve Babson, *Working Detroit: The Making of a Union Town* (1984).

Other general works offer diverse interpretive frameworks for the period covered by this book. James Green, *World of the Worker: Labor in Twentieth-Century America* (1980), posits an ill-defined but bold left-wing perspective and is especially strong on the social, gender, and racial aspects of working-class history. Michael Harrington, *Socialism* (1972), suggests a shrewd democratic socialist interpretation of labor's distinctive role in American politics. David Montgomery, *Workers' Control in America: Studies in the History of Work, Technology, and Labor Struggles* (1979), has been extraordinarily influential. The concluding essay, "American Workers and the New Deal Formula," poses a sharply different perspective from that found in the current book. David Brody, *Workers in Industrial America: Essays on the Twentieth Century Struggle* (1980), contains penetrating observations on key issues of the 1930s as well as path-breaking material on the post–World War II period.

More specialized works cover substantial segments of the period dealt with in the current book. Philip A. Taft, *The A.F. of L. from the Death of Gompers to the Merger* (1959), contains copious detail. Alice Kessler-Harris, *Out to Work: A History of Wage-Earning Women in the United States* (1982), Susan E. Kennedy, *If All We Did Was to Weep at Home: A History of White Working-Class Women in America* (1979), and James J. Kenneally, *Women and American Trade Unions* (1978), provide a strong introduction to the historical experiences of female workers. Philip S. Foner, *Organized Labor and the Black Worker, 1619–1973* (1974), is rich in detail, while William H. Harris, *The Harder We Run: Black Workers since the Civil War* (1982), is an excellent synthesis of recent scholarship. Two important collections provide a variety of good essays on black workers. They are John H. Bracey, Jr., August Meier, and Elliott Rudwick, eds., *Black Workers and Organized Labor* (1970), and Julius Jacobson, ed., *The Negro and the American Labor Movement* (1968). Irving Howe, *The World of Our Fathers* (1976), is excellent on Jewish workers and the needle trades unions. F. Ray Marshall, *Labor in the South* (1967), is useful, though careless in detail.

Studies of particular industries must also be consulted. Ronald Schatz, *The Electrical Workers: A History of Labor at General Electric and Westinghouse, 1923–1960* (1983), is superb. Vernon H. Jensen, *Heritage of Conflict: Labor Relations in the Nonferrous Metals Industry up to 1930* (1950) and *Nonferrous Metals Industry Unionism, 1932–1954* (1954), cover an important industrial sector. Robert R. Brooks, *As Steel Goes, . . .* (1940), and Clinton S. Golden and Harold J. Ruttenberg, *The Dynamics of Industrial Democracy* (1942), provide material on the steel industry. McAlister Coleman, *Men and Coal* (1943), conveys something of the mystique of coal mining and the UMW. Cletus Daniel, *Bitter Harvest: A History of California Farmworkers, 1870–1941* (1981), is an outstanding book. Joyce Shaw Peterson, "Auto Workers and Their Work, 1900–1933," *Labor History* 22 (1981): 213–36, is richly informative. David Brody, *The Butcher Workmen* (1964), is a detailed study of unionism in the meatpacking industry. Robert Ozanne, *A Century of Labor-Management Rela-*

tions at McCormick and International Harvester (1967), is based on unique documentary material.

White-collar employment is less well studied, but there are some fine accounts. John N. Schacht, *The Making of Telephone Unionism, 1920–1947* (1985), and Susan Porter Benson, " 'The Customers Ain't God': The Work Culture of Department-Store Saleswomen, 1890–1940," in Michael H. Frisch and Daniel J. Walkowitz, eds., *Working-Class America: Essays on Labor, Community, and American Society* (1983), 185–211, depict the worlds of important groups of women workers. Jurgen A. Kocha, *White-Collar Workers in America, 1900–1940* (1980), is informative. Harry Braverman, *Labor and Monopoly Capital: The Degradation of Work in the Twentieth Century* (1974), and Richard Edwards, *Contested Terrain: The Transformation of the Workplace in the Twentieth Century* (1979), are important Marxist critiques of modern work structures.

BIOGRAPHY AND MEMOIR

Biographies and autobiographies are also important sources for recent labor history. Melvyn Dubofsky and Warren Van Tine, *John L. Lewis: A Biography* (1977), ranks with the best of American lives. John Barnard, *Walter Reuther and the Rise of the Auto Workers* (1983), is an excellent introduction to its subject. Biographies by Joseph Goulden—*Meany* (1972) and *Jerry Wurf: Labor's Last Angry Man* (1982)—are based on extensive interviews with their subjects. Archie Robinson, *George Meany and His Times: A Biography* (1981), contains additional material. Matthew Josephson, *Sidney Hillman, Statesman of American Labor* (1952); Maxwell Raddock, *Portrait of an American Labor Leader: William L. Hutcheson* (1955); Thomas R. Brooks, *Clint: A Biography of a Labor Intellectual, Clinton S. Golden* (1978); Jervis Anderson, *A. Philip Randolph: A Biographical Portrait* (1973); and Charles P. Larrowe, *Harry Bridges: The Rise and Fall of Radical Labor in the United States* (1972, 1977), provide important material. Gary Fink, ed., *Biographical Dictionary of American Labor Leaders* (2d ed. 1984), is a useful compilation, while Charles Madison, *American Labor Leaders: Personalities and Forces in the Labor Movement* (1950), remains valuable, especially for its essays on Philip Murray and William Green. Murray Kempton, *Part of Our Time: Some Monuments and Ruins of the Thirties* (1955, 1967), contains portraits of Lee Pressman, Joseph Curran, and other 1930s labor activists.

Autobiographies and memoirs also contain vivid recollections, though their frequent reliance on unaided memory should encourage caution. Victor Reuther, *The Brothers Reuther and the Story of the UAW: A Memoir* (1976), is a vigorous defense of the Reuther legacy. See Frank Marquart, *An Auto Worker's Journal: The UAW from Crusade to One-Party Union* (1975), for a sharp contrast. Other memoir material emanating from the articulate ranks of the Autoworkers includes Clayton Fountain, *Union Guy* (1949); Wyndham Mortimer, *Organize! My Life as a Union Man* (1971); Claude E. Hoffman, *Sit-*

Down in Anderson: UAW Local 663, Anderson, Indiana (1968); and Charles Denby [Matthew Ward], *Indignant Heart: A Black Worker's Journal* (1978).

James Matles and James Higgins, *Them and Us: Struggles of a Rank-and-File Union* (1974), details the stormy history of the United Electrical Workers from the viewpoint of its pro-Soviet organization director. Also reflecting the views of activists in or close to the Communist party are Len De Caux, *Labor Radical—From the Wobblies to the CIO: A Personal History* (1970); Steve Nelson (with James R. Barrett and Rob Ruck), *Steve Nelson, American Radical* (1981); and Al Richmond, *A Long View from the Left: Memoirs of an American Revolutionary* (1973). Max Shachtman, "Radicalism in the Thirties: The Trotskyist View," in Rita James Simon, ed., *As We Saw the Thirties: Essays on Social and Political Movements of a Decade* (1967), 8–45, provides a fascinating contrast. David Dubinsky and A. H. Raskin, *David Dubinsky: A Life with Labor* (1977), contains vivid material on immigration, Communism, industrial unionism, foreign policy, politics, and the inner world of the labor movement. John Brophy, *A Miner's Life: An Autobiography,* ed. O. P. Hall (1964), is an important source for information on John L. Lewis, the UMW, and the CIO. Brophy and many others in the New Deal–era labor movement deposited oral history interviews, some quite lengthy and detailed, at the Columbia Oral History Project. Among those whose recollections are on file are Lee Pressman, Jacob Potofsky, Julius Emspak, R. J. Thomas, John P. Frey, John Edelman, and James B. Carey. See Louis Starr and Elizabeth Mason, eds., *The Oral History Collection of Columbia University* (1973, 1979). Published oral interviews with radical organizers appear in Alice and Staughton Lynd, eds., *Rank and File: Personal Histories of Working-Class Organizers* (1973). See Robert H. Zieger, "Memory Speaks: Observations on Personal History and Working-Class Culture," *Maryland Historian* 8 (1977): 1–13, for additional citations and commentary.

LABOR AND THE LEFT

Organized radicalism has been the subject of intense scholarly and polemical investigation. Those who would understand the 1930s and 1940s especially must attempt to get a handle on the ideologies, positions, and passions of the various left-wing organizations as they intersected with the labor movement at this critical juncture. Standard works on American socialism include David A. Shannon, *The Socialist Party of America: A History* (1955); Murray B. Seidler, *Norman Thomas: Respectable Rebel* (1961); W. A. Swanberg, *Norman Thomas: The Last Idealist* (1976); and Frank A. Warren, *An Alternative Vision: The Socialist Party in the 1930s* (1974).

The literature on Communism is abundant. Vivian Gornick, *The Romance of American Communism* (1977), contains credulous interviews with Party veterans and apostates. Joseph Starobin, *American Communism in Crisis, 1943–1957* (1972), is a mordant critique by a former Party member. Scholarly studies include Theodore Draper, *The Roots of American Communism* (1957); Harvey Klehr, *The Heyday of American Communism: The Depression Decade*

(1983); Maurice Isserman, *Which Side Were You On? The American Communist Party during the Second World War* (1982); and David A. Shannon, *The Decline of American Communism: A History of the Communist Party of the United States since 1945* (1959). Irving Howe and Lewis A. Coser, *The Communist Party of the United States* (1957, 1962), delivers a sharp socialist critique of the party, while William O'Neill, *A Better World—The Great Schism: Stalinism and the American Intellectuals* (1982), is a controversial effort to put the internecine struggles on the left in perspective. Constance A. Myers, *The Prophet's Army: Trotskyists in America, 1928–1941* (1976), and Robert Alexander, *The Right Opposition: The Lovestoneites and the International Communist Opposition of the 1930s* (1981), illuminate other phases of Marxist-Leninism.

The activities of the Communists in the labor movement continue to generate seemingly endless scholarly and polemical controversy. Standard discussions include David A. Saposs, *Communism in American Unions* (1959), stridently anti-Communist in content; Roger R. Keeran, *The Communist Party and the Auto Workers' Unions* (1980), far more sympathetic; and Bert Cochran, *Labor and Communism: The Conflict That Shaped American Unions* (1977), a biting critique of both the Communists and their liberal rivals. Maurice Zeitlin, ed., *Political Power and Social Theory*, vol. 4 (1984), contains articles and commentary reflecting diverse perspectives on the labor-and-Communism issue of the 1930s and 1940s. See also Theodore Draper, "American Communism Revisited," *New York Review of Books*, May 9 and 23, 1985.

CHAPTER 1

For the general economic, social, and political history of the 1920s, I relied most heavily on Arthur M. Schlesinger, Jr., *The Age of Roosevelt*, vol. 1, *The Crisis of the Old Order, 1919–1933* (1957), a brilliantly written and, despite inevitable correction by subsequent scholarship, enduring work. Older works by George Soule, *Prosperity Decade: From the War to the Depression, 1917–1929* (1947), and Broadus Mitchell, *Depression Decade: From the New Era through the New Deal, 1929–1941* (1947), both in the Economic History of the United States, stand up well. General histories of the 1920s of most value are William E. Leuchtenberg, *The Perils of Prosperity, 1914–1932* (1958), and John R. Hicks, *Republican Ascendancy, 1921–1933* (1960). John Kenneth Galbraith, *The Great Crash, 1929* (1955), remains the most lucid analysis of the cataclysm of 1929. Primary material of great value is found in President's Research Committee . . . , *Recent Social Trends in the United States,* 2 vols. (1933), and Robert S. Lynd and Helen Merrell Lynd, *Middletown: A Study in Modern American Culture* (1929). The best biography of Herbert Hoover is David Burner, *Herbert Hoover: The Public Life* (1978).

For labor history, the outstanding work is Irving Bernstein, *The Lean Years: A History of the American Worker, 1920–1933* (1960), a remarkable and wide-ranging achievement. Important articles include Frank Stricker, "Affluence for Whom? Another Look at Prosperity and the Working Class in the 1920s," *Labor History* 24 (1983): 5–33; Joyce Shaw Peterson, "Auto Workers

Confront the Depression, 1929–1933," *Detroit in Perspective* 6 (1982): 47–72; Alex Baskin, "The Ford Hunger March—1932," *Labor History* 13 (1972): 331–60; Steve Fraser, "Dress Rehearsal for the New Deal: Shop-Floor Insurgents, Political Elites, and Industrial Democracy in the Amalgamated Clothing Workers," in Frisch and Walkowitz, *Working-Class America* (1983), cited under "General Themes" above, 212–55; Daniel Nelson, "The Company Union Movement, 1900–1937: A Reexamination," *Business History Review* 56 (1982): 355–58; Gerald Zahavi, "Negotiated Loyalty: Welfare Capitalism and the Shoeworkers of Endicott Johnson, 1920–1940," *Journal of American History* 70 (1983): 602–20; Bernard Sternsher, "Victims of the Great Depression: Self-Blame/Non-Self-Blame, Radicalism, and the Pre-1929 Experience," *Social Science History* 1 (1977): 137–77; and Robert H. Zieger, "Herbert Hoover, the Wage-Earner, and the 'New Economic System,' " *Business History Review* 51 (1977): 161–89.

Specialized studies for the twenties and great crash period abound. Most useful for my purposes were Frances Fox Piven and Richard A. Cloward, *Poor People's Movements: Why They Succeed, How They Fail* (1977), on demonstrations by the unemployed and eviction protests; Walter I. Trattner, *From Poor Law to Welfare State: A History of Social Welfare in America* (1974, 1979), on relief policies and expenditures; Jordan A. Schwartz, *Interregnum of Despair: Hoover, Congress, and the Depression* (1970); and Donald Lisio, *The President and Protest: Hoover, Conspiracy, and the Bonus Riot* (1974). Robert H. Zieger, *Republicans and Labor, 1919–1929* (1969), examines government labor policy in the 1920s. Kristi Andersen, *The Creation of a Democratic Majority, 1928–1936* (1979), and David A. Burner, *The Politics of Provincialism: The Democratic Party in Transition, 1918–1932* (1968), are sophisticated accounts of depression-era politics.

CHAPTER 2

The classic work on labor in the 1930s is Irving Berstein, *The Turbulent Years: A History of the American Worker, 1933–1941* (1969), an outstanding achievement. Walter Galenson, *The CIO Challenge to the AFL: A History of the American Labor Movement, 1935–1941* (1960), is a strong institutional account. James O. Morris, *Conflict within the AFL: A Study in Craft versus Industrial Unionism, 1901–1938* (1958), is a useful analysis. Art Preis, *Labor's Giant Step: Twenty Years of the CIO* (1964, 1972), is the only general history of the CIO, though its usefulness is limited by its unrelentingly Trotskyist perspective. Christopher L. Tomlins, "AFL Unions in the 1930s: Their Performance in Historical Perspective," *Journal of American History* 65 (1979): 1021–42, ably defends the AFL record. The essays in Milton Derber and Edwin Young, eds., *Labor and the New Deal* (1957), remain useful, especially those on collective bargaining and legislation. Professor George Barnett's contemporary view of the labor movement in 1932 is quoted in David Brody, "The Expansion of the American Labor Movement: Institutional Sources of Stimulus and Restraint," in Stephen E. Ambrose, ed., *Institutions in Modern America* (1967), 11–36.

William E. Leuchtenberg, *FDR and the New Deal, 1932–1940* (1963), is a sound introduction to the thirties. Schlesinger, *The Age of Roosevelt,* vol. 2, *The Coming of the New Deal* (1959), and vol. 3, *The Politics of Upheaval* (1960), retain their brilliance and usefulness. Frank Freidel, *Franklin D. Roosevelt,* 4 vols. (1952–73), is the standard Roosevelt biography, but see also James MacGregor Burns, *Roosevelt: The Lion and the Fox* (1956). Robert S. McElvaine, *The Great Depression: America, 1929–1941* (1984), is a vivid recent account of the 1930s in which labor plays a major role. Challenging interpretations of the New Deal are offered in Theda Skocpol, "Political Response to Capitalist Crisis: Neo-Marxist Theories of the State and the Case of the New Deal," *Politics and Society* 10 (1980): 155–201; Paul K. Conkin, *The New Deal* (1967, 1975); and Barton J. Bernstein, "The New Deal: The Conservative Achievements of Liberal Reform," in Bernstein, ed., *Towards a New Past: Dissenting Essays in American History* (1968), 263–88. Melvyn Dubofsky, "Not So 'Turbulent Years': Another Look at the American 1930s," *Amerikastudien/American Studies* 24 (1979): 5–20, reexamines the meaning of labor's resurgence.

More specialized studies of unions and labor problems of the thirties abound. Those interested in legal and legislative matters should consult J. Joseph Huthmacher, *Senator Robert F. Wagner and the Rise of Urban Liberalism* (1971), for the background of New Deal labor policy. Irving Bernstein, *New Deal Collective Bargaining Policy* (1950), remains standard. James A. Gross, *The Making of the National Labor Relations Board: 1933–1937* (1974), is based on exhaustive research. Peter H. Irons, *The New Deal Lawyers* (1982), is generous in its treatment of the Wagner Act and the early NLRB, while Howell Harris, "The Snares of Liberalism? Politicians, Bureaucrats, and the Shaping of Federal Labour Relations Policy in the United States, ca. 1915–47," in Steven Tolliday and Jonathan Zeitlin, eds., *Shop Floor Bargaining and the State: Historical and Comparative Perspectives* (1985), 148–91, is richly illuminating. Richard C. Cortner, *The Wagner Act Cases* (1964) and *The Jones and Laughlin Case* (1970), trace constitutional issues. Karl Klare, "The Judicial Deradicalization of the Wagner Act and the Origins of Modern Legal Consciousness, 1937–1941," *Minnesota Law Review* 62 (1978): 265–339, raises important questions. But see also Matthew W. Finkin's ringing critique of Klare in "Revisionism in Labor Law," *University of Maryland Law Review* 43 (1984): 23–92. Jerold Auerbach, *Labor and Liberty: The La Follette Committee and the New Deal* (1966), and Patrick J. Maney, *"Young Bob": A Biography of Robert M. La Follette, Jr.* (1978), detail the work of the critical Senate labor hearings. Those interested in exploring the depth of corporate America's hostility towards unions would do well to consult the copious and fascinating records of this critical investigation, which are cited in the Auerbach and Maney books.

Studies of specific unions, strikes, and industries contain much of the labor history of the decade. See, e.g., Sidney Fine, *The Automobile under the Blue Eagle* (1963); Fine, *Sit-Down: The General Motors Strike of 1936–37* (1969), a labor history classic; Peter Friedlander, *The Emergence of a UAW Local, 1936–1939: A Study in Class and Culture* (1975); Raymond Boryczka, "Militancy and Factionalism in the United Auto Workers Union, 1937–1941,"

Maryland Historian 8 (1977): 13–25; Boryczka, "Seasons of Discontent: Auto Union Factionalism and the Motor Products Strike of 1935–36," *Michigan History* 61 (1977): 3–32; Roger R. Keeran, "The Communists and UAW Factionalism, 1937–1939," *Michigan History* 60 (1976): 115–36; and Steve Babson, "Pointing the Way: The Role of British and Irish Skilled Tradesmen in the Rise of the UAW," *Detroit in Perspective* 7 (1983): 75–96, for the automobile industry and the rise of the UAW. Charles P. Larrowe, "The Great Maritime Strike of '34," *Labor History* (1970): 403–51 and (1971): 3–37, is moving and authoritative.

For steel, Donald Sofchalk, "The Chicago Memorial Day Incident: An Episode of Mass Action," *Labor History* 6 (1965): 3–43, and James L. Baughman, "Classes and Company Towns: Legends of the 1937 Little Steel Strike," *Ohio History* 87 (1978): 175–92, contrast interestingly. See also Daniel J. Leab, "The Memorial Day Massacre," *Midcontinent American Studies Journal* 8 (1967): 3–17. John Bodnar, *Workers' World: Kinship, Community, and Protest in an Industrial Society, 1900–1940* (1982) and "Immigration, Kinship, and the Rise of Working-Class Realism in Industrial America," *Journal of Social History* 14 (1980): 45–65, provide grass-roots perspectives on the steel communities. Robert R. R. Brooks, *As Steel Goes, . . . Unionism in a Basic Industry* (1940), is dated but still useful. Max Gordon, "The Communists and the Drive to Organize Steel, 1936," *Labor History* 23 (1982): 254–65, contains vivid first-hand observations.

Daniel Nelson, "The Great Goodyear Strike of 1936," *Ohio History* 92 (1983): 6–36; Nelson, "Origins of the Sit-Down Era: Worker Militancy and Innovation in the Rubber Industry, 1934–1938," *Labor History* 23 (1982): 198–225; and Nelson, "The Rubber Workers' Southern Strategy: Labor Organizing in the New Deal South, 1933–1943," *The Historian* 46 (1984): 319–38, carefully probe the experience of a major early CIO affiliate. Harvey Schwartz, *The March Inland: Origins of the ILWU Warehouse Division, 1934–1938* (1978), is illuminating beyond the narrow confines of its title. Daniel Leab, *A Union of Individuals: The Formation of the American Newspaper Guild, 1933–1936* (1970), explores a neglected phase of union growth.

Joshua Freeman, "Catholics, Communists, and Republicans: Irish Workers and the Organization of the Transport Workers Union," in Frisch and Walkowitz, *Working-Class America* (1983), cited under "General Themes" above, 256–83, traces the origins of an exuberant left-wing union. Ronald L. Filippelli, "UE: The Formative Years, 1933–1937," *Labor History* 17 (1976): 351–71, and Ronald Schatz, "Union Pioneers: The Founders of Local Unions at General Electric and Westinghouse, 1933–1937," *Journal of American History* 66 (1979): 586–602, do the same for the electrical appliance and equipment industry. Robert H. Zieger, *Rebuilding the Pulp and Paper Workers' Union, 1933–1941* (1984), examines union rebirth in considerable detail.

Regional and ethnic themes are highlighted in Gary Gerstle, "The Mobilization of the Working-Class Community: The Independent Textile Union in Woonsocket, 1931–1947," *Radical History Review* 17 (1978): 161–72, and Bernard Sternsher, "Great Depression Labor Historiography in the 1970s: Middle-Range Questions, Ethno-Cultures, and Levels of Generalization," *Re-*

views in American History 11 (1983): 300–319, a perceptive critique despite its cumbersome title. See also Robert H. Zieger, *Madison's Battery Workers, 1934–1952: A History of Federal Labor Union 19587* (1977).

Lorin Lee Cary, "Institutionalized Conservatism in the Early C.I.O.: Adolph Germer, a Case Study," *Labor History* 13 (1972): 475–504, stresses continuity in union development. Several recent articles highlight early CIO political initiatives. See Hugh Lovin, "The Ohio 'Farmer-Labor' Movement in the 1930s," *Ohio History* 87 (Autumn 1978): 419–37, and "CIO Innovators, Labor Party Ideologues, and Organized Labor's Muddles in the 1937 Detroit Elections," *Old Northwest* 8 (1982): 223–43, as well as Kenneth Waltzer, "The Party and the Polling Place: American Communism and an American Labor Party in the 1930s," *Radical History Review* 23 (1980): 104–29. Daniel Nelson, "The CIO at Bay: Labor Militancy and Politics in Akron, 1936–1938," *Journal of American History* 71 (December 1984): 565–86, is particularly illuminating and significant. Carlos A. Schwantes, " 'We've Got 'em on the Run, Brothers': The 1937 Non-Automotive Sit-downs in Detroit," *Michigan History* 58 (1972): 179–200, describes the aftermath of the Flint sit-down. Steve Fraser, "From the 'New Unionism' to the New Deal," *Labor History* 25 (1984): 405–30, focuses on the social and economic thought of Sidney Hillman. Horace B. Cayton and George N. Mitchell, *Black Workers and the New Unions* (1939), a durable classic, is laced with rare interview material.

Accounts of activists and journalists vividly bring the turbulent thirties to life. Farrel Dobbs, *Teamster Rebellion* (1972) and *Teamster Power* (1973), recount the radical experiment of the Minneapolis truckers. Henry Kraus, *The Many and the Few: A Chronicle of the Dynamic Auto Workers* (1947), is a unique blend of scholarship and memoir by an articulate activist. Benjamin Stolberg, *The Story of the CIO* (1938), created a furor with its charges of Communist influence in the new labor federation, while Edward Levinson, *Labor on the March* (1938), sought to refute Stolberg. Ruth McKenny, *Industrial Valley* (1939), reconstructs the turbulent world of Akron's rubber workers, the shock troops of the early CIO, while Mary Heaton Vorse, *Labor's New Millions* (1938), captures the energy and enthusiasm of the CIO crusade.

CHAPTER 3

Irving Bernstein, *Turbulent Years*, and Preis, *Labor's Giant Step*, both cited for Chapter 2, contains excellent material on the 1939–41 period. Joel Seidman, *American Labor from Defense to Reconversion* (1953), is standard for the entire World War II era. Nelson N. Lichtenstein, *Labor's War at Home: The CIO in World War II* (1982), is a provocative recent analysis and rewards careful reading. Joshua Freeman, "Delivering the Goods: Industrial Unionism during World War II," *Labor History* 19 (1978): 570–94, and James Green, "Fighting on Two Fronts: Working-Class Militancy in the 1940's," *Radical America* 8 (1975): 7–48, are spirited brief introductions to the subject.

Martin Glaberman, *Wartime Strikes* (1980), mixes vivid firsthand information and a tendentious argument. Irving Howe and B. J. Widick, *The UAW and*

Walter Reuther (1949), provides an interesting contrast. Other aspects of the turbulent history of the automobile industry during the war are explored in Ed Jennings, "Wildcat! The Wartime Strikes in Auto," *Radical America* 9 (1975): 77–113; Lichtenstein, "Conflict over Workers' Control: The Automobile Industry in World War II," in Frisch and Walkowitz, *Working Class America* (1983), cited above, 284–311; and James R. Prickett, "Communism and Factionalism in the United Automobile Workers, 1939–1947," *Science and Society* 32 (1968): 257–77.

August Meier and Elliott Rudwick, *Black Detroit and the Rise of the UAW* (1979), is an important study that focuses on the explosive racial situation in Detroit during World War II. Other recent investigations of racial aspects of the war's labor history include Allan M. Winkler, "The Philadelphia Transit Strike of 1944," *Journal of American History* 59 (1972): 73–89; August Meier and Elliott Rudwick, "Communist Unions and the Black Community: The Case of the Transport Workers Union, 1934–1944," *Labor History* 23 (1982): 165–97; Donald T. Critchlow, "Communist Unions and Racism: A Comparative Study of the United Electrical, Radio, and Machine Workers and the National Maritime Union to the Black Question during World War II," *Labor History* 17 (1976): 230–44; and William H. Harris, "Federal Intervention in Union Discrimination: FEPC and West Coast Shipyards during World War II," *Labor History* 22 (1981): 325–47, an unusually detailed and important study.

There is an extensive literature relating to women's experiences during the war. Ruth Milkman, "Female Factory Workers and Industrial Structure: Control and Conflict over 'Women's Place' in Auto and Electrical Manufacturing," *Politics and Society* 12 (1983): 159–204, and Milkman, "Organizing the Sexual Division of Labor: Historical Perspectives on 'Women's Work' and the American Labor Movement," *Socialist Review* 49 (1980): 95–150, provide wide-ranging insights. Sharon Hartman Strom, "Challenging 'Woman's Place': Feminism, the Left, and Industrial Unionism in the 1930s," *Feminist Studies* 9 (1983): 359–86, adds needed background. Karen Anderson, *Wartime Women: Sex Roles, Family Relations, and the Status of Women during World War II* (1981), is standard. See also Anderson, "Last Hired, First Fired: Black Women Workers during World War II," *Journal of American History* 69 (1982): 82–97. William Chafe, *The American Woman: Her Changing Social, Economic, and Political Roles, 1920–1970* (1972); Paddy Quick, "Rosie the Riveter: Myths and Realities," *Radical America* 9 (1975): 115–32; Chester Gregory, *Women in Defense Work during World War II* (1974); Janice Trey, "Women in the War Economy: World War II," *Review of Radical Political Economy* 4 (1972): 42–57; Eleanor Straub, "U.S. Government Policy toward Civilian Women during World War II," *Prologue* 5 (1973): 240–54; and Alan Clive, "Women Workers in World War II: Michigan as a Test Case," *Labor History* 20 (1979): 44–72, offer diverse perspectives. Two articles by Nancy Gabin—"Women Workers and the UAW in the Post–World War II Period: 1945–1954," *Labor History* 21 (1979–80): 5–30, and " 'They Have Placed a Penalty on Womanhood': The Protest Actions of Women Auto Workers in Detroit-Area UAW Locals, 1945–1947," *Feminist Studies* 8 (1982): 373–98—analyze early postwar developments.

For overall material on economic and social conditions during the war, I have relied extensively on John Morton Blum, *V Was for Victory: Politics and American Culture during World War II* (1976); Richard Polenberg, *War and Society: The United States, 1941–1945* (1972); and Richard Lingeman, *Don't You Know There's a War On? The American Home Front, 1941–1945* (1970), a sprightly popular account. Polenberg, *One Nation Divisible: Class, Race, and Ethnicity in the United States since 1933* (1980), is good on statistical information and social issues. On the role of the federal government in labor affairs, see James MacGregor Burns, *Roosevelt: The Soldier of Freedom* (1970); George Q. Flynn, *The Mess in Washington: Manpower Mobilization in World War II* (1979); Albert A. Blum, *Drafted or Deferred: Practices Past and Present* (1967); and Fred Witney, *Wartime Experiences of the National Labor Relations Board, 1941–1945* (1949). Alan Clive, *State of War: Michigan in World War II* (1979), is outstanding. David Brody, "The New Deal and World War II," in John Braeman, Robert H. Bremner, and David Brody, eds., *The New Deal*, vol. 1, *The National Level* (1975), 267–309, is incisive. Paul A. C. Koistinen, "Mobilizing the World War II Economy: Labor and the Industrial-Military Alliance," *Pacific Historical Review* 42 (1973): 443–78, is filled with information and insights. Finally, two World War II novels—Harvey Swados, *Standing Fast* (1970), and Harriette Arnow, *The Dollmaker* (1954)—repay reading.

CHAPTER 4

Books by Seidman, Preis, and Lichtenstein, cited for Chapter 3, cover the 1945–46 strike wave. See also Barnard, *Walter Reuther*, and Dubofsky and Van Tine, *John L. Lewis*, cited above under "Biography and Memoir." P. K. Edwards, *Strikes in the United States, 1881–1974* (1981), throws a wealth of statistical and interpretive material at the reader. Articles by Barton J. Bernstein are careful and informative. See especially "Walter Reuther and the General Motors Strike of 1945–1946," *Michigan History* 49 (1965): 260–77; "The Truman Administration and Its Reconversion Wage Policy," *Labor History* 6 (1965): 214–31; and "The Truman Administration and the Steel Strike of 1946," *Journal of American History* 52 (1966): 791–803. Howell John Harris, *The Right to Manage: Industrial Relations Policies of American Business in the 1940s* (1982), is both balanced and provocative.

More general accounts of the postwar years include Eric Goldman, *The Crucial Decade, 1945–1955* (1956), and Joseph Goulden, *The Best Years, 1945–1950* (1976), which is rich in anecdotal material. George Lipsitz, *Class and Culture in Cold War America: "A Rainbow at Midnight"* (1981), mixes insight and radical romanticism. See also Arthur F. McClure, *The Truman Administration and the Problems of Postwar Labor, 1945–1948* (1969).

The best overall account of the Truman presidency is by Robert J. Donovan. See *Conflict and Crisis: The Presidency of Harry S. Truman, 1945–1947* (1977) and *Tumultuous Years: The Presidency of Harry S. Truman, 1949–1953* (1981). Alonzo Hamby, *Beyond the New Deal: Harry S. Truman and American Liberalism* (1973), is thorough and astute. Stephen Kemp Bailey, *Congress*

Makes a Law: The Story behind the Employment Act of 1946 (1950), focuses on the activities of the liberal-labor coalition.

There is no adequate account of the passage and impact of the Taft-Hartley Act. R. Alton Lee, *Truman and Taft-Hartley: A Question of Mandate* (1966), is informative but narrowly conceived. James Patterson, *Mr. Republican: A Biography of Robert A. Taft* (1972), overall an outstanding biography, is too credulous as to Taft's motives and actions. Congressman Fred Hartley, Jr., *Our New National Labor Policy: The Taft-Hartley Act and the Next Steps* (1948), is a bald declaration of conservative intent to reverse government labor policy. It contains a foreword by Senator Taft. James A. Gross, *The Reshaping of the National Labor Relations Board: National Labor Policy in Transition, 1937–1947* (1981), offers telling criticisms of the Taft-Hartley approach. Those interested in organized labor's detailed objections should consult the files of the AFL's monthly, *American Federationist,* and the CIO's *CIO News,* a weekly, for the 1946–50 period. Shrewd criticisms of the Taft-Hartley approach are found in James B. Atleson, *Values and Assumptions in American Labor Law* (1983), and Katherine Van Wezel Stone, "The Post-War Paradigm in American Labor Law," *Yale Law Review* 90 (1981): 1509–80. See also Harris, "Responsible Unionism," cited for Chapter 2 above, and Christopher L. Tomlins, *The State and the Unions: Labor Relations, Law, and the Organized Labor Movement in America, 1880–1960* (1985).

Fortune magazine's paeans to American capitalism are summarized in its publication *USA: The Permanent Revolution* (1951). There is no adequate account of postwar collective bargaining gains, but see Taft, *Organized Labor,* cited above under "General Themes," for basic information. The pages of *Fortune,* whose labor editor, Daniel Bell, was an astute observer, and of the *New York Times,* which had several able reporters on the labor beat, brim with information about labor's objectives and postwar contracts. The radical publication *Labor Action* also covered negotiations in basic industry very capably. Maeva Marcus, *Truman and the Steel Seizure Case: The Limits of Presidential Power* (1977), is informative on the 1952 steel strike, while Jack Stieber, "Labor's Walkout from the Korean War Wage Stabilization Board," *Labor History* 21 (1980): 239–60, illuminates an important episode.

The CIO's political efforts after the war are ably covered in James C. Foster, *The Union Politic: The CIO Political Action Committee* (1974). Joseph Gaer, *The First Round* (1944), is an excellent compilation of pamphlets and documents pertaining to the early efforts of PAC. Arthur Kornhauser et al., *When Labor Votes: A Study of Auto Workers* (1956), is a pioneering electoral analysis. Seymour Martin Lipset, *Political Man: The Social Bases of Politics* (1960), contains important material on working-class voting behavior. Samuel Lubell, *The Future of American Politics* (3d ed. 1965), is standard. John W. Jeffries, *Testing the Roosevelt Coalition: Connecticut Society and Politics in the Era of World War II* (1979), helps place labor's political efforts in perspective, as does David M. Oshinsky, *Senator McCarthy and the American Labor Movement* (1976).

Curtis D. MacDougall, *Gideon's Army*, vol. 3, *The Campaign and the Vote* (1965), contains important material on laborite support for Wallace in 1948. Norman D. Markowitz, *The Rise and Fall of the People's Century: Henry A. Wallace and American Liberalism, 1941–1948* (1973), is critical of mainstream labor's support for Truman, while Hamby, *Beyond the New Deal*, cited above, stresses the limits of third-party politics. Mike Davis, "The Barren Marriage of American Labour and the Democratic Party," *New Left Review* 124 (1980): 43–84, is a ringing critique of organized labor's thralldom to the Democracy. Kenneth Waltzer, "The FBI, Congressman Vito Marcantonio, and the American Labor Party," in Athan Theoharis, ed., *Beyond the Hiss Case: The FBI, Congress, and the Cold War* (1982), 176–214, focuses on a successful pro-Soviet politician.

The postwar anti-Communist crusade, both foreign and domestic, has produced a veritable library of books and articles. Memoirs, polemics, dispassionate treatises, explanations, and exculpations abound. For contrasting but not entirely incompatible overviews, see Earl Latham, *The Communist Controversy in Washington: From the New Deal to McCarthy* (1969), and Athan Theoharis, *Seeds of Repression: Harry S. Truman and the Origin of McCarthyism* (1969). The articles in Robert Griffith and Athan Theoharis, eds., *The Specter: Original Essays on the Cold War and the Origins of McCarthyism* (1974), provide a sampling of revisionist writing. The publication of and controversy surrounding Allen Weinstein, *Purjury: The Hiss-Chambers Case* (1978), and Ronald Radosh and Joyce Milton, *The Rosenberg File: A Search for the Truth* (1983), indicate the enduring legacy of this period.

Books and articles noted above under "Labor and the Left" provide the basic bibliography for this subject. Harvey A. Levenstein, *Communism, Anti-Communism, and the CIO* (1981), is a good survey of the postwar phase. In addition to Saposs, *Communism in American Unions*, Max Kampelman, *The Communist Party vs. the CIO* (1957), stridently reflects classic anti-Communist liberalism. John Earl Haynes, *Dubious Alliance: The Making of Minnesota's DFL Party* (1984), is a balanced study of the Communist versus anti-Communist fight in a critical state. Mary Sperling McAuliffe, *Crisis on the Left: Cold War Politics and American Liberals, 1947–1954* (1978), is harsh in its treatment of liberal-labor anti-Communists. David M. Oshinsky, "Labor's Cold War: The CIO and the Communists," in Griffith and Theoharis, *The Specter*, cited above, 116–51, is also critical of CIO actions. Other accounts emphasizing the violations of democratic procedure and the illiberal consequences of the CIO ouster of the pro-Soviet unions include William D. Andrew, "Factionalism and Anti-Communism: Ford Local 600," *Labor History* 20 (1979): 227–55; Frank Emspak, "The Breakup of the CIO," in Zeitlin, *Political Power and Social Theory*, cited under "Labor and the Left" above, 101–39; and Mark McCulloch, "White-Collar Unionism, 1940–1950," *Science and Society* 46 (1982–83): 405–19. James R. Prickett, Walter Galenson, and Irving Howe conducted an acrimonious debate on this subject in the pages of *Industrial Relations* (1974): 219–43; (1975): 270–72; (1976): 349–54. Thomas R. Brooks, "Rewriting History: The Labor Myth," *The American Federationist* (1978): 11–15, upholds traditional liberal-labor anti-Communism. C. Wright Mills, *The New Men of Power: America's Labor Leaders* (1948), seeks to define a democratic radical anti-Communist perspective, while the pages of the short-lived *Labor and Nation* (1945–49) are dominated by this theme.

Roy Godson, *American Labor and European Politics: The AFL as a Transnational Force* (1976), details laborite anti-Communism. Julius Braunthal, *History of the International,* vol. 3, *1943–1968* (1971, 1980), provides a needed multinational context. Neil Betten, *Catholic Activism and the Industrial Worker* (1976); Douglas P. Seaton, *Catholics and Radicals: The Association of Catholic Trade Unionists and the Labor Movement, from Depression to Cold War* (1981); and Schatz, *Electrical Workers,* cited under "General Themes" above, discuss the important Roman Catholic component in laborite anti-Communism. David Caute, *The Great Fear: The Anti-Communist Purge under Truman and Eisenhower* (1978), contains fascinating material on antiradicalism run amok in and around the labor movement. Material in Ronald W. Reagan and Richard G. Hubler, *Where Is the Rest of Me?* (1965), on the Communism issue in Hollywood in the late forties is of more than ordinary interest, but see also Nancy Lynn Schwartz (with Sheila Schwartz), *The Hollywood Writers' Wars* (1982).

CHAPTERS 5 AND 6

General histories of the 1950s and 1960s include Geoffrey Perrett, *A Dream of Greatness: The American People, 1945–1963* (1979), and William Manchester, *The Glory and the Dream: A Narrative History of America, 1932–1972,* vol. 2 (1974). Godfrey Hodgson, *America in Our Time* (1976), is a penetrating overview. James Gilbert, *Another Chance: Postwar America, 1945–1968* (1981), and Frederick F. Siegel, *Troubled Journey: From Pearl Harbor to Ronald Reagan* (1984), teem with shrewd insights. Douglas T. Miller and Barbara Marion Novak, *The Fifties: The Way We Really Were* (1977), is informative but drips with disdain for its subject, while Paul A. Carter, *Another Part of the Fifties* (1983), is an episodic glimpse at the decade. The decade of the sixties has been served better by historians. William L. O'Neill, *Coming Apart: An Informal History of America in the 1960s* (1971), is a remarkable achievement. Allen J. Matusow, *The Unravelling of America: A History of Liberalism in the 1960s* (1984), is solid and provocative.

For working-class life in the 1950s and 1960s, there is a cornucopia of material. Daniel Bell, *The End of Ideology: On the Exhaustion of Political Ideas in the Fifties* (rev. ed. 1962), contains his sparkling essay "Work and Its Discontents," along with others on crime, trade unionism, and politics that are infallibly challenging. Lipset, *Political Man,* cited for Chapter 4 above, surveys the theme of working-class authoritarianism, as does his article "Working-Class Authoritarianism," in Paul Blumberg, ed., *The Impact of Social Class* (1972). Richard Hamilton, *Class and Politics in the United States* (1972), provides a sharp critique. See also Louis Lipsitz, "Working-Class Authoritarianism: A Reevaluation," *American Sociological Review* (1965): 103–10.

Bennett Burger, *Working-Class Suburb: A Study of Auto Workers in Suburbia* (1960); Mirra Komarovsky, *Blue-Collar Marriage* (1962); and Eli Chinoy, *Automobile Workers and the American Dream* (1955), stress the limitations of working-class life in the 1950s. William Kornblum, *Blue-Collar Community* (1974), is an important study of steelworkers. Joseph T. Howell, *Hard Living on Clay Street: Portraits of Blue-Collar Families* (1973), is sensitive and informative. Barbara Garson, *All the Livelong Day: The Meaning and Demeaning of Routine Work* (1975); Elinor Langer, "Inside the New York Telephone Company," in William L. O'Neill, ed., *Women at Work* (1972); B. J. Widick, ed., *Auto Work and Its Discontents* (1976); and Robert Blauner, *Alienation and Freedom: The Factory Worker and His Industry* (1964), examine workers' attitudes toward work and authority. See Robert Dubin, "Industrial Workers' Worlds: A Study of the 'Central Life Interests' of Industrial Workers," *Social Problems* 3 (1956): 131–42; Martin Meissner, "The Long Arm of the Job: A Study of Work and Leisure," *Industrial Relations* 10 (1971): 239–60; and George Strauss and Eliezer Rosenstein, "Workers' Participation: A Critical View," *Industrial Relations* 9 (1970): 197–214, for perceptive commentary on this theme.

Several excellent collections offer insights into working-class life. They are Arthur B. Shostak and William Gomberg, eds., *Blue-Collar World* (1964); Sar A. Levitan, ed., *Blue-Collar Workers: A Symposium on Middle America* (1971); and, especially, Irving Howe, ed., *The World of the Blue-Collar Worker* (1972). Ferdinand Zweig, *The Worker in an Affluent Society* (1961), and Michael Harrington, *The Other America: Poverty in the United States* (1962), examine economic aspects. The best single book on working-class life in the 1960s is Andrew Levison, *The Working-Class Majority* (1974). See also Brendan Sexton and Patricia C. Sexton, *Blue Collars and Hard Hats* (1971).

Studs Terkel, *Working* (1972), lets workers speak for themselves. Harvey Swados, *On the Line* (1957), and Eric Hoffer, *Working and Thinking on the Waterfront: A Journal, June 1958– May 1959* (1969), offer contrasting reports by worker-intellectuals. Dennis Smith, *Report from Engine Co. 82* (1972), is a vivid narrative of a firefighter's work. Several outstanding novels depict the lives of American workers in this period. See especially Alfred Maund, *The International* (1961); Clancy Sigal, *Going Away* (1962); John Sayles, *Union Dues* (1977); and Lawrence Swaim, *Waiting for the Earthquake* (1977).

The special circumstances of black workers are ably recounted in books by Harris and Foner, cited under "General Themes" above. See also F. Ray Marshall, *The Negro and Organized Labor* (1965). Herbert Hill's indictment of organized labor's racial policies is found in *Black Labor and the American Legal System: Race, Work, and the Law* (1974), while William Gould, *Black Workers in White Unions* (1977), is an outstanding scholarly study. B. J. Widick, *Detroit: City of Race and Class Violence* (1972), depicts the Motor City's racial tensions. Brooks, *Toil and Trouble*, cited under "General Themes" above, has good material on the DRUM phenomenon. See also James A. Geschwender, *Class, Race, and Worker Insurgency* (1977), and John C. Leggett, *Class, Race, and Labor: Working-Class Consciousness in Detroit* (1968). Goulden, *Meany;* Barnard, *Reuther;* and Anderson, *Randolph,* all cited under "Biography and Memoir" above, have important material on blacks and the labor movement. Essays in Julius Jacobson, ed., *The Negro and the American Labor Movement* (1968), are strong on post–World War II developments; see especially Harold M. Baron and Bennett Hymer, "The Negro Worker in the Chicago Labor Market," 232–85 for an early statement of the "segmented labor markets" thesis. Michael Piore, *Birds of Passage: Migrant Labor and Industrial Societies* (1979), develops this theme brilliantly. A series on black workers in diverse industries, "The Racial Policies of American Industry," edited by Herbert R. Northrup for the Wharton School at the University of Pennsylvania (1968–74), contains reams of solid material.

As noted above, the historical literature on collective bargaining in the postwar period is spotty. Those interested in unfolding developments should consult the *New York Times, John Herling's Labor Letter,* and such scholarly publications as the *Monthly Labor Review, Industrial and Labor Relations Review, Industrial Relations,* and the annual *Proceedings of the . . . Industrial Relations Research Association.* Michael Piore, "Can the American Labor Movement Survive Re-Gomperization?" *Proceedings of the Thirty-Fifth Annual Meeting* [of the Industrial Relations Research Association] (1983): 30–39, provides an arresting overview. Arthur Kornhauser, Robert Dubin, and Arthur M. Ross, eds., *Industrial Conflict* (1954), is an excellent book of readings, examining a broad range of industrial relations matters as they appeared in the mid-1950s. David Brody, "The Uses of Power, I: The Industrial Battleground," in Brody, *Workers in Industrial America* (cited under "General Themes" above), 173–214, is outstanding on contract evolution through the postwar era. Edward R. Livernash, *Collective Bargaining in the Basic Steel Industry: A Study of the Public Interest and the Role of Government* (1976), and Robert M. Macdonald, *Collective Bargaining in the Automobile Industry: A Study of Wage Structure and Competitive Relations* (1963), are able studies by economists. See also Lloyd G. Reynolds and Cynthia H. Taft, *The Evolution of Wage Structure* (1956). Richard A. Lester, *As Unions Mature: An Analysis of the Evolution of American Unionism* (1958), has been influential. Atleson, *Values and Assumptions in American Labor Law,* and Stone, "Post-War Paradigm," both cited for Chapter 4 above, are critical of the drift of contractual developments. Finkin, "Revisionism in Labor Law," however, cited for Chapter 2, takes sharp issue with Stone. Steven Tolliday and Jonathan Zeitlin, "Shop Floor Bargaining, Contract Unionism, and Job Control: An Anglo-American Comparison," in Nelson Lichtenstein and Stephen Meyer, eds., *The American Automobile Industry: A Social History* (1986), gives the UAW high marks for its workplace efforts. Hugh Mosley, "Corporate Social Benefits and the Underdevelopment of the American Welfare State," *Contemporary Crises* 5 (1981): 139–54, is a perceptive analysis focusing on the UAW's contracts with General Motors.

For the merger of the AFL and CIO, biographies of Meany and Reuther, frequently cited above, supply basic information. Arthur J. Goldberg, *AFL-CIO: Labor United* (1956), contains important documents. Taft, *Organized Labor,* cited above under "General Themes," provides a brief narrative. For Reuther's growing disillusionment, see Frank Cormier and William J. Eaton, *Reuther* (1970), and Victor Reuther, *The Brothers Reuther,* cited under "Biography and Memoir."

Public employee unionism is treated well in Brooks, *Toil and Trouble* (see "General Themes"). The entries in Gary M. Fink, ed., *Labor Unions* (1977), are very helpful. Goulden, *Wurf,* cited under "Biography and Memoir," is basic for AFSCME. The teachers' unions are covered in Philip A. Taft, *United They Teach: The Story of the United Federation of Teachers* (1974), a sympathetic account, and Robert J. Braun, *Teachers and Power: The Story of the American Federation of Teachers* (1972), unrelentingly hostile to the AFT. Richard N. Billings and John Grenya, *Power to the Public Worker* (1974), is a brief overview of public employee unionism. Peter Rachleff and the Work Environment Project, *Moving the Mail: From a Manual Case to Outer Space* (1982), introduces the problems of work and unionism in the U.S. Postal Service. For the 1968 Memphis garbage strike, see Gerald D. McKnight, "The 1968 Memphis Sanitation Strike and the FBI: A Case Study in Urban Surveillance," *South Atlantic Quarterly* 83 (1984): 138–56.

In the fifties and sixties, critics of the labor movement abounded. Paul Jacobs, *The State of the Unions* (1963), is a sober look at corruption, racial injustice, and union bureaucracy. Like Jacobs a former union staff member, Stanley Aronowitz, in *False Promises: The Shaping of American Working Class Consciousness* (1973), flails away at the unions but from a neo-Marxist perspective. The editors of the leftist publication *root and branch* [sic] published a volume entitled *Root and Branch: The Rise of the Workers' Movements* (1975), which chronicles the rank-and-file strikes of the early 1970s and lambasts the bureaucratic leadership of the established labor movement. Essays by Jeremy Brecher, Stanley Aronowitz, Paul Mattick, Jr., and others make for lively reading. Burton Hall, ed., *Autocracy and Insurgency in Organized Labor* (1972), is an excellent compilation of articles by Hall, Stan Weir, Herbert Hill, Sidney Lens, and others, attacking organized labor's bureaucratization, corruption, and support for militarism. Walter Sheridan, *The Fall and Rise of Jimmy Hoffa* (1972), and Ralph and Estelle James, *Hoffa and the Teamsters: A Study of Union Power* (1965), recount the sorry story of the Teamsters. Arthur M. Schlesinger, Jr., *Robert F. Kennedy and His Times* (1978), contains excellent material on the union corruption hearings of the 1950s. See also John Hutchinson, *The Imperfect Union: A History of Corruption in American Trade Unions* (1970), on this subject. Other works highlighting the less savory side of postwar unionism include Vernon H. Jensen, *Strife on the Waterfront: The Port of New York since 1945* (1974), a careful scholarly study, and Brit Hume, *Death and the Mines: Rebellion and Murder in the United Mine Workers* (1971), an outstanding example of labor reportage which focuses on the sad decay of the United

Mine Workers. William Serrin, *The Company and the Union: The "Civilized Relationship" of the General Motors Corporation and the United Automobile Workers* (1973), reflects the prevalent anti-union atmosphere of the early seventies in its dismissive approach to the UAW.

The unions had few ardent defenders. Haynes Johnson and Nick Kotz, *The Unions* (1972), despite occasional sensationalism, is a balanced treatment. Thomas R. Brooks, *Communications Workers of America: The Story of a Union* (1977), is a sympathetic study. John Herling, *Right to Challenge: People and Power in the Steelworkers' Union* (1972), is a tough-minded but ultimately edifying account of a kind of union democracy in action. Derek C. Bok and John T. Dunlop, in *Labor and the American Community* (1970), give organized labor good marks for effectiveness, responsibility, and public-mindedness. Everett Kassalow and Benjamin Martin, eds., *Labor Relations in Advanced Industrial Societies: Issues and Problems* (1980), helps place American developments in perspective.

Conservative critics of the labor movement have not been particularly prolific aside from ephemeral and journalistic attacks. Sylvester Petro, *Labor Policy of the Free Society* (1957); Petro, *Power Unlimited—The Corruption of Union Leadership: A Report on the McClellan Committee Hearings* (1959); Petro, *The Kohler Strike: Union Violence and Administrative Law* (1961); and Petro, *The Kingsport Strike* (1967), are doctrinaire. Terry Catchpole, *How to Cope with COPE: The Political Operations of Organized Labor* (1968), admires labor's political efficiency but detests its goals in a lucid critique.

Organized labor's foreign policy operations are scathingly attacked from the left in Ronald Radosh, *American Labor and United States Foreign Policy: The Cold War in the Unions from Gompers to Lovestone* (1969), and Henry Berger, "Organized Labor and American Foreign Policy," in Irving Louis Horowitz, John C. Leggett, and Martin Oppenheimer, eds., *The American Working Class: Prospects for the 1980s* (1979). Peter Weiler, "The United States, International Labor, and the Cold War: The Breakup of the World Federation of Trade Unions," *Diplomatic History* 5 (1981): 1–22, and Howard Schonberger, "American Labor's Cold War in Occupied Japan," *Diplomatic History* 3 (1979): 249–72, are critical of labor's anti-Communist priorities. Roy Godson, *American Labor and European Politics*, cited above for Chapter 4, is vigorously sympathetic to the AFL's postwar European operations. Goulden, *Meany*, contains much information on labor and foreign policy, much of it in Meany's and Lovestone's words. Victor Reuther, *The Brothers Reuther*, cited above, outlines the foreign policy aspects of the Meany-Reuther split. Arnold Beichman, "Free Unionism in Postwar Europe," *American Federationist* 84 (1977): 21–24, defends labor's traditional approach. Finally, the well-edited social democratic publication *The New Leader* is a storehouse of laborite anti-Communist foreign policy perspectives. The independent left *New Politics* can be read for contrast.

On labor's political operations in the Kennedy-Johnson years, see the Goulden and Barnard biographies, frequently cited above, as well as Schlesinger, *Robert Kennedy*, also cited above. James L. Sundquist, *Dynamics of the Party System: Alignment and Realignment of Political Parties in the United*

States (1973), provides excellent material on Democratic strength through the 1950s. Ronnie Dugger, *The Politician: The Life and Times of Lyndon Johnson* (1982), contains fascinating material on the anti-union milieu in which the pre-presidential Johnson flourished. See also Carl Solberg, *Hubert Humphrey: A Biography* (1984). Great Society social programs are contrastingly assessed in Matusow, *The Unravelling of America,* cited above, and John E. Schwarz, *America's Hidden Success: A Reassessment of Twenty Years of Public Policy* (1983). Stephen B. Oates, *The Trumpet Soundeth: A Biography of Dr. Martin Luther King* (1983), is magnificent.

Brody, "The Uses of Power, II: Political Action," in Brody, *Workers in Industrial America* (cited above), 215–57, is a shrewd discussion of labor politics of the fifties and sixties. The standard work is J. David Greenstone, *Labor in American Politics* (1969). Catchpole, *How to Cope with COPE,* cited above, contains useful documentary material. The best account of the 1968 election is Lewis Chester, Godfrey Hodgson and Bruce Page, *An American Melodrama: The Presidential Campaign of 1968* (1969), a book brimming with insights and information. Michael Harrington, *Socialism* (1972) and *Towards a Democratic Left: A Radical Program for a New Majority* (1968), convey the ever-recurring hopes of the American democratic left.

EPILOGUE

Much of the material in this chapter is based on a course that Douglas Fraser and I conducted in the winter of 1985 at Wayne State University. A syllabus is available through the Department of History, Wayne State University. While Mr. Fraser is in no way responsible for the content of this chapter, his ideas, experiences, and insights have been invaluable. "Working for the Union: An Interview with Douglas A. Fraser by William Serrin," *American Heritage,* January–February 1985, 57–64, surveys the career of one of the country's outstanding trade unionists.

The only general historical account of the 1970s now available is Peter N. Carroll, *It Seemed Like Nothing Happened: The Tragedy and Promise of America in the 1970s* (1982). Its chapter on labor is disappointing. A. H. Raskin, "A Reporter at Large: A Unionist in Reaganland," *The New Yorker,* September 7, 1981, 54–113, supplies a lively overview. Of the daily press, the *New York Times* and the *Wall Street Journal* have the best labor coverage, while *John Herling's Labor Letter* contains important documentary material. The independent socialist periodical, *In These Times,* covers labor issues and economic problems generously.

For the economic context, Gus Tyler, "The Other Economy: America's Working-Class Poor," *The New Leader* 61 (May 10, 1978): 3–35, is an excellent snapshot as of the late seventies. Lester C. Thurow, *The Zero-Sum Society: Distribution and the Possibilities of Economic Change* (1980), is thoughtful, while Barry Bluestone and Bennett Harrison, *The Deindustrialization of America* (1982), analyzes recent developments. Robert Kuttner, *The Economic Illusion: False Choices between Prosperity and Justice* (1984), and frequent articles and reviews in *Dissent, New Republic,* and *Atlantic Monthly* by the same author provide keen analysis of economic developments and union problems. Robert Z. Lawrence, *Can America Compete?* (1984), and James Fallows, "America's Changing Economic Landscape," *Atlantic Monthly* 255 (March 1985): 47–68, offer more optimistic assessments. Andrew Hacker, "Women vs. Men in the Labor Force," *New York Times Magazine,* December 9, 1984, is a good summary.

Richard B. Freeman and James L. Medoff, *What Do Unions Do?* (1984), is an important book covering a wide range of contemporary issues. Louis A. Ferman, ed., "The Future of American Unionism," *Annals of the American Academy of Political and Social Science,* vol. 473 (May 1984), contains useful summaries of current research and perspectives. See especially Markley Roberts, "The Future Demographics of American Unionism," 23–32; Sar A. Levitan and Clifford M. Johnson, "The Changing Work Place," 116–27; Freeman and Medoff, "Trade Unions and Productivity: Some New Evidence on an Old Issue," 149–64; Thomas A. Kochan and Michael J. Piore, "Will the New Industrial Relations Last? Implications for the American Labor Movement," 177–89; and Charles M. Rehmus, "Labor and Politics in the 1980s," 40–51. Thomas B. Edsall, *The New Politics of Inequality* (1984), is a brilliant analysis with a splendid chapter on labor's decline and its implications. See also Piore, "Can American Labor Survive Re-Gomperization?" Paul Weiler, "Promises to Keep: Securing Workers' Rights to Self-Organization under the NLRA," *Harvard Law Review* 96 (June 1983): 1769–1827, contains both technical analysis and important general insights.

Stanley Aronowitz, *Working-Class Hero: A New Strategy for Labor* (1983), sets a provocative agenda for a revitalized labor movement. A. H. Raskin, "Labor's Grand Illusions," *New York Times Magazine,* February 10, 1985, 52–54, 67–68, and David Moberg, "New AFL-CIO Report Outlines Labor Revival," *In These Times,* March 13–19, 1985, 5, 11, assess labor's self-examination. Kuttner, "The State of the Unions," *New Republic,* March 25, 1985, 25–30, raises key questions. The AFL-CIO report itself is AFL-CIO Committee on the Evolution of Work, *The Changing Situation of Workers and Their Unions* (February 1985). David Halle, *America's Working Man: Work, Home, and Politics among Blue-Collar Property Owners* (1984), is a penetrating study of contemporary workers.

Index

The Johns Hopkins University Press

AMERICAN WORKERS, AMERICAN UNIONS, 1920–1985

This book was composed in Times Roman by Professional Book Compositors, Inc., from a design by Martha Farlow. It was printed on 50-lb. Sebago Eggshell Cream Offset paper and bound by The Maple Press Company.